AF380484

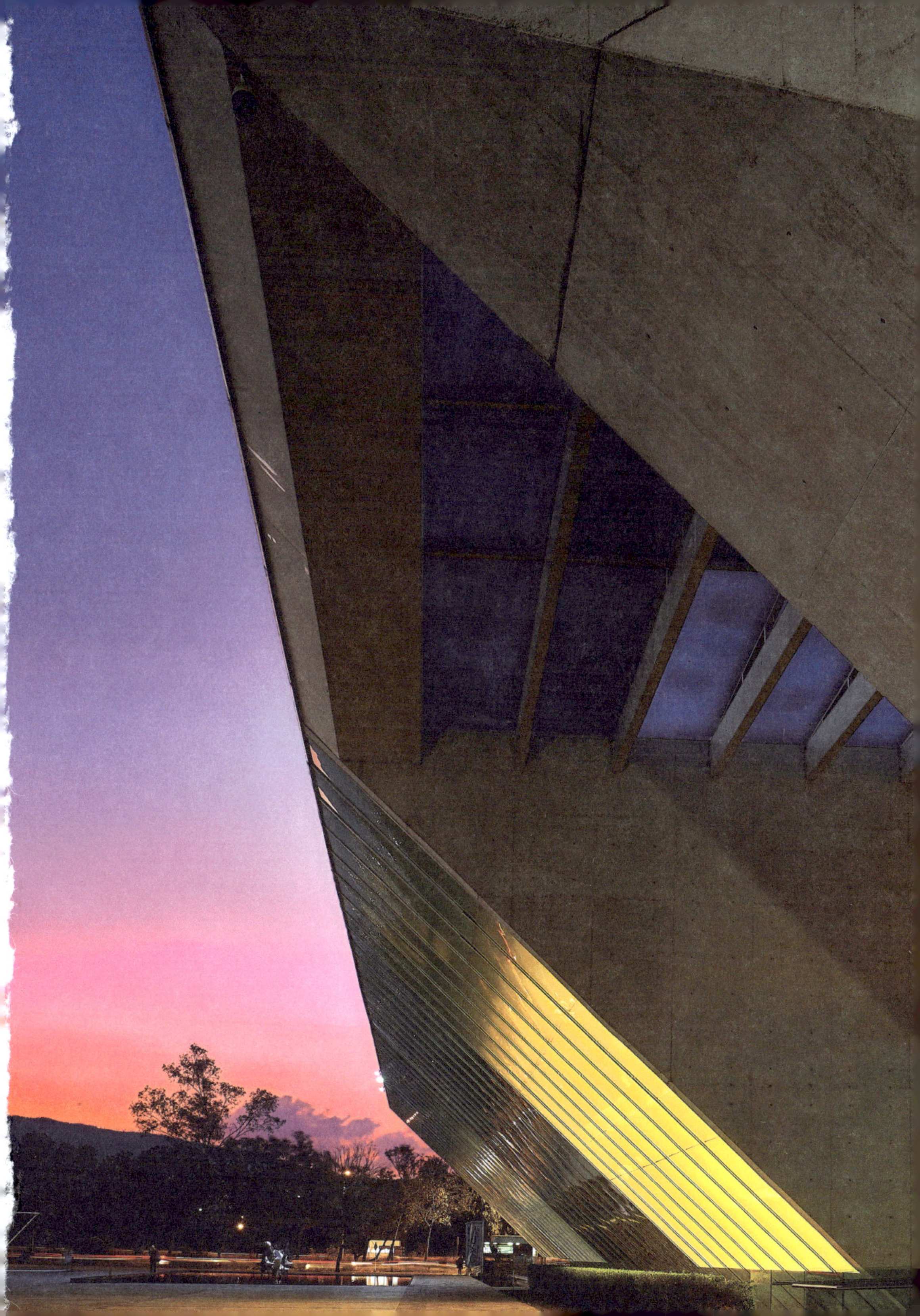

Texts and Curatorship
Mónica Amieva (M. A.) · IIE
Andrea de Caso (A. d. C.) · MUAC
Pilar García (P. G.) · MUAC
Julio García Murillo (J. G. M.) · MUAC
Amanda de la Garza · DiGAV, MUAC
Jaime González Solís (J. G. S) · MUAC
Sol Henaro (S. H.) · MUAC
Alejandra Labastida (A. L.) · MUAC
Cuauhtémoc Medina (C. M.) · MUAC, IIE
Elva Peniche (E. P.) · MUAC
Virginia Roy Luzarraga (V. R. L.) · MUAC

Curatorial Coordination
Pilar García

Translation
Robin Myers

Editorial Direction
Ekaterina Álvarez · MUAC

Editorial Coordination
Ana Xanic López · MUAC
Vanessa López · MUAC

Proofreading
Ana Xanic López · MUAC
Vanessa López · MUAC
Juan E. Tovar
Julianna Neuhouser

Copyright Managment
Lourdes Padilla

Design
Cristina Paoli · Periferia Taller Gráfico

Design Assistant
Raquel Achar Cohen

First edition 2020
D.R. © 2020 UNAM, Universidad Nacional Autónoma de México
Av. Universidad 3000, Ciudad Universitaria, Coyoacán, 04510, Mexico City
MUAC, Museo Universitario Arte Contemporáneo, UNAM
Insurgentes Sur 3000, Centro Cultural Universitario, 04510, Mexico City

D.R. © the authors for the texts
D.R. © the translator for the translations
D.R. © the authors for the images
© 2020, Editorial RM, S.A. de C.V./ Córdoba 234-7, Roma Norte. 67000, Mexico City
© RM Verlag S.L.C/Loreto 13-15 Local B, 08029, Barcelona, Spain
www.editorialrm.com
418

ISBN RM Verlag 978-84-17975-63-0
ISBN UNAM 978-607-30-3832-4

All rights reserved.
This publication may not be photocopied nor reproduced in any medium or by any method, in whole or in part, without the written authorization of the editors.

Printed and made in Mexico.

Cover: *Zócalo, Ciudad de México, 22 de mayo, 1999* [*Zócalo, Mexico City, May 22, 1999*], 1999–2017. Still, p.18

MUAC
One Hundred Works

MUAC · Museo Universitario Arte Contemporáneo, UNAM

Foreword

—

Amanda de la Garza

To collect, many distinguished texts and authors would have us believe, means to impose order and meaning on the world. This psychology of collecting is rooted in the European mannerist and baroque idea of *Wunderkämmer*: an assortment of objects that symbolizes the structure of reality. However, this exorbitant and accumulative project bears little resemblance to the experience of institutional collecting today. A museum storage space is a landscape of disordered fragments. Museum collections, no matter how young, are never a map, but a rocky topography marked by surprising formations: a territory shaped over time by actions, accidents, and divergent projects, unconcluded lines and hollows, where wills and generations have settled like sediment into a whole that grows in value precisely by refusing to adapt to a single comprehensive vision. A project that promises constant reformulation, always considering and reconsidering the past; a project whose very nature as a set means that it can never be entrapped in a given present.

Collections are a construction of heterogeneity, which is why exhibitions and publications so naturally respond to them by pursuing a selective, anthologizing goal. A collection measures its lives in time by the succession of provisional orders gleaned from shuffling and reassessing their content. They are not only an open, infinite project; their representation also calls for the continual reconfiguration—and critical revision—of the canon. Returning to our image of a collection as a rich landscape within a complex geological history, an exhibit from a collection is the presentation of complexity submerged under the surface. A productive chaos, enveloped in an order as provisional as it is passionate and evocative.

Compounding this struggle is the complexity entailed by the apprehension with which all contemporary art collections prepare to greet the public. Such terrain acknowledges itself as new ground, recent earth; it is unstable, ever-shifting. Besides the risk that governs the works in their possession, contemporary art museums must also confront the challenge of how to establish a sense of conclusiveness in their catalogs. For one thing, they are plagued by concern that the present moment will overvalue the immediate. For another, they are also beset by the uncertainty—which is inherent to aesthetic risk—of publicly sharing passions that are convictions in their place of issuance, but which invariably come off as tentative and controversial in dialogue. Another concern is to ensure, amid the momentum of strengthening the collection by apprehending the artistic present, that genealogy-forging moments won't be forgotten along the way.

A frequent decision, one that has long dominated exhibition policy in the MUAC collection (DiGAV, UNAM) is to avoid selection altogether. In this approach, collections are presented as raw material for themed exhibitions, which are then evaluated for the proximity and relevance of their reference points and content more than for the quality of the works themselves. With *MUAC: One Hundred Works,* the museum is taking the opposite risk: embracing its collection and offering it to the public as an object that contains multitudes. An object that is largely capable of establishing a certain conviction with respect to its own content —guided not by theme but by the relevance that particular works and artists already have in our awareness of contemporary art in Mexico. In this book, we then seek to provide the viewer with an array of works we see as essential to the history of recent art.

This selection, in turn, invokes the future: the preponderant role to be played by collections in the exhibition program as the museum—founded over a little more than a decade ago—continues to develop. In fully recognizing its heterogeneous nature, the museum must advance not only in its exhibitions, but also in its research and documentation. In this sense, such processes invite the collections' gaze to be subject, too, to a review of the canon and its determinations, to a critique of its historical biases. Exhibitions from the collection not only contribute to reassessing that canon, but also to circulating its works beyond the University itself. Themed exhibitions from the collection have toured public and private museums in many states across Mexico, offering a panorama of one of our most important public reserves of contemporary art.

As the custodian of an artistic legacy, the museum must carry out crucial technical processes for the sake of its conservation and future archaeology, including restoration and other challenges demanded by works of contemporary art and the materials they employ. At the same time, other essential tasks include cataloging work in compliance with international standards and, over the medium term, honoring the desire to make the collection available to the public online.

In its first decade, amid obstacles, accidents, and constantly fluctuating resources and possibilities, the MUAC collection has managed to achieve a substantial representation of art produced in Mexico after 1952 (a date marked by the construction of Ciudad Universitaria as a modernizing project), especially following the political, social, and cultural shakeup of 1968. The museum has amassed its collection through a range of sources and alliances: the resources provided by the UNAM, the Patronato MUAC, the artists who entrust the MUAC with their work through donations and a payment-in-kind program, as well as commissions for the exhibition program. The collection is protected by the University; at the same time, it belongs to the local art world and, ultimately, to the nation itself.

This is a landscape with a complex stratigraphy. From 2004 to 2008, Olivier Debroise established a "founding collection" for the MUAC, selecting standout works from the compendium that the UNAM's Dirección General de Artes Visuales had been accumulating for decades. Now—nearly 12 years after the museum was founded and 16 after having regulated art acquisitions through collegiate bodies—we pause to rethink the role of these artistic objects that have become touchstones in the MUAC collection. Debroise set out to fulfill a foundational mission: not only to endow the University with a public collection of contemporary art, but also to "put local production in global perspective" and regulate and systematize the art acquisition process. Each work in this book is defined not by generation or narrative sequence, but by being able to tell its own story about the MUAC collection.

Over the next 12 years, two curator colleagues, Pilar García and Sol Henaro, have taken turns cultivating the reasoned growth of two collections: the art collection and the documentary archive collection. Both have nourished an increasingly substantial assemblage of works by artists working in and about Mexico. *MUAC: One Hundred Works* presents a selection of key pieces from those collections. The selection was made collectively by the museum's curatorial staff—a process that has lasted over a year. We trust that these works will become an object of

   AMANDA DE LA GARZA

vital interest for researchers and students, a reference point in the future artistic battles to be fought across the region, and a companion the public in the everyday lives of our public.

The texts that accompany these works of art have been stylistically standardized. However, their authorship, which is distributed among the members of the MUAC's curatorial team, has been identified with initials that the reader will find alongside the authors' names on the legal page. The curatorial team has long sought to forge a stronger bond with the museum collection both through curatorship and through research. The goal, in this sense, was to dismantle the stratigraphy of a disjointed relationship between the temporary exhibition program and the collection.

We have organized these works in alphabetical order by the artist's last name or the name of the collective: a conventional and intentionally neutral method that will allow for easier searching through the volume. As luck would have it, this edition has coincided with our hundredth issue of Folios MUAC, our editorial collection. In addition to chronicling our projects from diverse critical and documentary standpoints, the Folios MUAC series has enabled us to build a new relationship with our audiences, one in which promoting a culture of contemporary art isn't tantamount to printing opulent, arbitrary books. And so we have two simultaneous causes for celebration: the public maturity of our collections, and the trajectory of an editorial project that has become a point of reference.

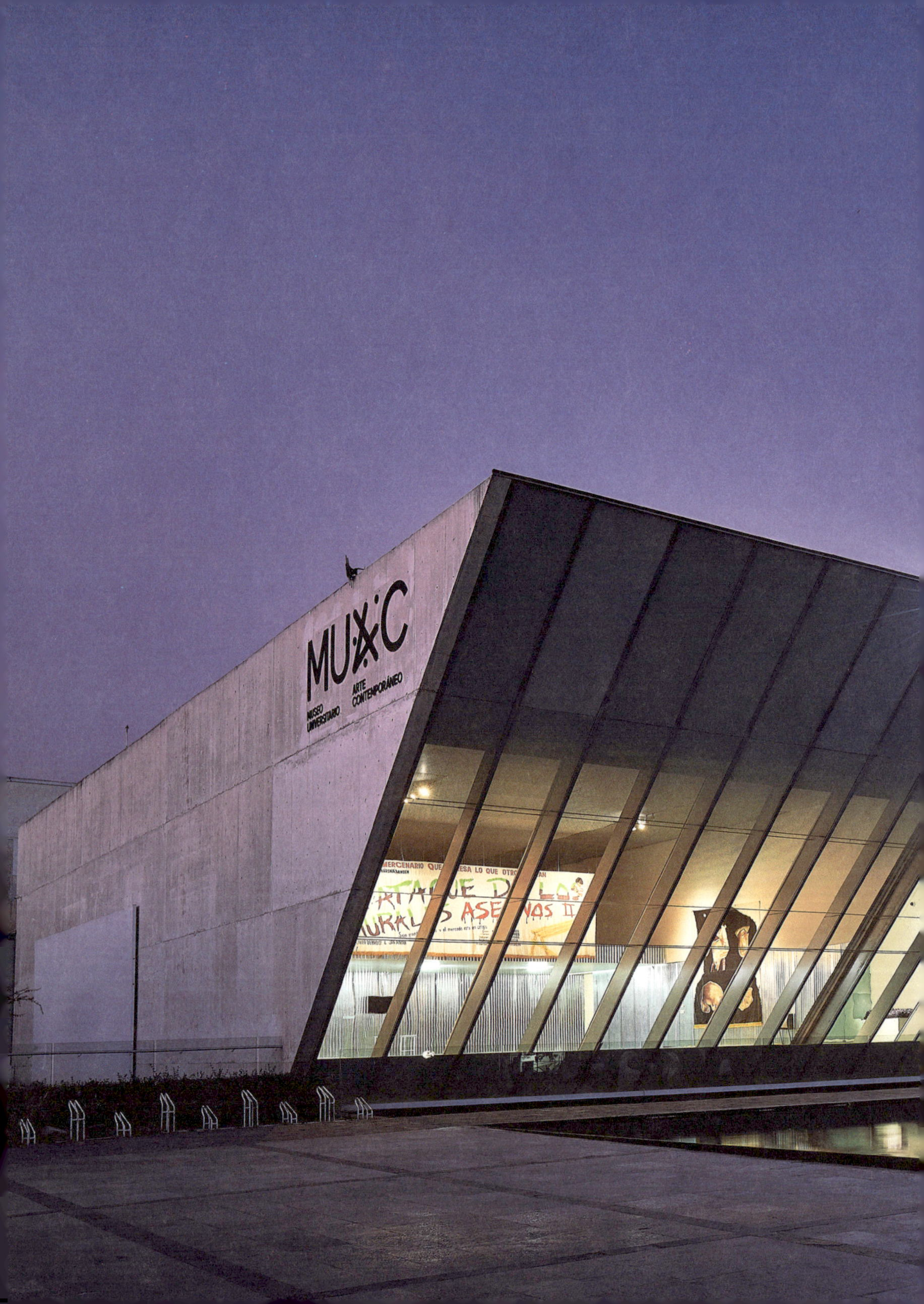

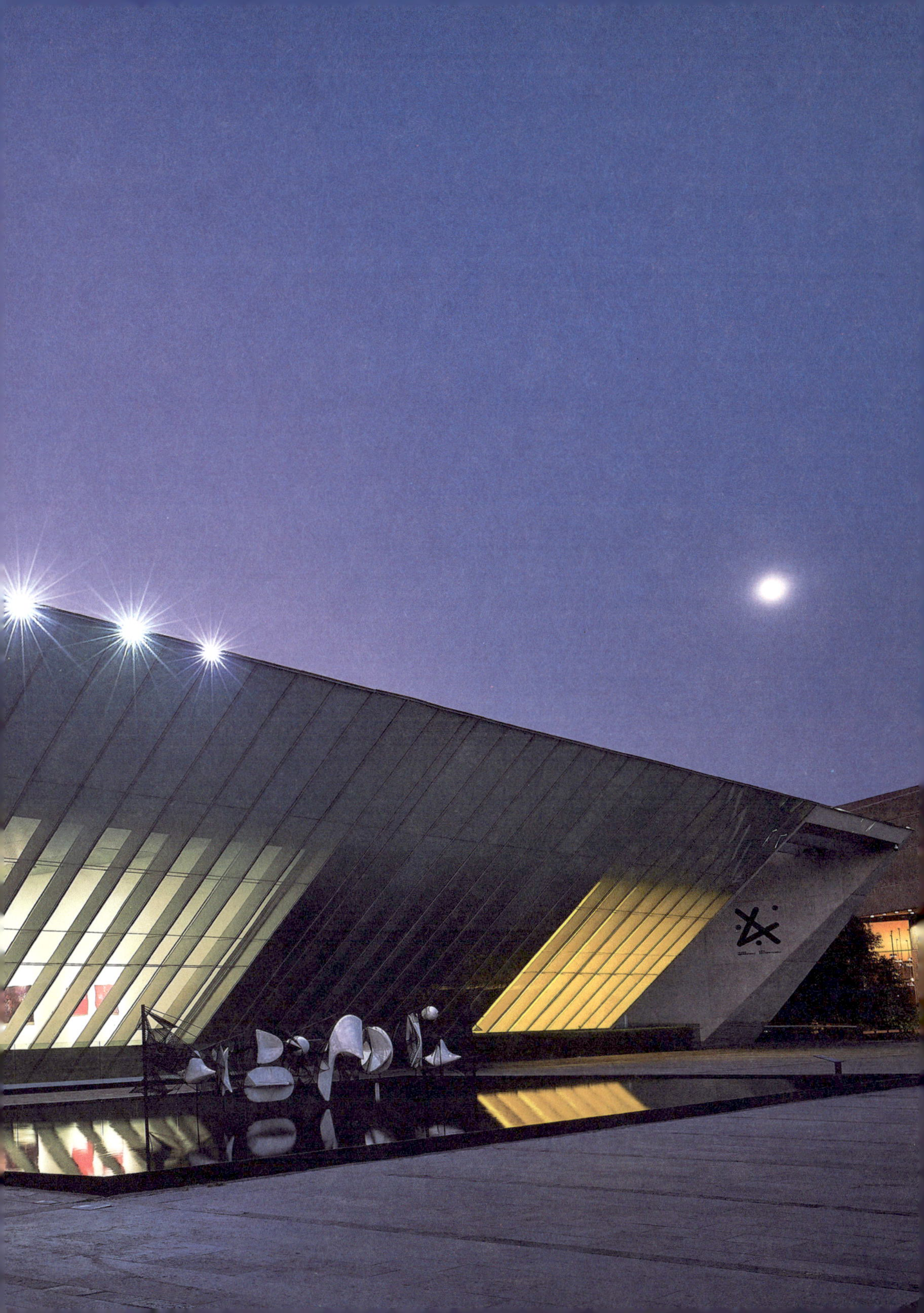

Carlos Aguirre

Acapulco, Mexico, 1948

Name of Dead, 2006–2010

Installation. 1139 newspaper clippings (obituaries)
150 × 600 cm
Gift of the artist, 2011

For five years, Carlos Aguirre cut out and collected obituaries published in *The New York Times.* Under the headline "Names of the Dead," the United States Department of Defense systematically confirmed the deaths of US soldiers in the Iraq War.

The installation of 1139 newspaper clippings—affixed only with thumbtacks, arranged one after the other—condemns the handling of information related to the war. Drawing on notions of data collection and the archive, Aguirre exposes the long list of names of dead soldiers—names often excluded from the official discourse. In this way, the artist grants materiality to these lists, transforming information into a graphic object of protest.

A. d. C.

Detail

The Department of Defense has identified 1,714 American service members who have died since the start of the Iraq war. It confirmed the death of the following Americans yesterday:

CRUMPLER, Adam J., 19, Lance Cpl., Marines; Charleston, W.Va.; Second Marine Division.
HARRIS, Noah, 23, First Lt., Army; Ellijay, Ga.; Third Infantry Division.
LONG, William A., 26, Cpl., Army; Lilburn, Ga.; Third Infantry Division.

Names of the Dead

The Department of Defense has identified 1,718 American service members who have died since the start of the Iraq war. It confirmed the deaths of the following Americans:

COMETA, Anthony S., 21, Specialist, Army National Guard; Las Vegas; 1864th Transportation Company, 106th Transportation Battalion.
HORRIGAN, Robert M., 40, Master Sgt., Army; Austin, Tex.; Headquarters, Special Operations Command.
KILPATRICK, Christopher R., 18, Pfc., Army; Columbus, Tex.; 603rd Transportation Company, 142nd Corps Support Battalion, Warrior Brigade.
McNULTY, Michael L., 36, Master Sgt., Army; Knoxville, Tenn.; Headquarters, Special Operations Command.

Names of the Dead

The Department of Defense has identified 1,722 American service members who have died since the start of the Iraq war. It confirmed the deaths of the following Americans yesterday:

HOSKINS, Christopher L., 21, Specialist, Army; Danielson, Conn.; Second Infantry Division.
IDALSKI, Nicholas R., 23, Specialist, Army; Crown Point, Ind.; Second Infantry Division.
STEWART, James D., 29, Sgt., Army; Chattanooga, Tenn.; 10th Mountain Division.
VAUGHN, Brian A., 23, Specialist, Army; Pell City, Ala.; Second Infantry Division.

Names of the Dead

The Department of Defense has identified 1,724 American service members who have died since the start of the Iraq war. It confirmed the deaths of the following Americans yesterday:

DUPLANTIER, Arnold II, 26, Sgt., Army National Guard; Sacramento; First Battalion, 184th Infantry.
TACKETT, Joseph M., 22, Sgt., Army; Whitehouse, Ky.; Third Infantry Division.

Names of the Dead

The Department of Defense has identified 1,726 American service members who have died since the start of the Iraq war. It confirmed the death of the following Americans this week:

CHARETTE, Bolly A., 21, Lance Cpl., Marines; Cranston, R.I.; Second Marine Division.
PINEDA, Carlos, 22, Cpl., Marines; Los Angeles, Second Marine Division.

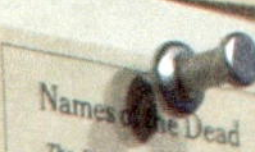

Army; Vega Baja, P.R.; 390th Transportation Company, 88th Corps Support Company, 43rd Area Support Group.

Names of the Dead

The Department of Defense has identified 2,045 American service members who have died since the start of the Iraq war. It confirmed the deaths of the following Americans this week:

CAHILL, Joel E., 34, Capt., Army; Norwood, Mass.; Third Infantry Division.
FEGLER, Jason A., 24, Staff Sgt., Army; Virginia Beach; 101st Airborne Division.
HAYES, James F., 48, Sgt. First Class, Army; Barstow, Calif.; 101st Airborne Division.
SORENSEN, Ryan J., 26, Lance Cpl., Marines; Boca Raton, Fla.; Second Marine Division.
WREN, Thomas A., 44, Lt. Col., Army Reserve; Lorton, Va.; Multi-National Security Transition Command.

...has identified 2,049 American service members who have died since the start of the Iraq war. It confirmed the deaths of the following Americans yesterday:

FREEMAN, Brian L., 27, Staff Sgt., Army; Lucedale, Miss.; Third Squadron, Third Armored Cavalry.
POPE, Robert C. II, 22, Specialist, Army; East Islip, N.Y.; Third Squadron, Third Armored Cavalry.
REYES, Mario A., 19, Pfc., Army; Las Cruces, N.M.; Third Squadron, Third Armored Cavalry.
SMITH, Justin S., 28, First Lt., Army; Lansing, Mich.; Third Squadron, Third Armored Cavalry.

Names of the Dead

The Department of Defense has identified 2,051 American service members who have died since the start of the Iraq war. It confirmed the deaths of the following Americans this week:

BOATMAN, Darrell W., 38, Gunnery Sgt., Marines; Fayetteville, N.C.; Eighth Engineer Support Battalion, Second Marine Logistics Group, Second Marine Expeditionary Force.
TAMBURELLO, Jeremy P., 19, Lance Cpl., Marines; Denver; First Marine Division.

Names of the Dead

The Department of Defense has identified 2,052 American service members who have died since the start of the Iraq war. It confirmed the death of the following American on Saturday:

CASHE, Alwyn C., 35, Sgt. First Class, Army; Oviedo, Fla.; Third Infantry Division.

Names of the Dead

The Department of Defense has identified 2,056 American service members who have died since the start of the Iraq war. It confirmed the deaths of the following Americans yesterday:

CHISHOLM, Tyrone L., 27, Army; Savannah, Ga.; Squadron, Third Armored Cavalry.
FISHER, Donald E. II, Army; Avon, Mass.; portation Company, Support Battalion, Support Group.
MENDEZ SANCHEZ, Pfc., Army; Rincon Transportation Co Corps Support Bat Corps Support Group.
PARROTT, Michael Sgt., Army Natio nath, Colo.; Join quarters.
SUTHERLAND, Staff Sgt., Army N.J.; Fourth Sq alry, 172nd Str bat Team.
TERANDO, Jo Army Nationa Ill., 28th Infa

Names of the Dead

The Department of Defense has identified 2,342 American service members who have died since the start of the Iraq war. It confirmed the death of the following American yesterday:

ROGERS, Gregory S., 42, Sgt. First Class, Army; Cincinnati; 101st Airborne Division.

Names of the Dead

The Department of Defense has identified 2,348 American service members who have died since the start of the Iraq war. It confirmed the deaths of the following Americans yesterday:

GARDNER, James W., 22, Specialist, Army; Glasgow, Ky.; 101st Airborne Division.
LOVE, Joseph L., 22, Pfc., Army; North Pole, Alaska; 94th Engineer Combat Battalion, Eighth Sustainment Command.
MISSILDINE, Jody W., 19, Pvt., Army; Plant City, Fla.; First Armored Division.
NAVARROARELLANO, Juana, 24, Lance Cpl., Marines; Ceres, Calif.; Ninth Engineer Support Battalion, Third Marine Logistics Group, Third Marine Expeditionary Force.
TAYLOR, Bryan N., 20, Lance Cpl., Marines; Milford, Ohio; Second Marine Division.
WALLER, Richard P., 22, Cpl., Marines; Fort Worth; First Battalion, First Marines, First Marine Expeditionary Force.

Names of the Dead

The Department of Defense has identified 2,350 American service members who have died since the start of the Iraq war. It confirmed the deaths of the following Americans on Tuesday:

COLLINS, David S., 24, Sgt., Army; Jasper, Ga.; 101st Airborne Division.
LAMBERSON, Randall L., 36, Sgt. First Class, Army; Springfield, Mo.; 101st Airborne Division.

Names of the Dead

The Department of Defense has identified 2,356 American service members who have died since the start of the Iraq war. It confirmed the deaths of the following Americans yesterday:

BLANCO, Joseph A., 25, Cpl., Army; Bloomington, Calif.; Fourth Infantry Division.
COSTELLO, James F. III, 27, Pfc., Army; St. Louis; Fourth Infantry Division.
CREIGHTON, Shawn R., 21, Specialist, Army; Windsor, N.C.; Fourth Squadron, 14th Cavalry, 172nd Stryker Brigade Combat Team.
HESS, Kenneth D., 26, Specialist, Army; Asheville, N.C.; Fourth Squadron, 14th Cavalry, 172nd Stryker Brigade Combat Team.
PALMISANO, Eric A., 27, Lance Cpl., Marines; Florence, Wis.; First Transportation Support Battalion, First Marine Logistics Group, First Marine Expeditionary Force.
ROEHL, George R. Jr., 21, Pfc., Army; Manchester, N.H.; Fourth Infantry Division.

BANDHOLD, Scott M., 27, Specialist, Army; North Merrick, N.Y.; Fourth Infantry Division.
CALDERON-ASCENCIO, Roland 21, Pfc., Army; Miami; Fourth Infantry Division.
GLIMPSE, Marcus S., 22, Lance Cpl., Marines; Huntington Beach, Calif.; First Marine Division.
MARTINI, Philip J., 24, Lance Cpl., Marines; Lansing, Ill.; First Marine Division.

Names of the Dead

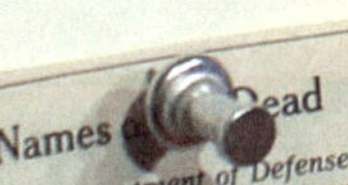

The Department of Defense has identified 2,617 American service members who have died since the start of the Iraq war. It confirmed the deaths of the following Americans yesterday:

WEIMORTZ, David G., 28, Cpl., Marines; Irmo, S.C.; Second Marine Division.
ZAYAS, Edgardo, 29, Specialist, Army; Dorchester, Mass.; 101st Airborne Division.

...died since the start of the Iraq war. It confirmed the deaths of the following Americans yesterday:

ALMAZAN, David J., 27, Sgt., Army; Los Angeles; First Armored Division.
BENSON, Darry, 46, Sgt., Army National Guard; Winterville, N.C.; 730th Quartermaster Battalion.
CHAMPLIN, Donald E., 28, Lance Cpl., Marines; Natchitoches, La.; Second Marine Division.
CROSS, Kenneth M., 21, Specialist, Army; Superior, Wis.; Second Infantry Division.
DOLAN, Daniel G., 19, Pfc., Army; Roy, Utah; Second Infantry Division.
HANSEN, Jeffrey J., 31, Staff Sgt., National Guard; Cairo,

Names of the Dead

The Department of Defense has identified 2,626 American service members who have died since the start of the Iraq war. It confirmed the death of the following American yesterday:

SCHNEIDER, Matthew E., 23, Specialist, Army; Gorham, N.H.; First Armored Division.

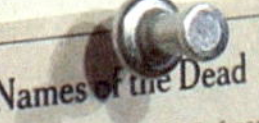

war. It the d the following American y day:

WARNDORF, Christopher Cpl., Marines; Burlington Second Marine Division.

ALEX, Eugene n., Army; Bay City, Mich.; Fourth Squadron, 14th Cavalry, 172nd Stryker Brigade Combat Team.
DEASON, Michael L., 28, Staff Sgt., Army; Farmington, Mo.; 101st Airborne Division.
GOLLA, Cliff K., 21, Lance Cpl., Marines; Charlotte, N.C.; Second Marine Division.
HARRIS, Shane P., 23, Lance Cpl., Ma

David Alfaro Siqueiros

Ciudad Camargo, Mexico, 1896*–Cuernavaca, Mexico, 1974

El pueblo a la Universidad. La Universidad al pueblo.
Por una cultura nuevohumanista de profundidad universal,
[***The People to the University, the University to the People:***
For a New Humanist Culture of Universal Depth], *ca.* 1952

Study for mural
Acrylic on wood chipboard
46.5 × 162.5 cm
Acquisition, 2005

*There are discrepancies with respect to his place and date of birth

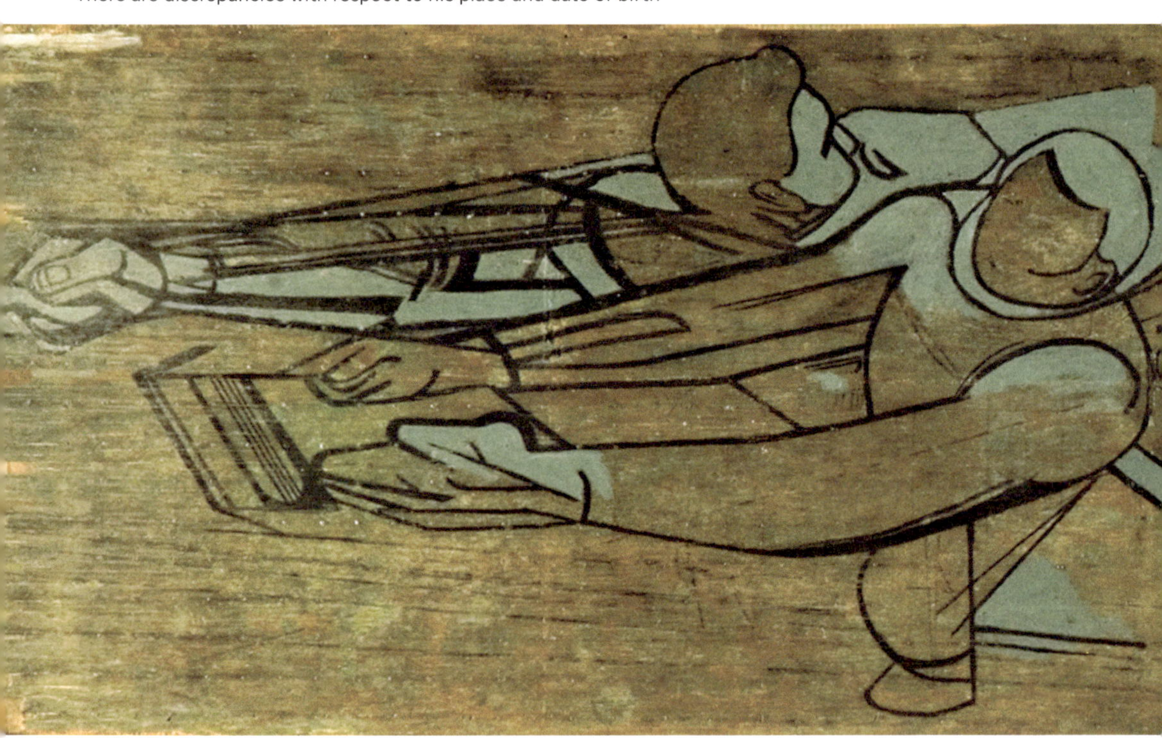

Siqueiros created a mural committee to create the pieces comissioned for Ciudad Universitaria. After negotiating with the architects of the building complex, he was hired to decorate all four façades of the Sala de Consejo Universitario at the Rectoría. This sketch corresponds to the south wall, the only one he finished: five students, bearing symbols of books and writing/drawing implements, deliver their knowledge to the people. The geometrical synthesis of the sketch marked the mural's inception from 1952 to 1954; in the latter year, the construction of mosaic-covered concrete volumes began. The incorporation of three-dimensional elements, which Siquieros defined as "sculpture-painting," as well as the mural's polyangular composition, built in relation to multiple vanishing points, sought to depict movement—especially for the cars driving along Insurgentes Avenue, in a simultaneous critique and appropriation of billboard advertisements.

J. G. M.

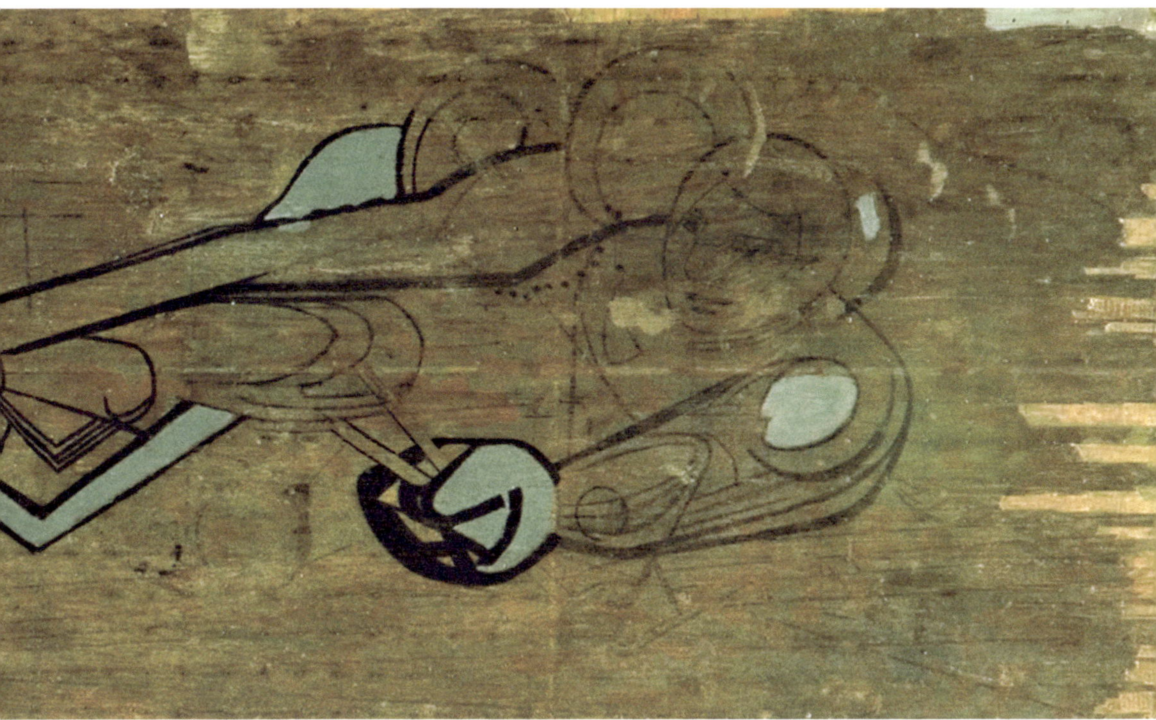

Francis Alÿs

—

Antwerp, Belgium, 1959

Colector, 1990–1992

In collaboration with Felipe Sanabria
6 magnetized metal dogs on wheels, video, photographs,
maps, sketches, and documentary materials
Variable dimensions
Acquisition, 2007

Francis Alÿs has grounded some of his artistic practice in movement and walks around the city. His wanderings and actions in public space offer new forms of contact with the urban sphere and are presented as a novel way of inhabiting and experiencing the environment.

Colector is the first project Alÿs created for a walking routine. First, he created a magnetic toy dog; the MUAC possesses the entire series of prototypes for this object. Then the artist brought the toy on various walks around downtown Mexico City. Along the way, scraps of metal from the street adhered to the dog, forming a kind of inventory. Following the surrealist logic of the found object, the residue acts as a social record, revealing aspects of the city's identity.

The piece would prompt the creation of *Zapatos magnéticos* [*Magnetic Shoes*] (Havana Biennial, 1994), in which the artist walked the streets of Havana wearing magnet-outfitted shoes.

V. R. L.

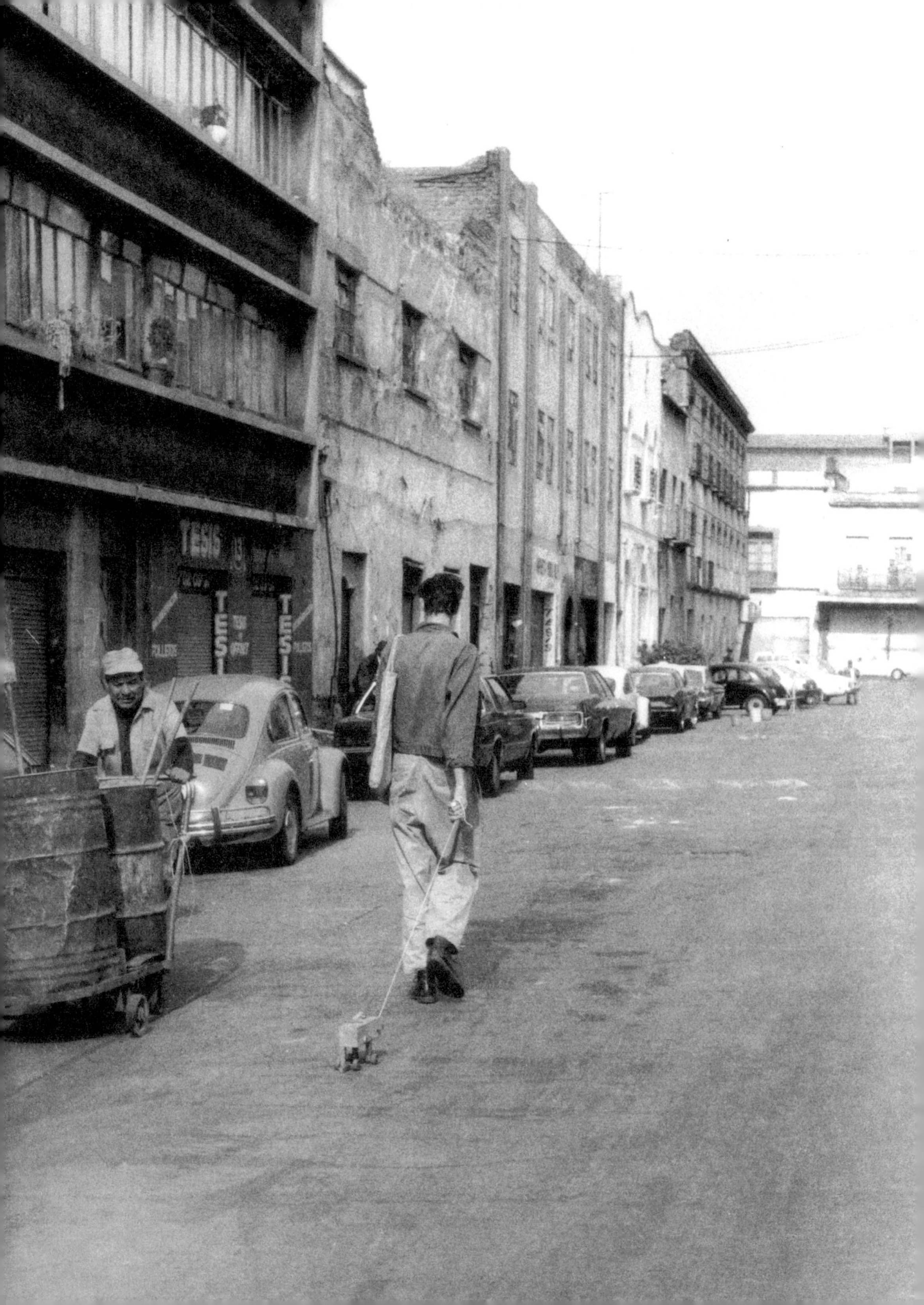
TESIS
TESIS

Francis Alÿs

—

Antwerp, Belgium, 1959

Zócalo, Ciudad de México, 22 de mayo, 1999
[***Zócalo, Mexico City, May 22, 1999***], 1999–2017

Video installation. 36 pieces
Color video, stereo sound, 2 speakers,
drawings and photographs
12 h
Ed. photograph: 1 AP + 7, ed. video: 1/2 AP + 4
Acquisition through the SHCP
Pago en Especie program, 2018

In the late twentieth century, Alÿs combined symbolic actions
and interventions based on urban routes by documenting sculptural social situations derived from the interplay among streets,
bodies, and objects. Most of these works took place in the privi-
leged theater of downtown Mexico City. Within this quadrant, the
symbolism of power clashes with a lifestyle that resists, in practice, to the authoritarian economic rationalization and the empire
of the motor vehicle by staging a different kind of modernity.

    Zócalo is the icon of how Alÿs transformed downtown Mexico
City into an extension of his art studio, as well as into a conceptual theater. On May 22, 1999, in collaboration with filmmaker
Rafael Ortega, Alÿs filmed the city's main square in order to
document a previously unconscious social form: the way in which
passers-by, seeking shelter in the shade cast by the flagpole,
form a human line that functions as a virtual sundial, which shifts
by three degrees every 12 hours of sunlight. This seeming mir-
acle has become an enduring image of contemporary art in the
region—and a key example of how Alÿs sought to transform
community life through the emergence of an urban myth.

C. M.

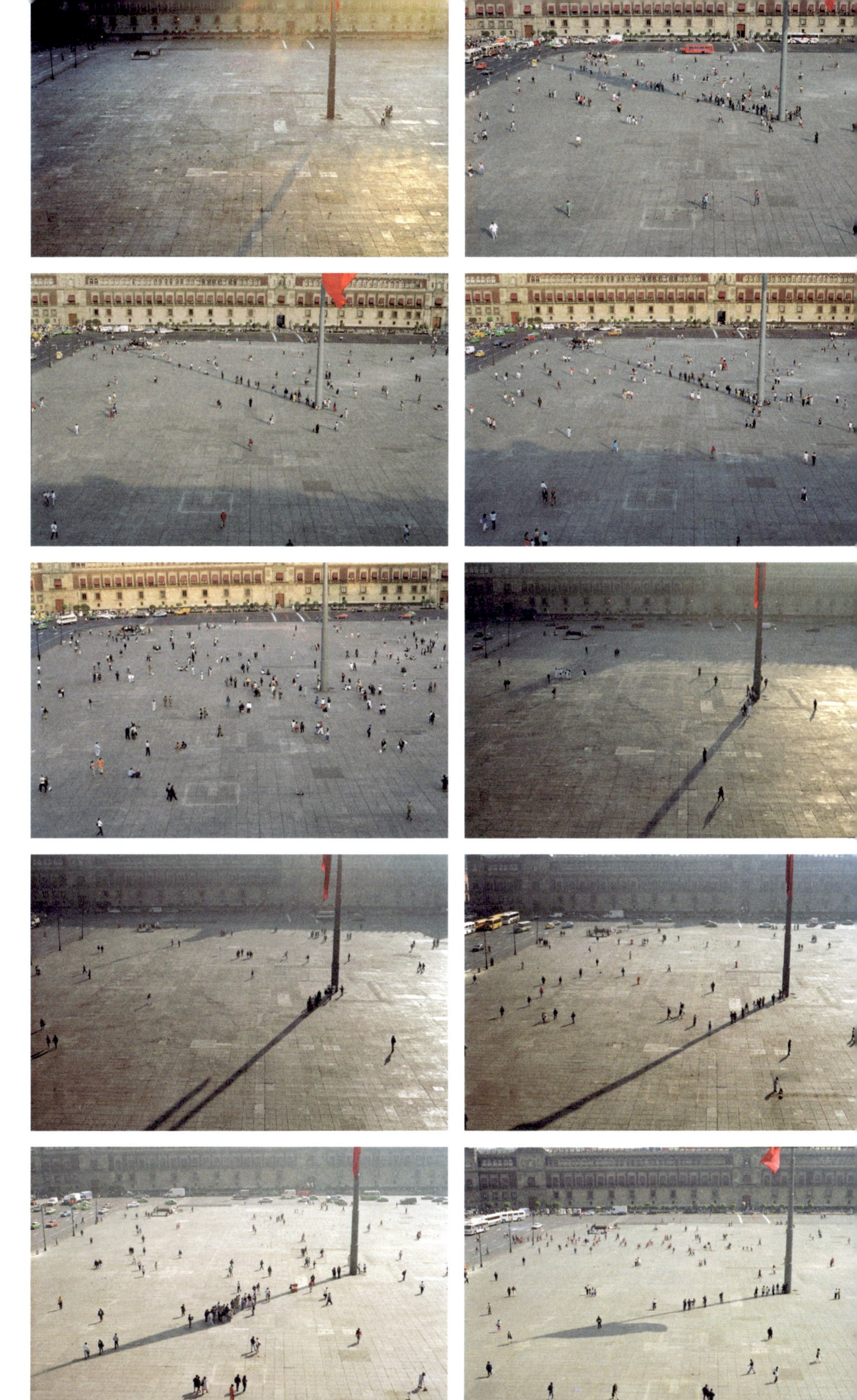

Carlos Amorales

Mexico City, Mexico, 1970

Drifting Star, 2001

Installation. 750 plexiglass hanging elements
Variable dimensions
Acquisition through the SHCP
Pago en Especie program, 2015

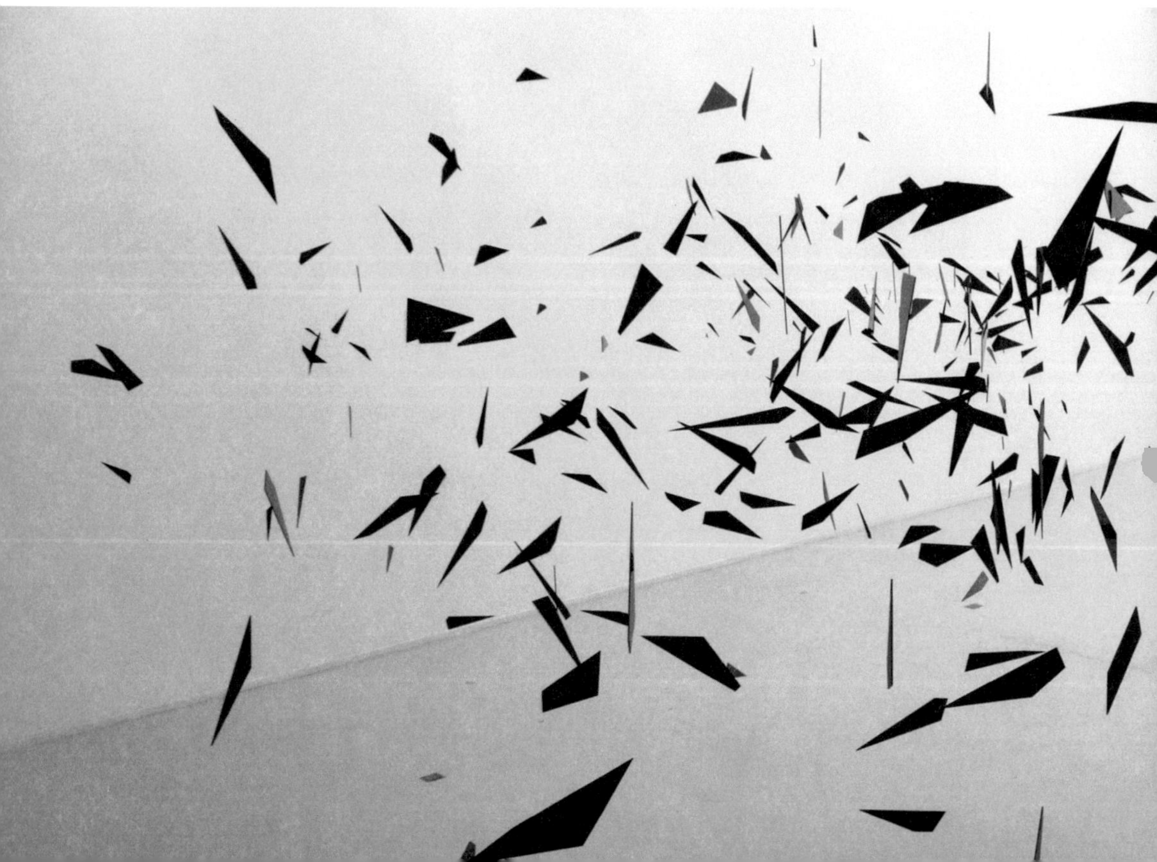

Starting in 1998, and for nearly two decades thereafter, Amorales developed most of his work through a database of vector drawings, which offered him a vocabulary both constrained in its elements and infinite in its possible variations and applications. The installation *Drifting Star* is especially illustrative of the different translation and production processes that emerged from this project. The hundreds of black Plexiglass pieces hanging in the exhibition hall bring the first scene of his video *Dark Mirror* (2004) into the viewer's space. This video, in turn, emerged from two acts of authorial transfer: the delegation of the artist's film, which is about an animator who made freewheeling use of the archive's vector images, and a pianist specialized in improvising incidental music for cinema. In this sense, *Drifting Star* should be experienced as a third- or fourth-generation appropriation, which nonetheless returns like a visual boomerang to an essential scene in Amorales's work on the twenty-first century: the cascades of rubble and glass forming sculptural nebulae in the 2001 attack on the Twin Towers, in New York.

C. M.

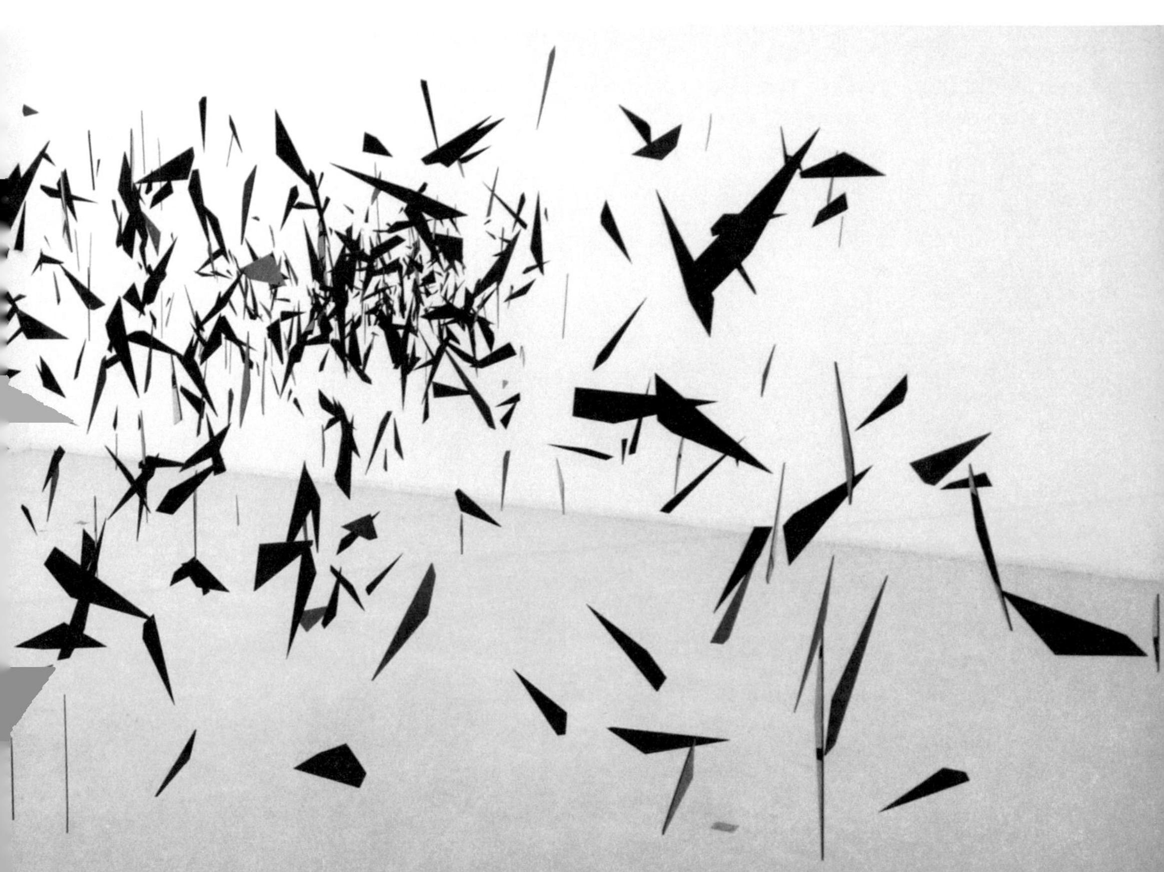

Carlos Amorales

Mexico City, Mexico, 1970

Veremos cómo todo reverbera [*We'll
See How Everything Reverberates*], 2012

Installation. 3 hanging mobiles with
cymbals. Steel, copper, and epoxy paint
570, 520, and 480 cm Ø
Ed. 1/3
Acquisition with funds from the Presupuesto
de Egresos de la Federación, 2016

Amorales made this mobile during a residency at Atelier Calder
in Saché, France, the American sculptor's final studio. The piece
does far more than reinterpret Calder's sculptural vision in terms
of an assembly of cymbals: in fact, it presents the spectator
with a non-predetermined situation, in which the artist does not
explicitly indicate whether the instrument should or shouldn't be
touched through the cowhides included in the installation. The
reverberation proposed by Amorales alludes both to the musical
instrument and to the evocation of Calder's work, as well as to
the transferal of decision-making onto the audience, which
must then confront and resolve—all by itself—both the prospect
of its freedom and the anxiety of its uncertainty.

C. M.

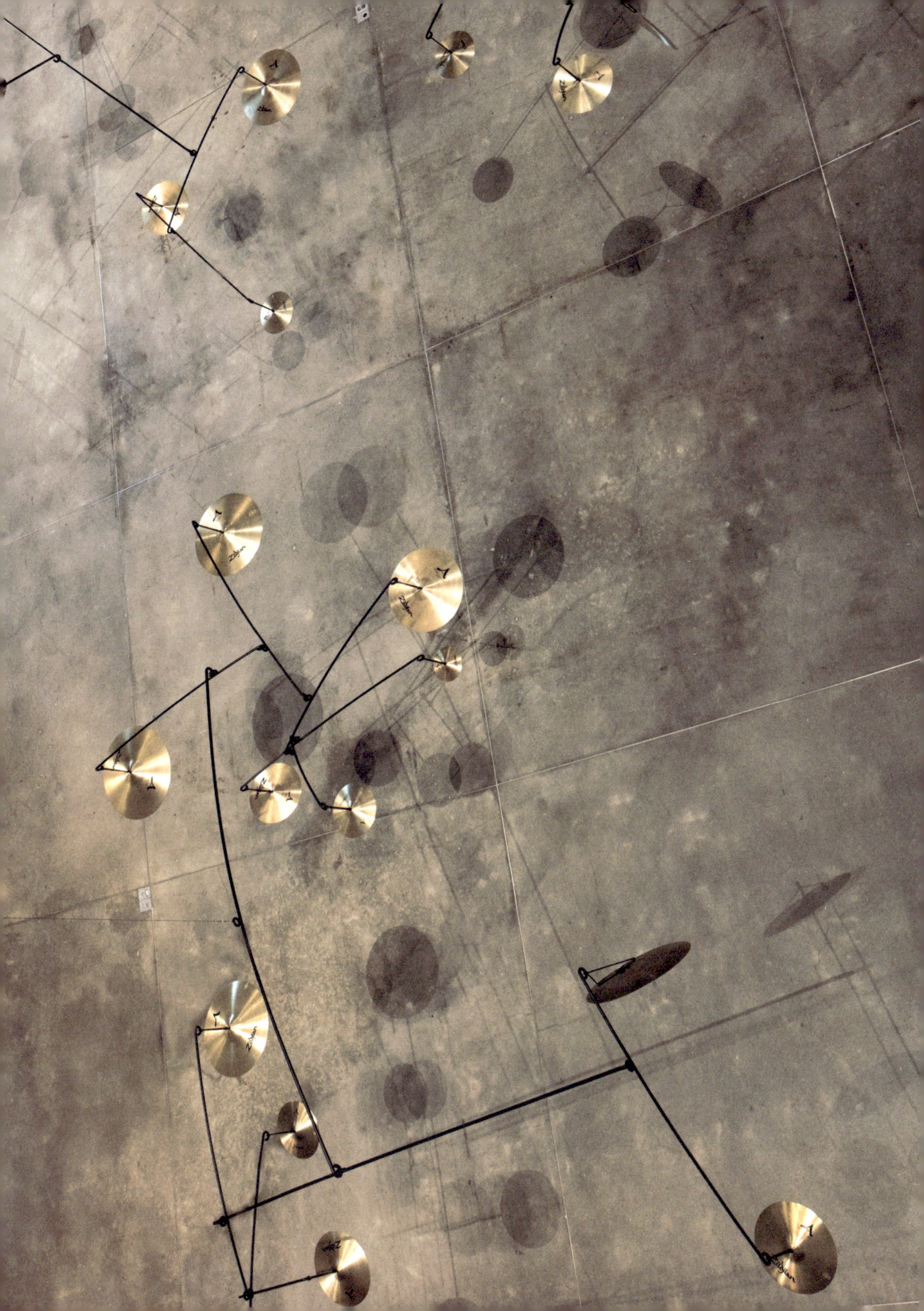

Julieta Aranda

—

Mexico City, Mexico, 1975

The Tale of the Tiger Is Longer
Than the Tiger's Tail, 2011

Installation. Resin, concrete, polymer-
filled cardboard, varnished wood, neon
lamp, wood with vinyl paint, bricks, mortar,
photo print on mirror, and metal plate
Variable dimensions
Acquisition with funds from the Presupuesto
de Egresos de la Federación, 2016

In this installation, Aranda addresses how the Televisa media
corporation has intervened in the indoctrination of Mexican
society, as well as the company's historical political affiliation
with the Mexican government. The metal plate in the installation
displays a quote from a 1993 speech in which Emilio "el Tigre"
Azcárraga cynically declared that the TV company only cared
about entertaining a "truly screwed lower class that will never be
less screwed." The loss of symbolic power undergone by Televisa,
Mexico's media empire and monopoly, is invoked by the way in
which its original logo is disassembled; its strips look piled-up
in space, like a heap of junk and remnants.

J. G. S.

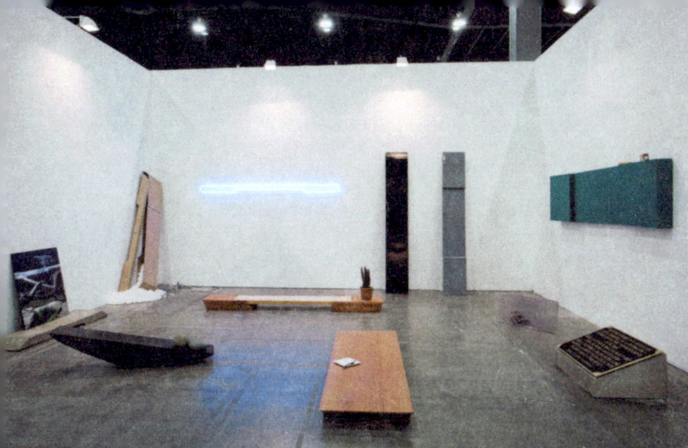

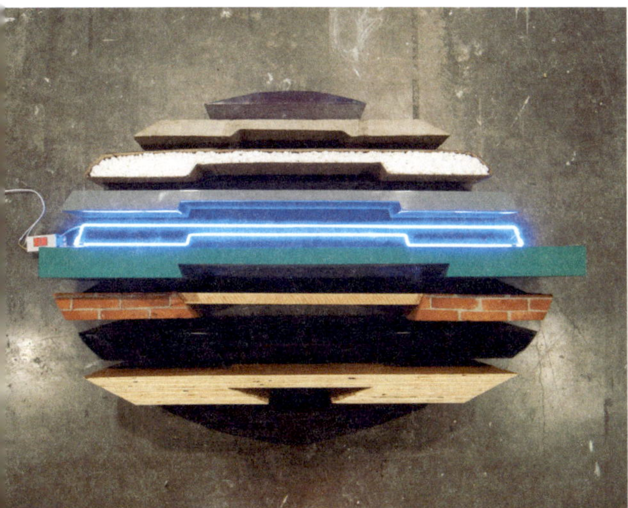

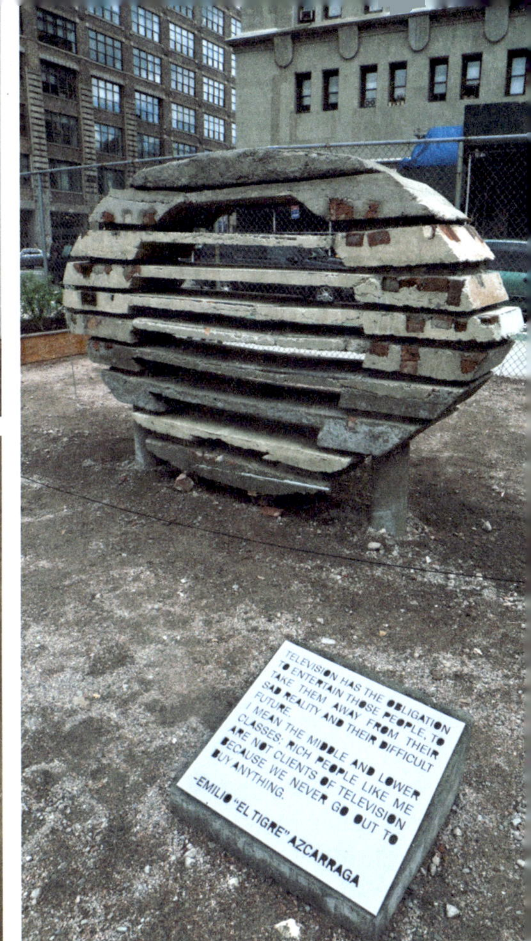

TELEVISION HAS THE OBLIGATION
TO ENTERTAIN THOSE PEOPLE, TO
TAKE THEM AWAY FROM THEIR
SAD REALITY AND THEIR DIFFICULT
FUTURE. THE MIDDLE AND LOWER
CLASSES: RICH PEOPLE LIKE ME
ARE NOT CLIENTS OF TELEVISION
BECAUSE WE NEVER GO OUT TO
BUY ANYTHING.
-EMILIO "EL TIGRE" AZCARRAGA

Carlos Arias Vicuña

Santiago, Chile, 1964

Familia [*Family*], 1995–1996

Embroidery on cloth
174 × 105 cm
Gift of the artist, 2016

Since the 1990s, Carlos Arias Vicuña shifted from painting to embroidery to question two fundamental phenomena: genre, in the sense of artistic disciplines, and the sexual gender of representation. *Familia* depicts identity as a set of knotted threads: the bond of the umbilical cord that connects the child's bodily fluids to the image of a phallic mother, suggesting the impossibility of escaping the flow of genealogical ghosts and identifications. An allegory of the painful path that always tries to return to the source, helpless to stop connecting the artistic with the sexual, and the political.

C. M.

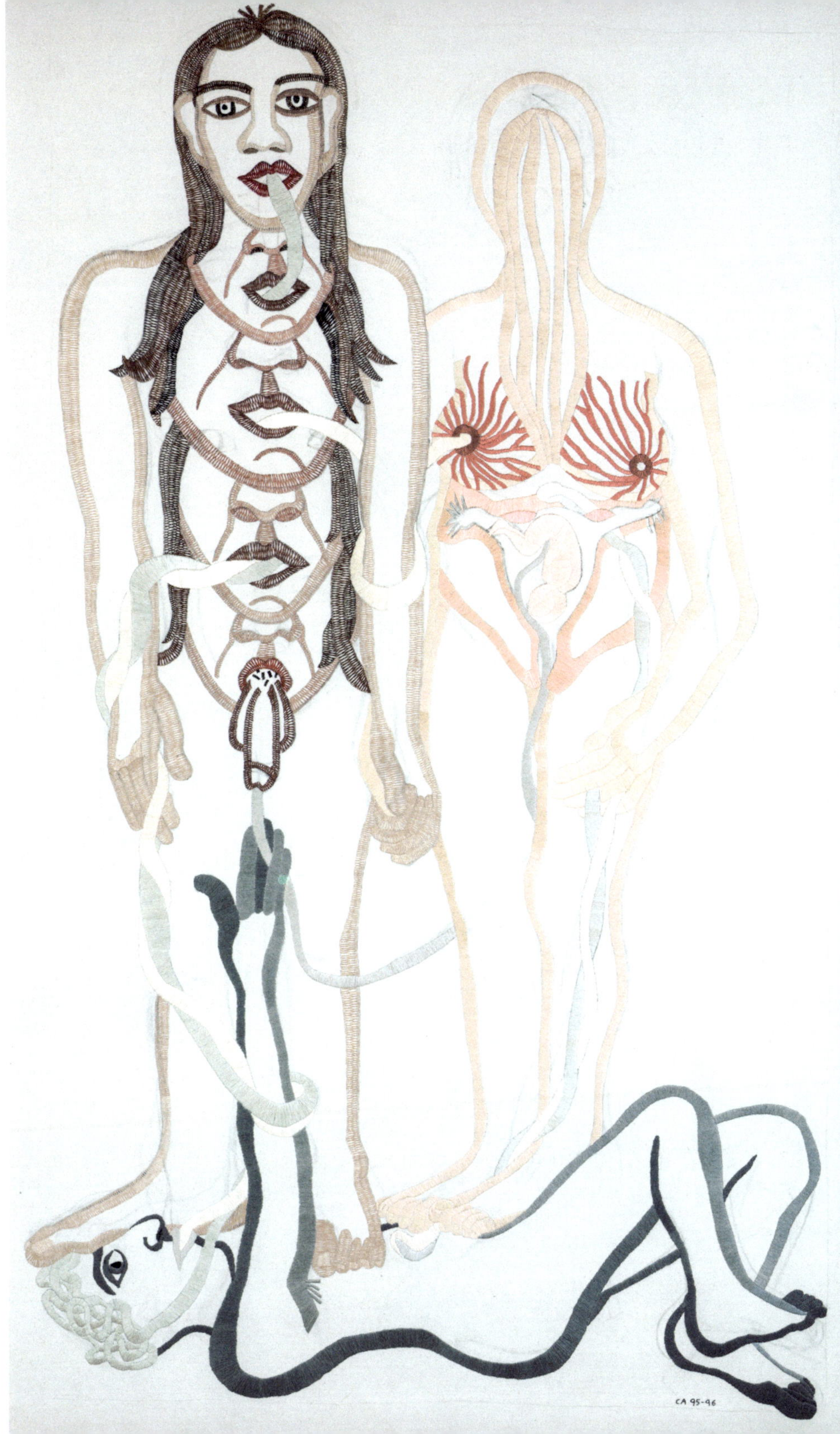
CA 95-96

Marcela Armas

Durango, Mexico, 1976

Exhaust, 2009

Video recording and photographic print
5' 50"
91.2 × 115 cm
Edition 1 ⁄ 3
Acquisition through the SHCP
Pago en Especie program, 2015

In the late 2000s, several of Armas's pieces incorporated the presence of fossil fuels as forces acting on the urban landscape. In *Exhaust,* a plastic wrapper inflates with gas produced by the combustion of six cars, its structure taking the form of a vehicular bridge. Armas is part of a generation of artists who explore technology as a material basis for their work, seeking to understand both its collaborative possibilities and the danger it poses to human beings. In this series, she conjures the implications of our habits and logics of consumption amid the everyday violence enacted on the environment we inhabit.

A. L.

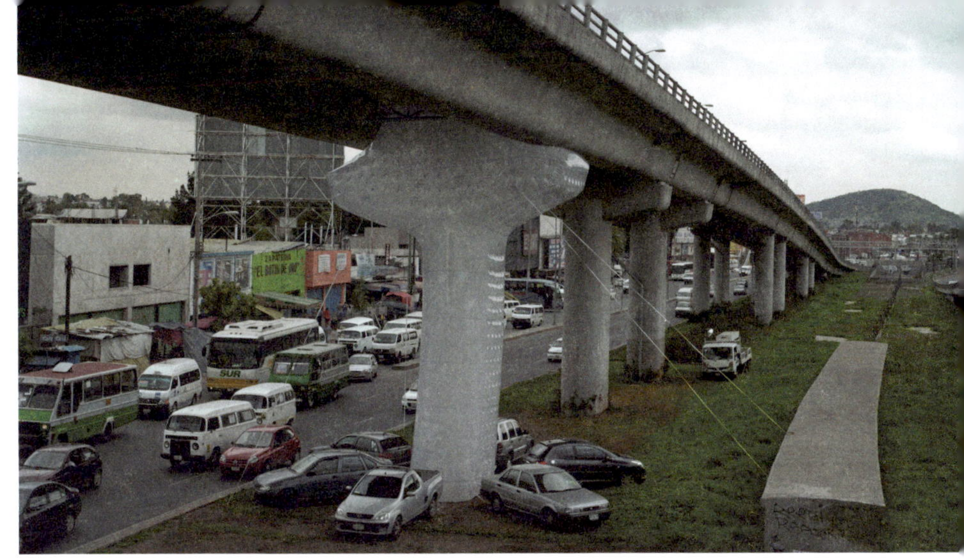

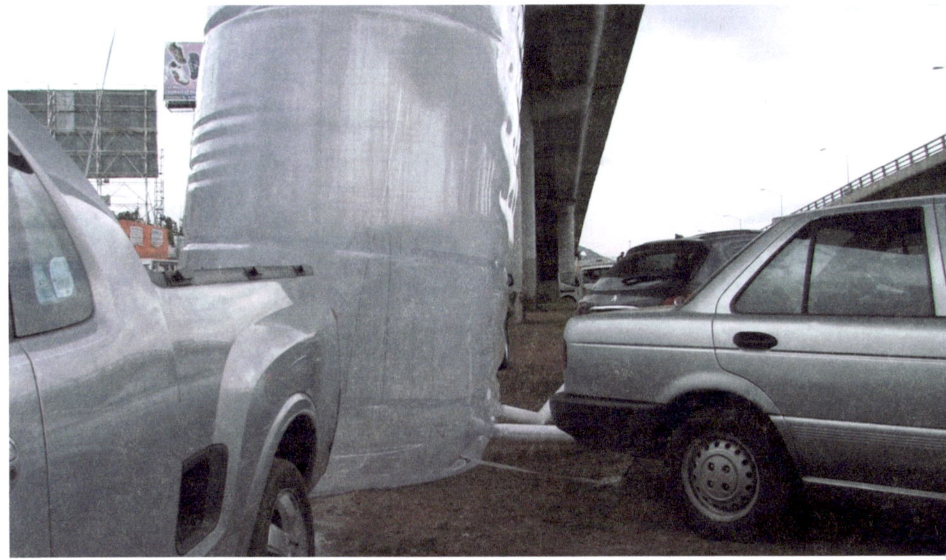

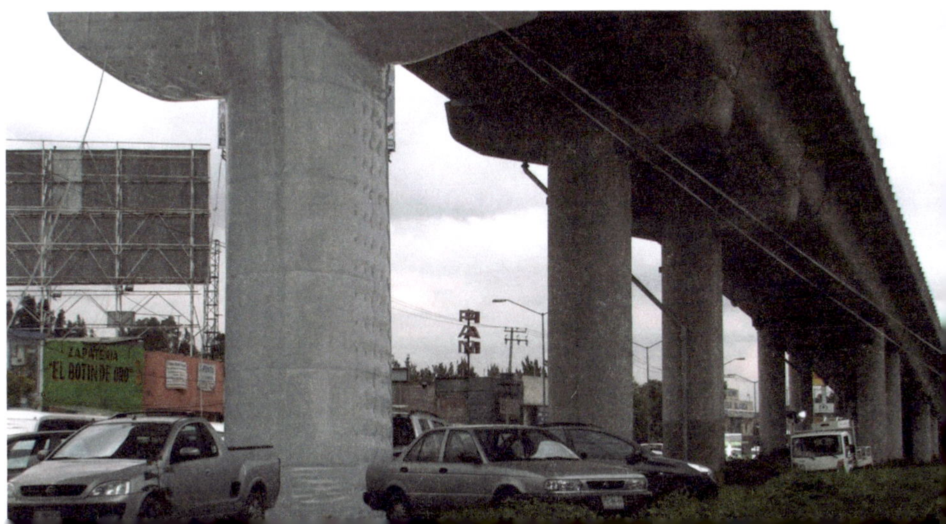

François and Bernard Baschet

Paris, France, 1920–2014; Paris, France, 1917–2015

Monumento de percusión. Escultura musical
[***Percussion Monument: Musical Sculpture***], 1964

Aluminum sheets and metal rods
330 × 400 × 200 cm
Gift of the artists, 1968

Monumento de percusión combines three innovative aspects of
the 1960s art scene: questioning the object, experimenting with
sound, and audience participation. The goal of French sculptor
François Baschet and his brother Bernard, a sound engineer, was
to expand the territory of music into new sound formats that
would more faithfully reproduce nature, the industrial era, and
the ambient noise of major cities.

Following John Cage's precepts on the need to test our ears'
immediate experience, the Baschet brothers turned to materials rarely found in musical sculptures (glass grilles, metal bars
as vibration elements, aluminum-sheet amplifiers, and plastic
balloons) so as to foster a complex experience of the sound
spectrum. Here, metals could be rubbed with wet fingers,
cotton swabs, and rubber-coated drumsticks, not simply struck.
The common denominator of these experiences was the viewer's
own participation in discovering new kinds of sound.

Monumento de percusión was part of the exhibition *Estructuras
musicales* [*Musical Structures*] at the UNAM's Museo de Ciencias
y Arte in March 1966, following a stint at MoMA in New York.
Monumento de percusión joined the museum collection after
this exhibition.

P. G.

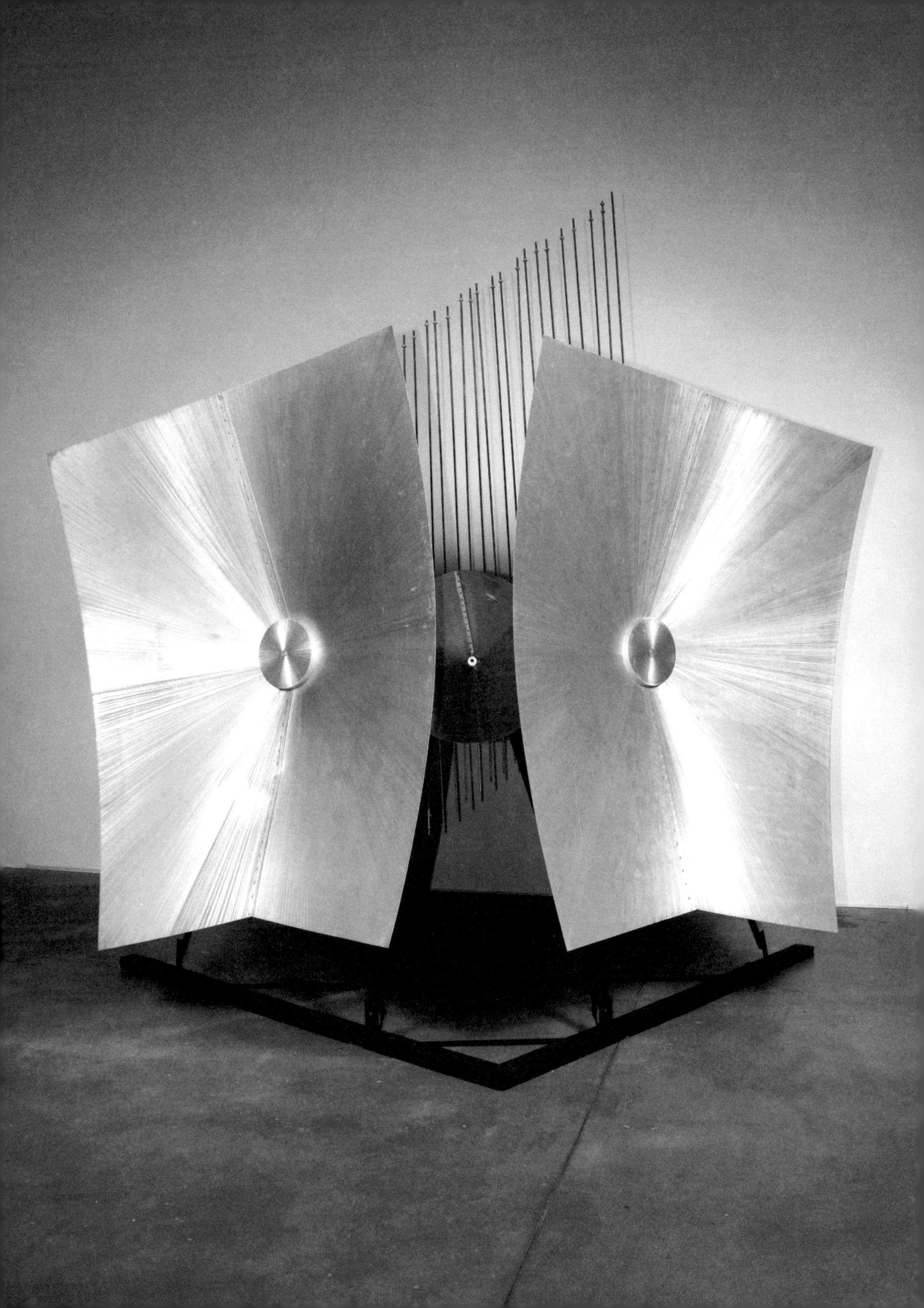

Erick Beltrán

—

Mexico City, Mexico, 1974

Atlas Eidolon, 2014

Installation. 1100 PVC photographs, spherical
metal structure, 14 photocopied diagrams
Variable dimensions
Gift of the artist, 2016

This piece was inspired by the systems at work in the art of
Medieval and Renaissance memory, such as *Ars combinandi,*
by Ramón Llull and Giordano Bruno, and the image theory put
forth by Aby Warburg, the pioneer of iconology, in his *Atlas
Mnemosyne*. In contrast to these ancient models of memory,
however, Beltrán replaces magical and astral symbols with public
figures, placing the viewer inside the debate over the repetition
of political models and their appearance in the public sphere.
The piece is structured as a dynamic sculpture with a system of
revolving rings, their concentric movements producing repetitive,
hypnotic visual effects, and a series of diagrams with images
and animations that form a pavilion. Its objective is to display
the networks of power and genealogy of the Enrique Peña Nieto
presidency (2012–2018).

In this reading machine, diagrams and animations constitute
a system of persistent image-mapping in which a certain order
of appearance and the rearrangement of the journalistic archive
activate the collective psyche. In doing so, they show how the
actors in the Mexican political system, even when the individual
officials change, are a ghostly formula that comes back to life
with every new presidency—in such a way that history continually
repeats itself. The piece was produced specifically for the Museo
Tamayo, and its presentation was subject to questioning and
political interference.

M. A.

Detail

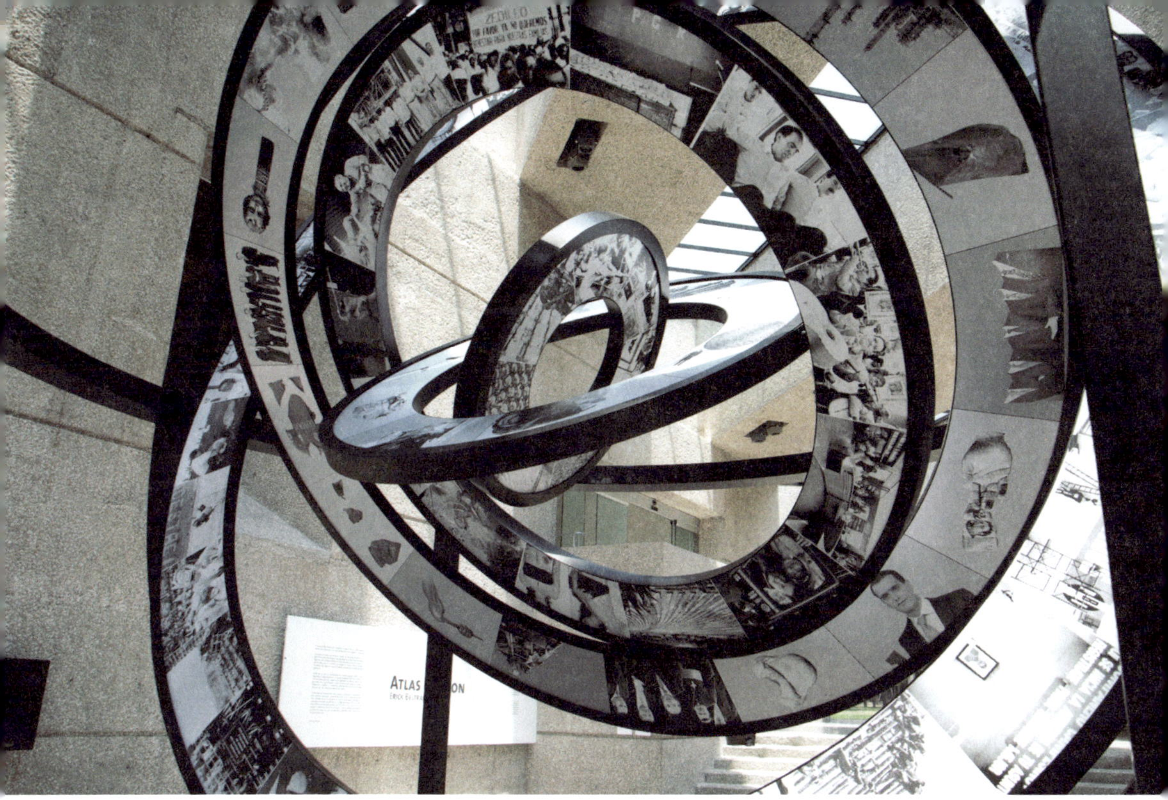

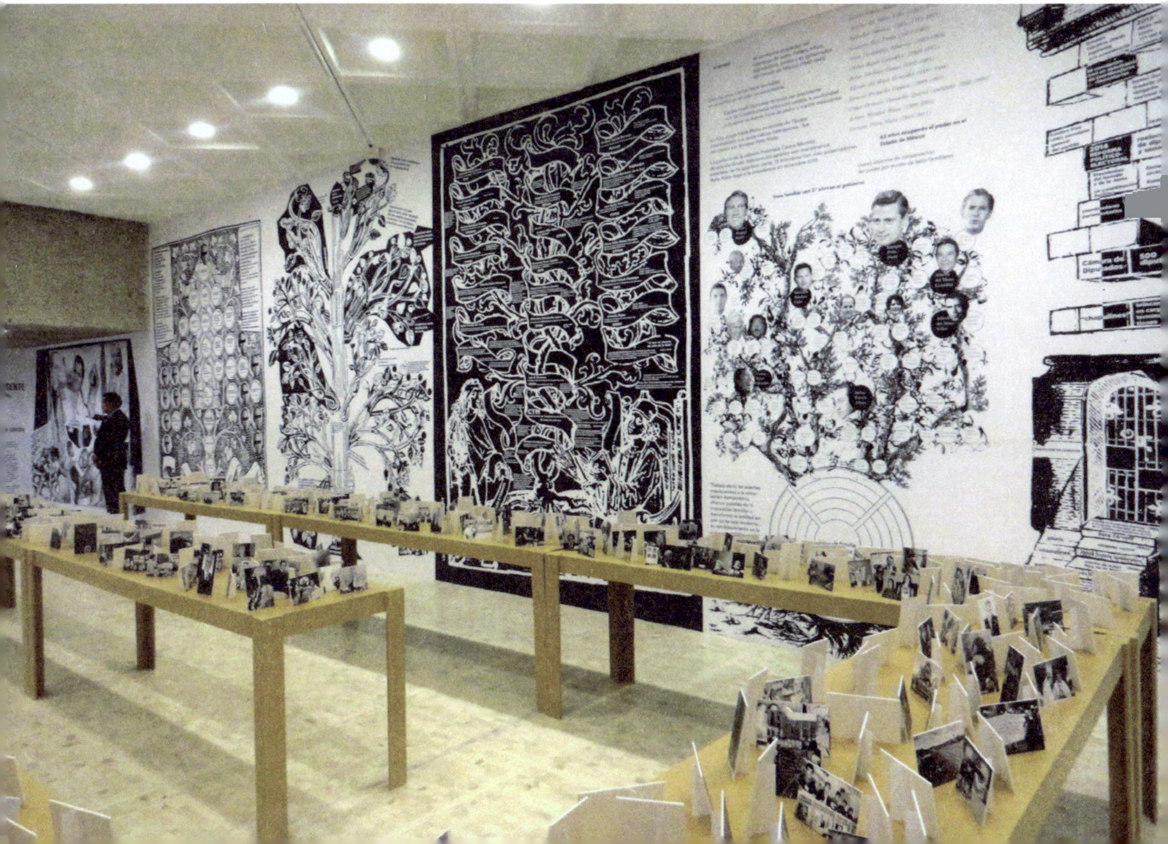

Maris Bustamante

Mexico City, Mexico, 1949

El pene como instrumento de trabajo
[*para quitarle a Freud lo macho*]
[*The Penis as an Instrument of Labor/*
To Make Freud Un-Macho], 1982

Mask. Print on cardboard
42.2 × 25 cm
Fondo No-Grupo, Centro de Documentación
Arkheia MUAC (DiGAV-UNAM)
Acquisition, 2012

Combining humor with provocation, Maris Bustamente's many feminist works are representative of the No-Grupo in its final stage. This mask was used by Bustamante at a *Montaje de Momentos Plásticos* [*Exhibition of Visual Moments*]. Acerbically and incisively challenging the phallocracy and prevailing sexism, it constitutes the artist's response to the Freudian theory of "penis envy." The work is now rightly considered an artistic milestone of gender critique in Mexico.

S. H.

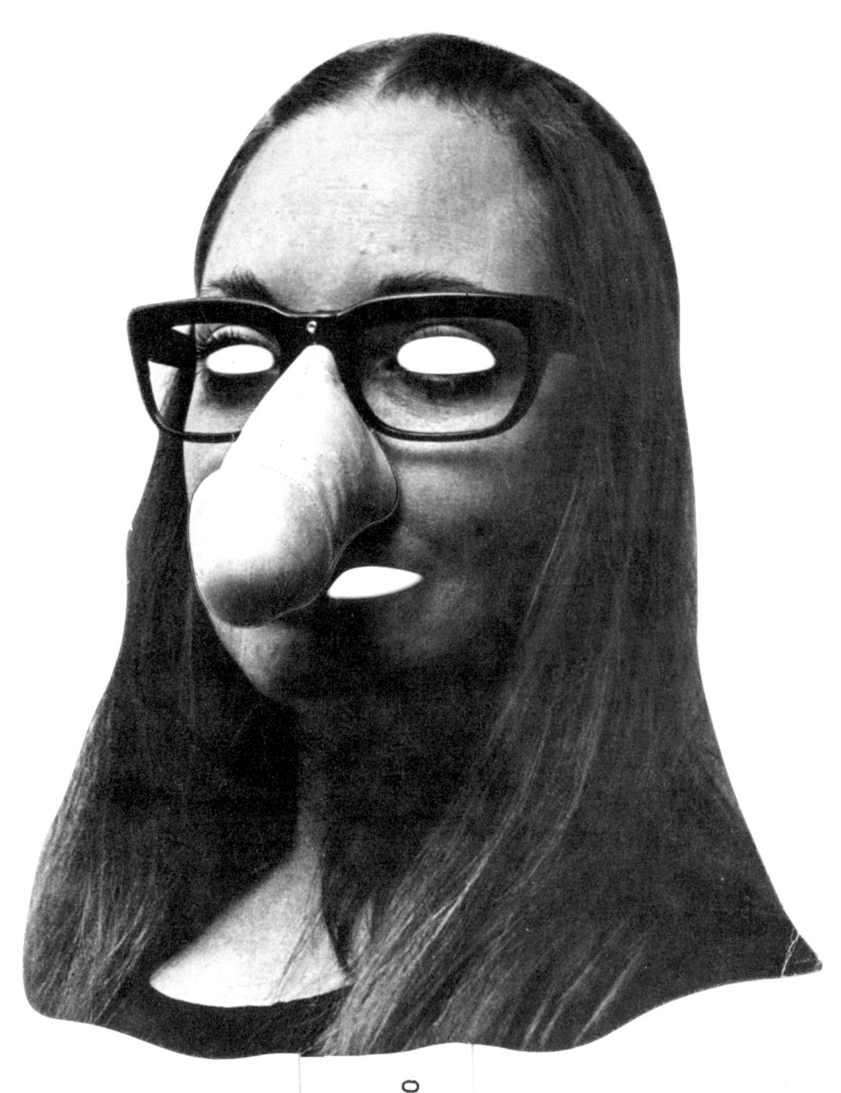

maris bustamante
DEL NO GRUPO

Tania Candiani

Mexico City, Mexico, 1974

Pausa [*Pause*], 2012

Video installation. Single-channel video
divided into 2 screens, stereophonic sound.
4:3 format, and 18 typed pages
Typed pages: 31 x 24.5 cm each
Acquisition through the SHCP
Pago en Especie program, 2018

A group of writers convened by Candiani tell stories directly into
the ear of a scribe, who takes down each narrative by hand as a
first draft, a translation process that culminates in a final type-
written version and in the artist's own video record.

This project combines Candiani's fascination with oral history
and cartographies of memory with her research, driven by her
interest in obsolescence and technological reminiscence, into
artifacts and machines. Characteristically, many of these works
involve sound materials. In fact, the artist had already documented the figure of the scribe for her action *Otras narrativas*
[*Other Narratives*] (2009), in which she used a sewing machine to
record the words whispered by spectators to their lovers during
intercourse. In *Pausa,* the main sound emission comes from the
scribe's hands and the typewriter. The image shifts from an initial
frontal shot of the two participants, where the writer is speaking,
to other shots in which their bodies disappear and the written
language is relegated to background: we can't make out more
than a scattering of words, and we have no access to the scribe's
final interpretation of the story. In any case, Candiani offers
us the dance of the typewriter keys as a way to access sound,
including the silences that allude to the act of thought.

A. L.

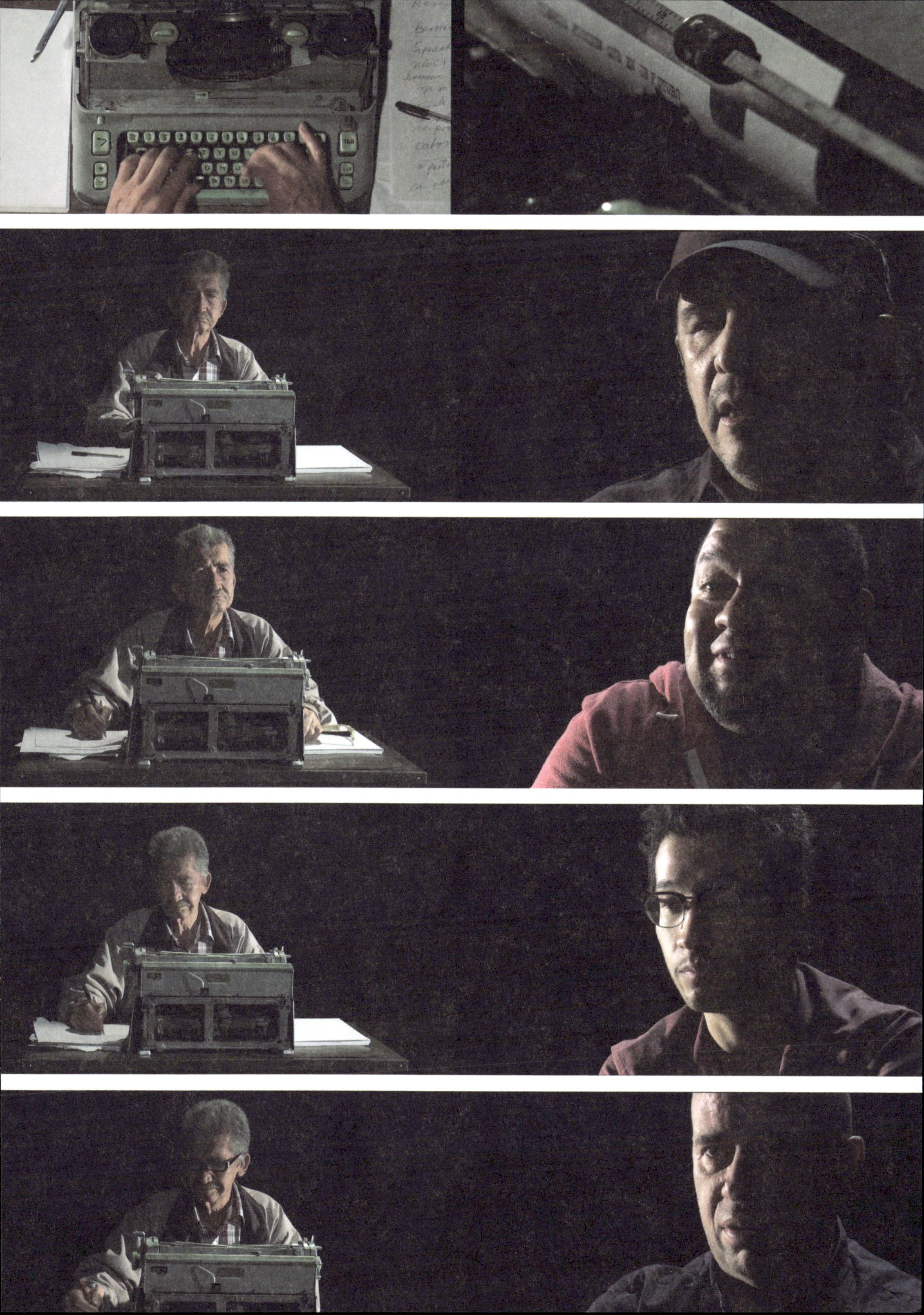

Mónica Castillo

Mexico City, Mexico, 1961

Tríptico [*Triptych*], 1990

Oil on canvas with tinplate frame
55 × 132 × 25 cm
Gift of Rocío Mireles, 2020

The series *Presentación en sociedad* explores the boundaries
between painting and installation by addressing the archetypes of femininity and its rituals, such as the celebration of
quinceañeras. The iconography of the crown of thorns, evoking
the humiliation and the wound of the Catholic Passion to which
female bodies are also subjected, joins the object that frames
the painted image to intensify the iconic correlation between
the frame itself and sharp-edged objectuality. At the same time,
it addresses the self-portrait as yet another setting of patriarchal
and heteronormative violence.

M. A.

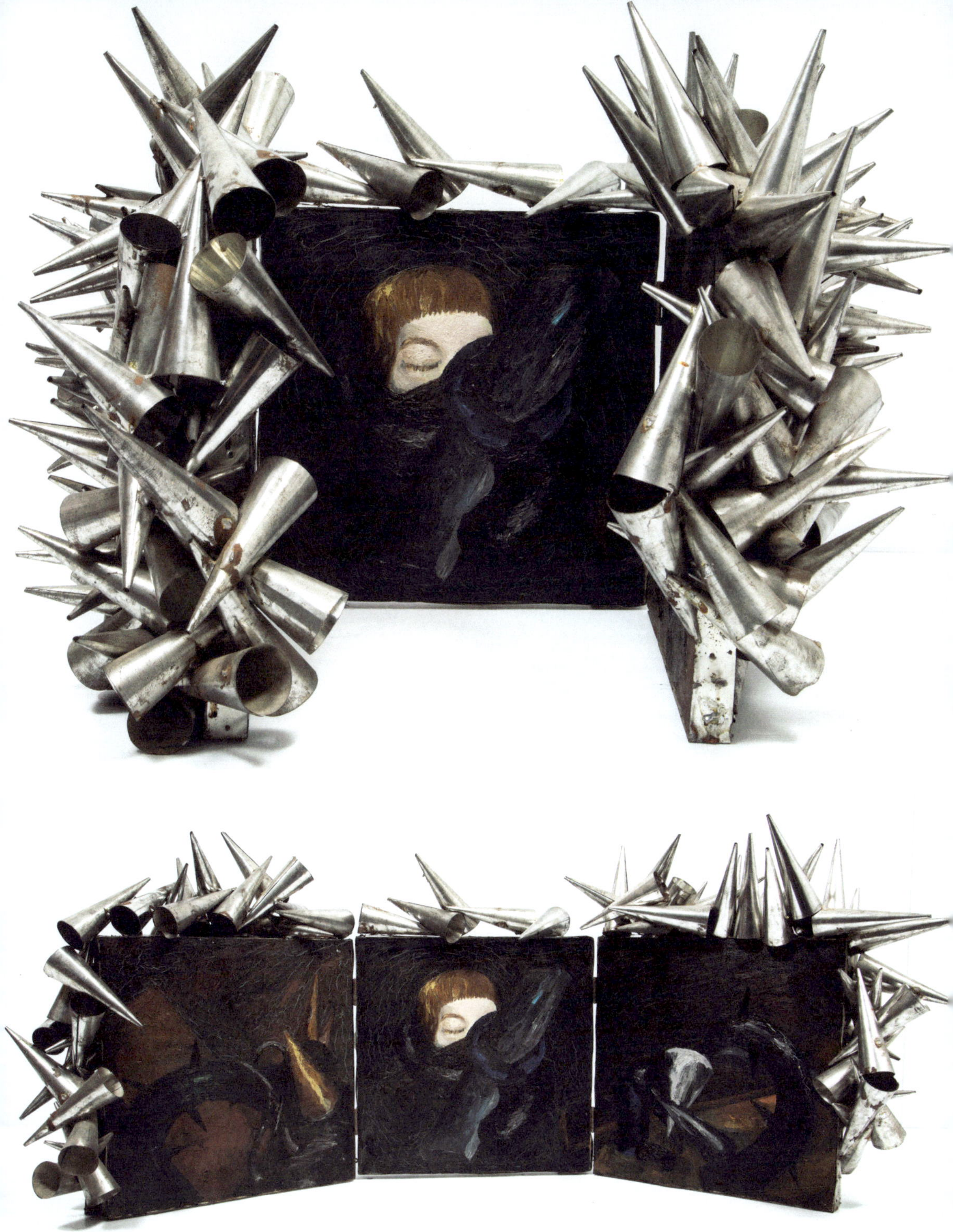

Miguel Castro Leñero

Mexico City, Mexico, 1956

Barco [*Ship*], 1997

Oil on canvas
160 × 160 cm
Acquisition, 1999

Juan García Ponce praised Miguel Castro Leñero for his "pictures in which the painting shows the painting." Castro Leñero typically counterposes images made with pure, elemental strokes onto surfaces created through accidents and exercises with the material itself. The association they awaken is innocent, idyllic. In the words of Alberto Blanco: "There is nothing to understand: it's enough to look with your eyes wide open. Or, if you will, you need to approach what's there to understand with a child's fresh gaze." *Barco* dates from the period when Castro Leñero's work found special relevance among Mexican audiences and markets, in the sense that it suggested an emancipation from all cultural and political impositions.

C. M.

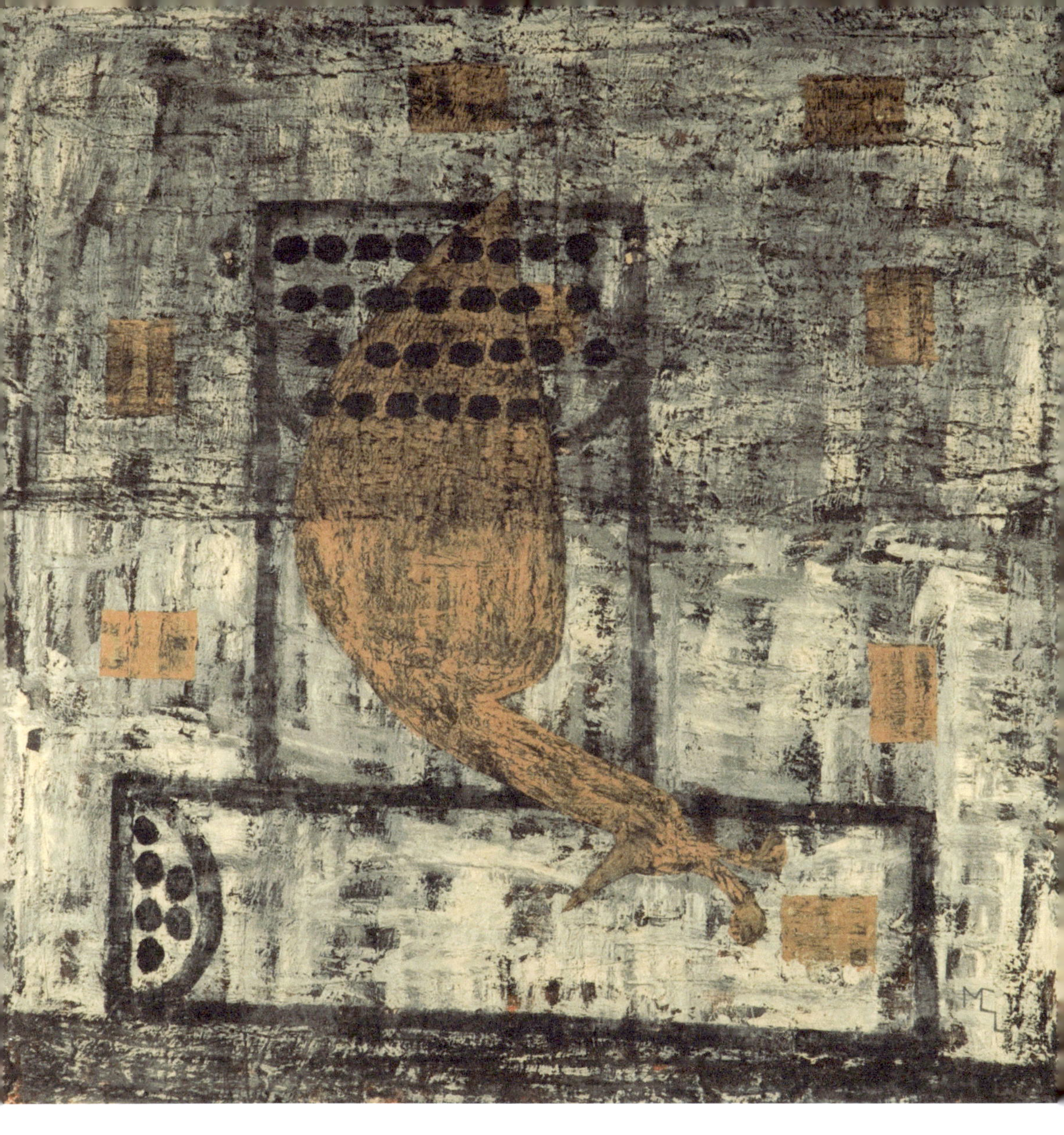

Arnaldo Coen

Mexico City, Mexico, 1940

El comienzo, el cimiento, la simiente latente
[*The Beginning, the Basis, the Latent Seed*], 1968

3 elements. Acrylic on wood
184.5 × 21 × 21.5 cm
Acquisition through the SHCP
Pago en Especie program, 2014

In 1967, after a trip to Paris, Arnaldo Coen invoked a recurring element in his work: the female torso. The visible faces of this three-dimensional piece, which consists of 3 wooden prisms piled up on top of each other, exemplify his obsession. Each side reveals a different sculptural treatment of the torso, with flat colors and geometric elements consistent with pop and op: visual vocabularies that the artist would incorporate into his work in the late '60s and '70s.

The piece is strikingly playful, allowing the viewer to rearrange all parts and faces to produce different combinations. It shares an affinity with the structuralist exploration that its title borrows from the first lines of *Blanco* (1967) by Octavio Paz.

A. d. C.

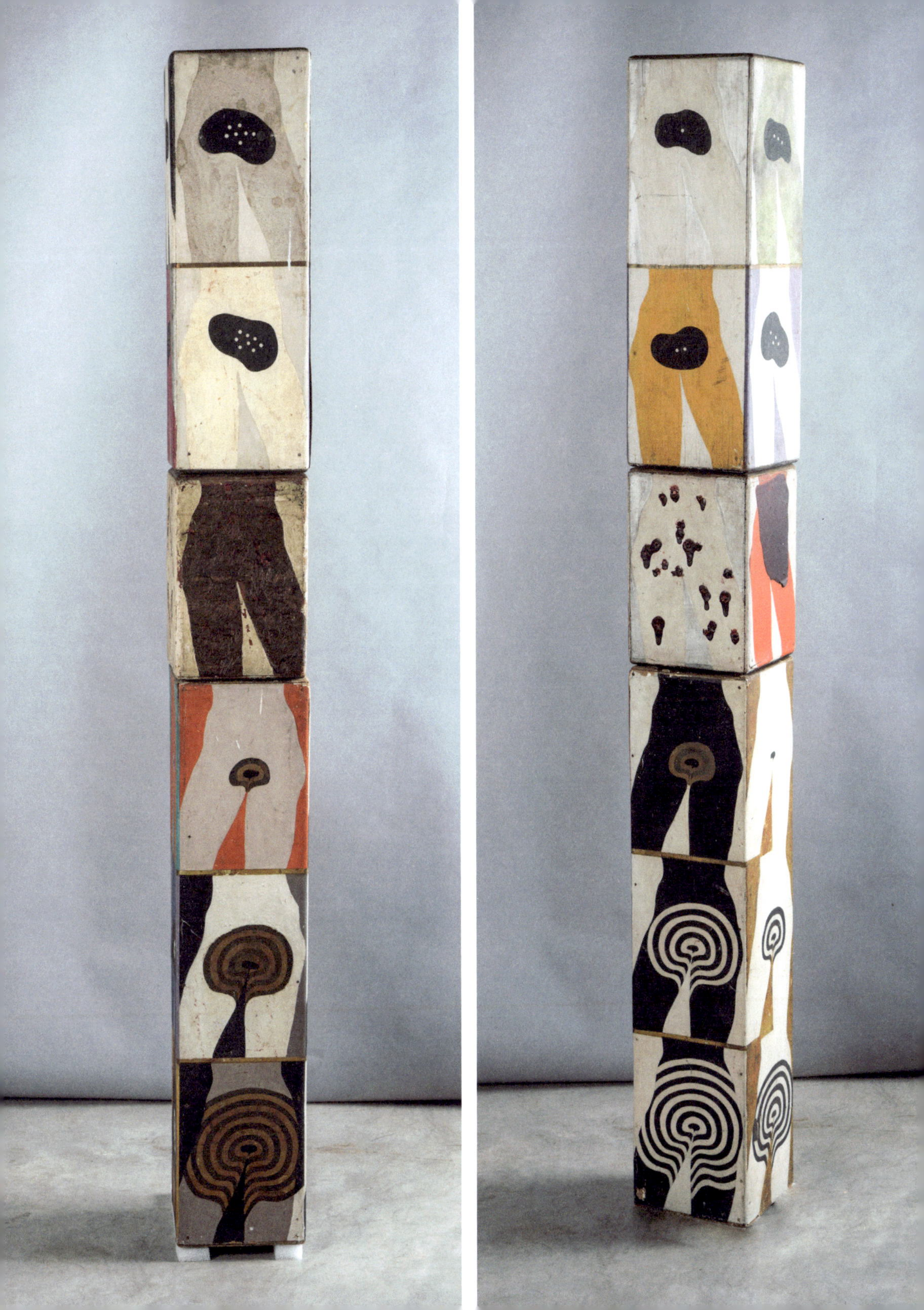

Armando Cristeto Patiño

Mexico City, Mexico, 1957

Untitled, 1978–1979

From the series *El condón* [*The Condom*]
Gelatin silver print
20.5 × 11 cm
Acquisition with funds from the Presupuesto
de Egresos de la Federación, 2013

Throughout his career as a photographer, Cristeto has explored and documented the affective dimension of youth communities and homosexual eroticism. This series shows male bodies without necessarily revealing the identity of each subject, spotlighting instead the prophylactics they hold and handle. With this series, made long before the so-called "AIDS crisis," the photographer heralded the role of latex in the new sexual reality that began with the onset of the pandemic, which first hit Mexico in 1983. Here, Cristeto perceptively spotlights the condom as the inter-face between prevention and an aseptic enjoyment of sexuality.

S. H.

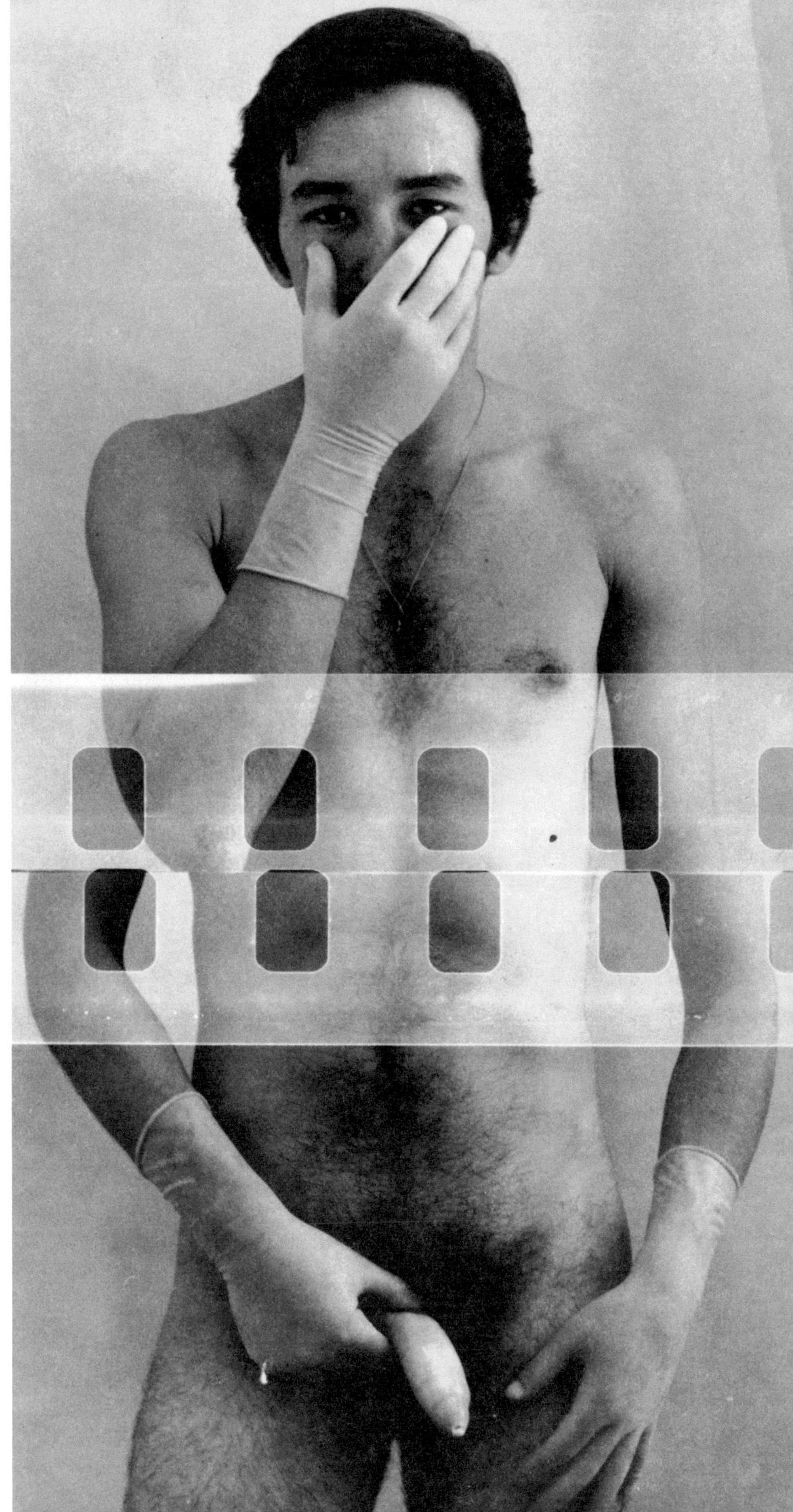

Minerva Cuevas

Mexico City, Mexico, 1975

Arqueología política
[*Political Archaeology*], 2000

16 digital prints on rigid
aluminum structure
60 × 40 cm each
Ed. 1/3
Acquisition, 2007

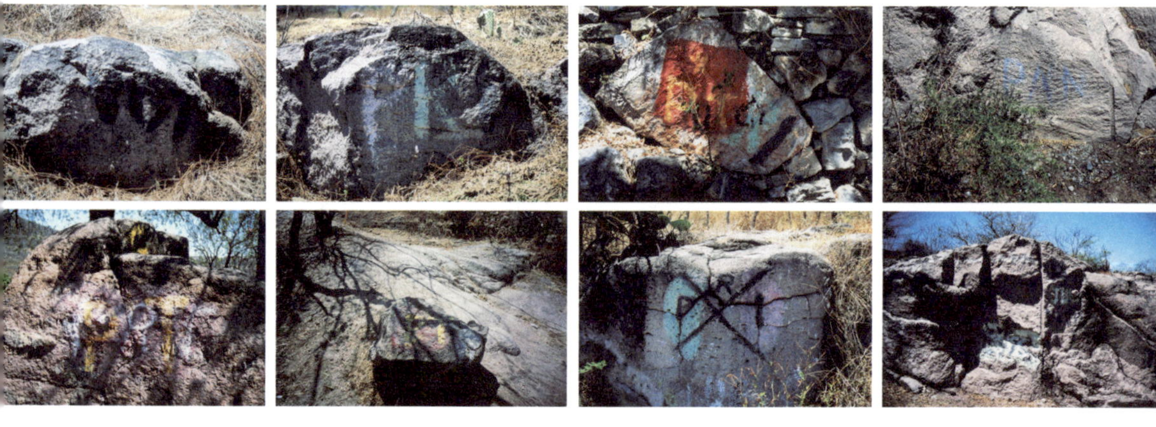

Grounded in humor and criticism, the work of Minerva Cuevas has often appropriated the language of advertising to introduce critical content into the circulation and saturation of images in consumer society.

In *Arqueología política,* the artist photographed a series of signs and emblems for Mexican political parties that had been painted on rocks, a longstanding form of political advertising in public spaces. The images, taken in states near Mexico City, are from 2000, just before Vicente Fox of the Partido Acción Nacional was elected to the presidency.

In a country where partisanship is measured in almost filial loyalty, seeing these blotted-out traces set against humdrum landscapes invites us to rethink the role of politics and its association with citizenship and the imaginary.

V. R. L.

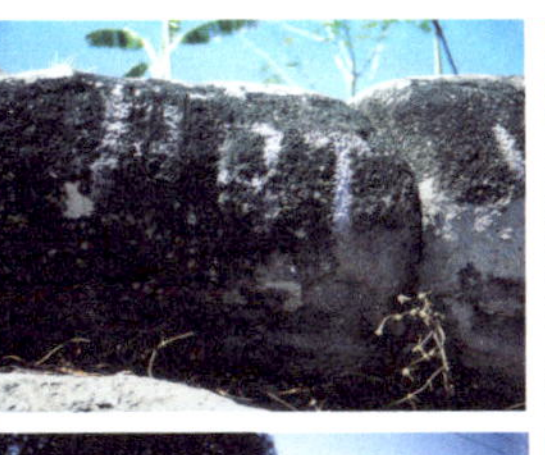
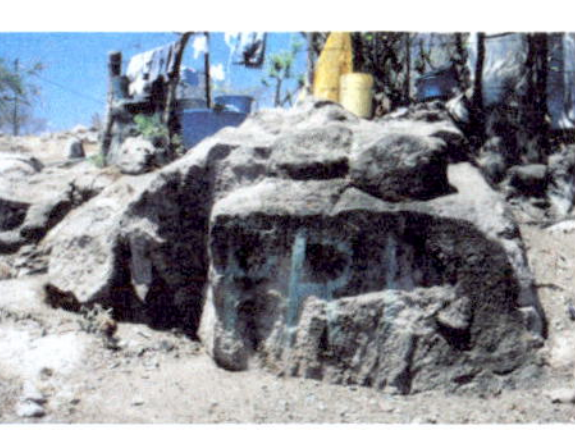
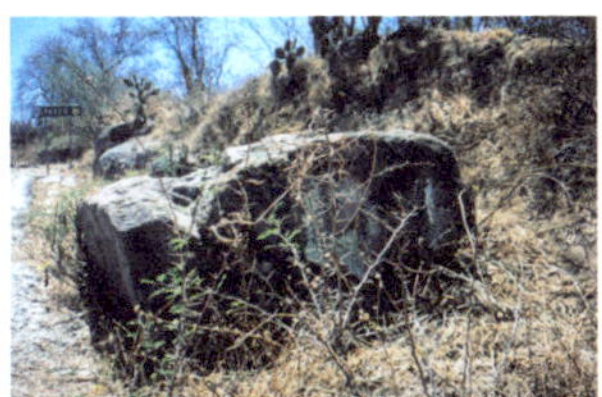
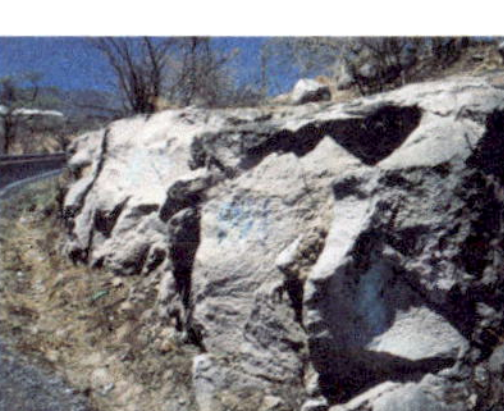
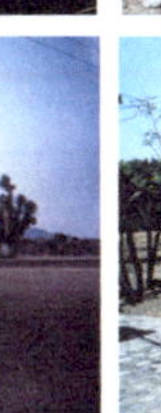

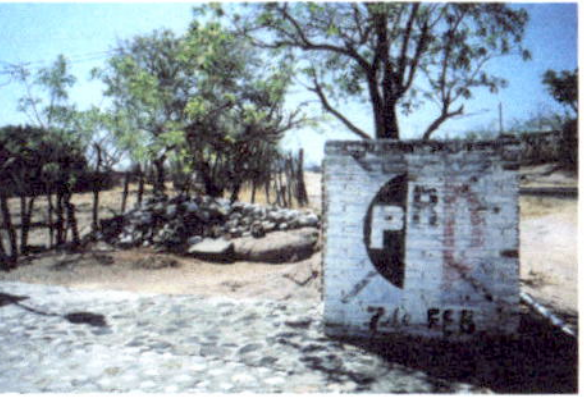

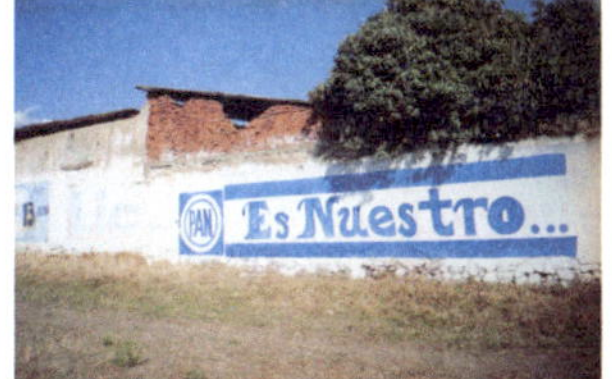

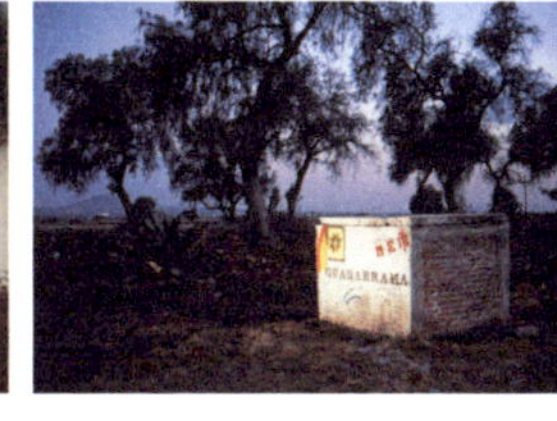

Ximena Cuevas

Mexico City, Mexico, 1963

Natural Instincts, 1999

From the series *Dormimundo*
DVD video
3' 6"
Acquisition with funds from the Presupuesto
de Egresos de la Federación, 2013

This video uses material from Mexican television to fashion a horror musical, encapsulating the racism deeply entrenched in national culture. Inserted into a billboard, the images of a screaming mother—horrified at the sight of her newborn's dark skin—become a mirror. The piece is part of the series *Dormimundo,* in which Cuevas employs humor and parody to address the lies we tell ourselves as a society. In this case, the work explores the "whitening" fantasies that accompanied the aspirational cultural of neoliberalism in the late twentieth century.

A. L.

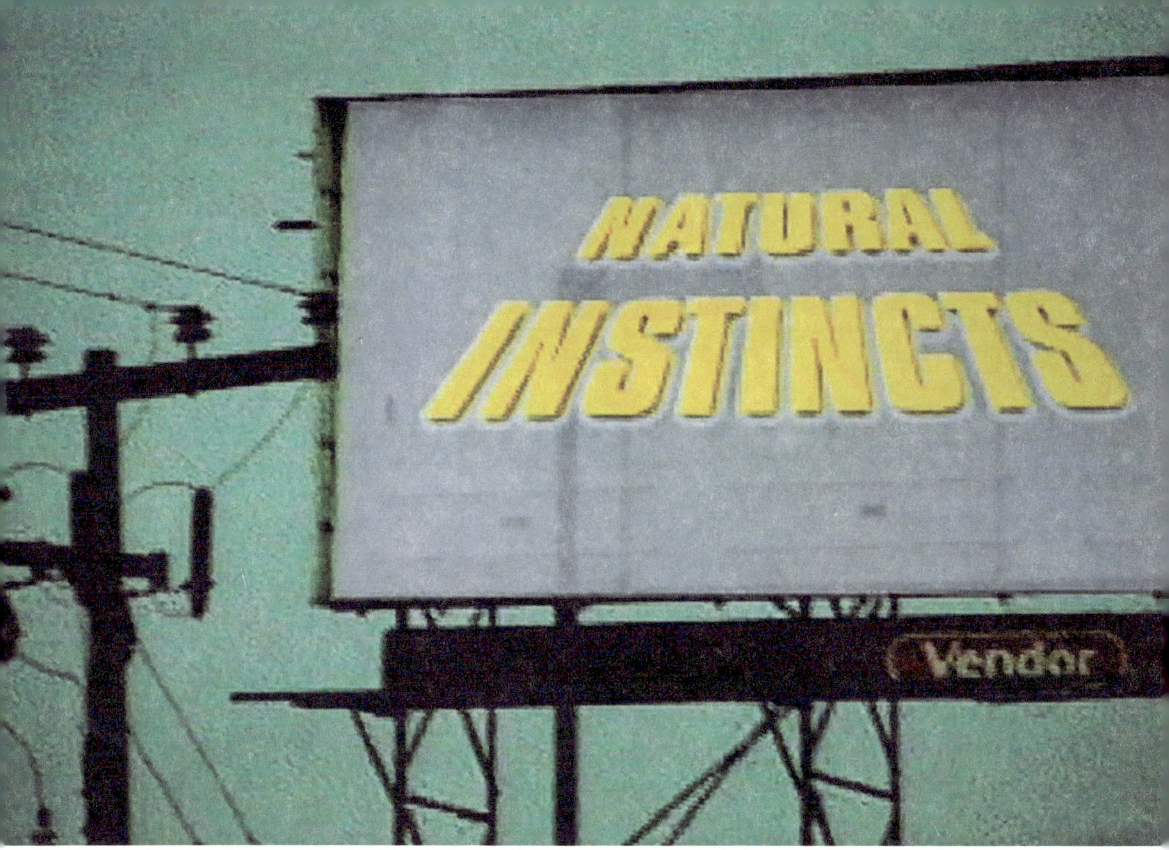

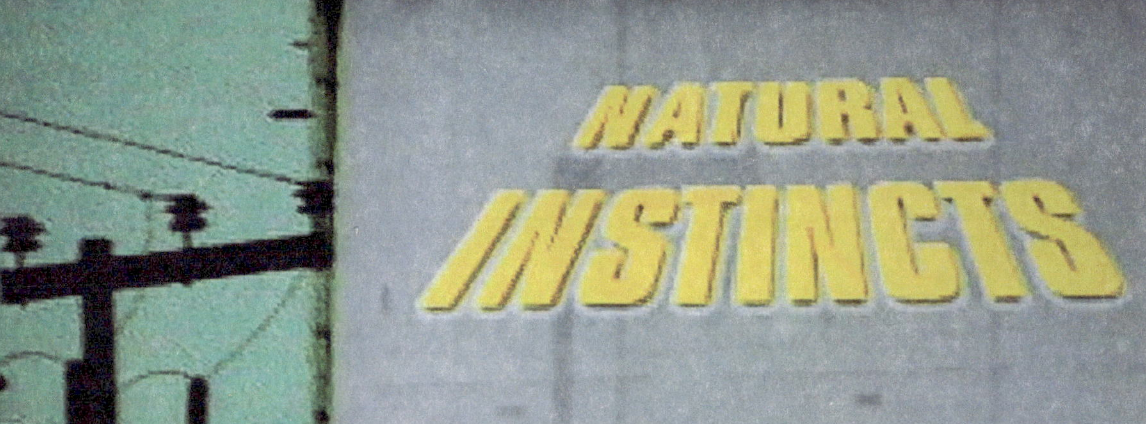
NATURAL
INSTINCTS
Vendor
Vendor

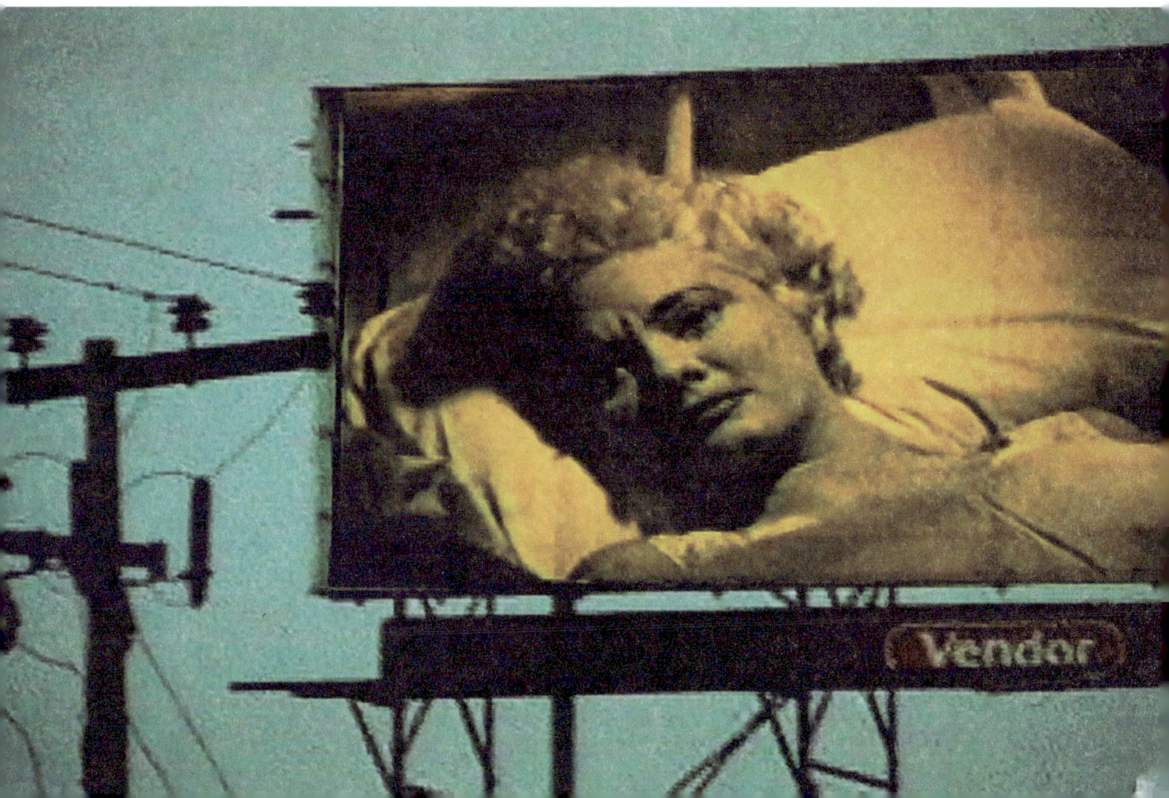

Iván Edeza

Mexico City, Mexico, 1967

Contador [*Meter*], 2012

DVD-NTSC digital video
10"
Ed. 5/5 + 1 AP
Gift of the artist, 2013

Edeza's work delves into the depiction of violence and its framing within a systemic structure of representation. This frequently takes place by means of formal research into the medium itself as texture, where Edeza questions the many different filters of the image and self-censorship.

    Contador shows a ten-second countdown that marks the murder statistics during the presidential administration of Felipe Calderón, who declared "war on drugs." The numbers combine the artist's speculations with figures from the weekly periodical *Zeta;* the final statistic is the journalistic projection of deaths for the fifth year of Calderón's administration. The piece was made in the last year of his presidency; the total number of murders ultimately exceeded these estimates.

V. R. L.

3,007
asesinatos

Felipe Ehrenberg

Mexico City, Mexico, 1943–Ahuatepec, Mexico, 2017

Arte conceptual [*Conceptual Art*], 1968

Acrylic on chipboard
200 × 180 × 5.5 cm
Gift of the artist, 1990

In the second exhibition held by the *Salón Independiente* in 1969 at the Museo de Ciencias y Arte, Felipe Ehrenberg presented *Arte conceptual,* mounted below another piece titled *La caída* [*The Fall*]. The title of this piece, despite its pop-imagery orientation, inaugurates the artist's interest in the conceptualisms he would revisit and definitively explore while living in London years later. *Arte conceptual* comes from a series of "wood constructions" shown by the artist at Jacks Misrachi's newly opened gallery in 1968. Ehrenberg's proximity to southern pop art modalities weren't limited to painting: as a contributor to the magazine *El Corno Emplumado* [*The Plumed Horn*], he published many drawings that incorporated images from advertising campaigns. These boxes, painted with stencils and acrylic paint, depict flat, brightly colored female forms with well-defined borders, poster-style, provocatively surrounded by signs like arrows.

P. G.

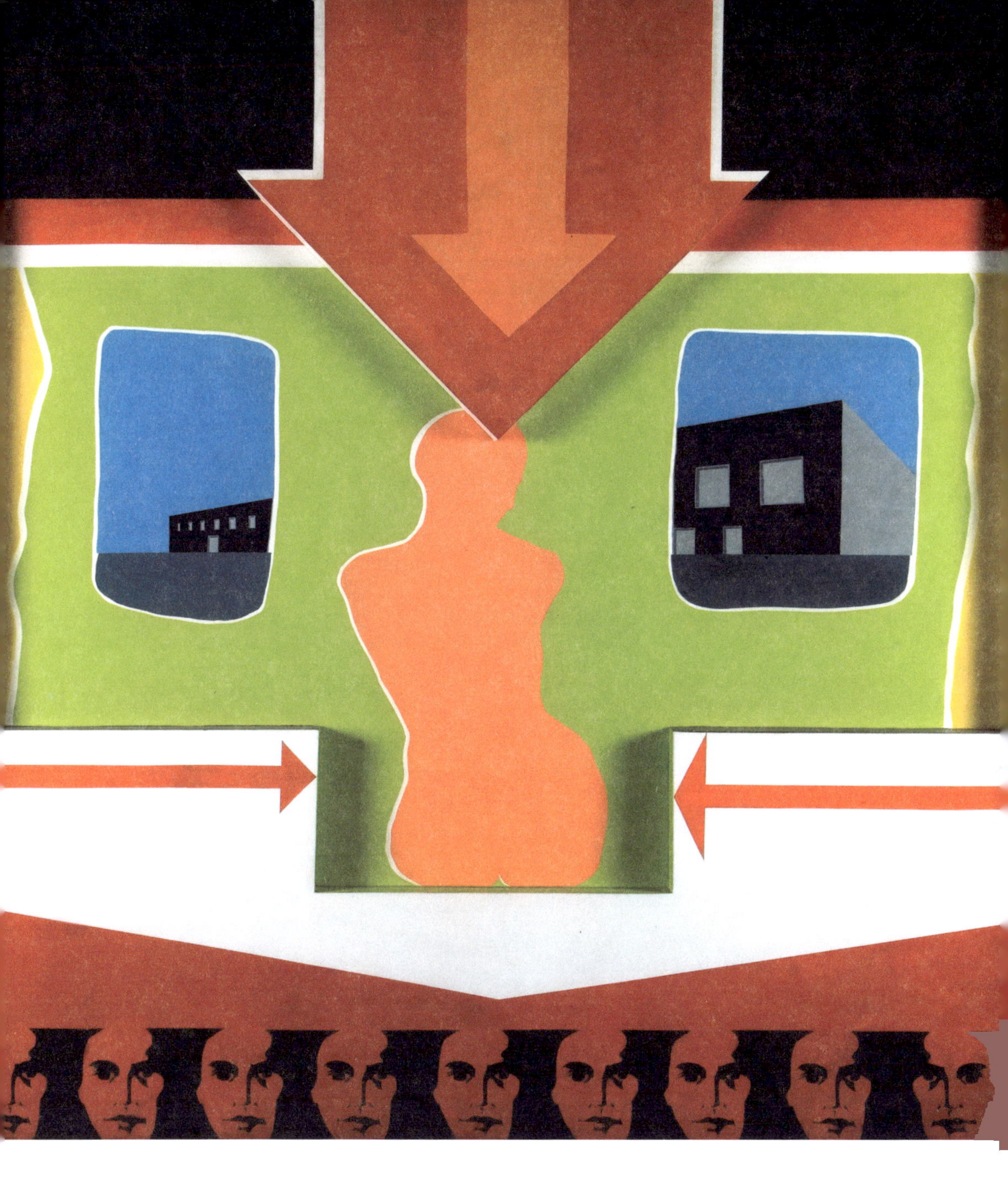

Juan Francisco Elso

Havana, Cuba, 1956–1988

Corazón de América [*Heart of the Americas*], 1987

Fragment of the installation *Transparencia
de Dios* [*The Transparency of God*]
Branches, wax, ash, and dry grass
230 × 170 cm Ø
Acquisition, 2005

Corazón de América is part of the project *Por América* [*Because
of the Americas*], which Juan Francisco Elso intended to exhibit
in the Museo de Arte Carrillo Gil in Mexico City, but was can-
celled due to the artist's illness and death in 1988 before being
reconstructed posthumously in 1990. It was part of the installation *Transparencia de Dios,* comprising three elements—*Corazón
de América, El rostro de Dios* [*The Face of God*], and *La mano de
Dios* [*The Hand of God*]—in which Elso encoded his goal of producing the emotional nucleus of the American continent, fusing
Amerindian and Afro-American spiritual traditions.

In response to his enlightened reading of texts by Miguel
León-Portilla and Alfredo López Austin, Elso proposed to activate
the Nahua concept *in ixtli in yolotl* (translated by experts as *face
or eye and heart*) as an indigenous metaphor for what is essential to human beings, clasping the maker's own creative hand.
With a sculptural technique based on materials found in nature
and inherited from ancestral rites, Elso aimed to do more than
simply carry out a symbolic operation; he wanted to intervene on
a political-teleological plane. *Corazón de América,* more than a
representation, is an attempt to constitute the power and desire
of a new culture that must replace Western hegemony.

Along with José Bedia and Ricardo Rodríguez Brey, Elso was a
member of the first wave of the Cuban avant-garde, the Volumen I
[Volume 1] group. Driven by its Afro-Cuban affiliation, this group
set out to engage systematically with indigenous Mexican culture.

C. M.

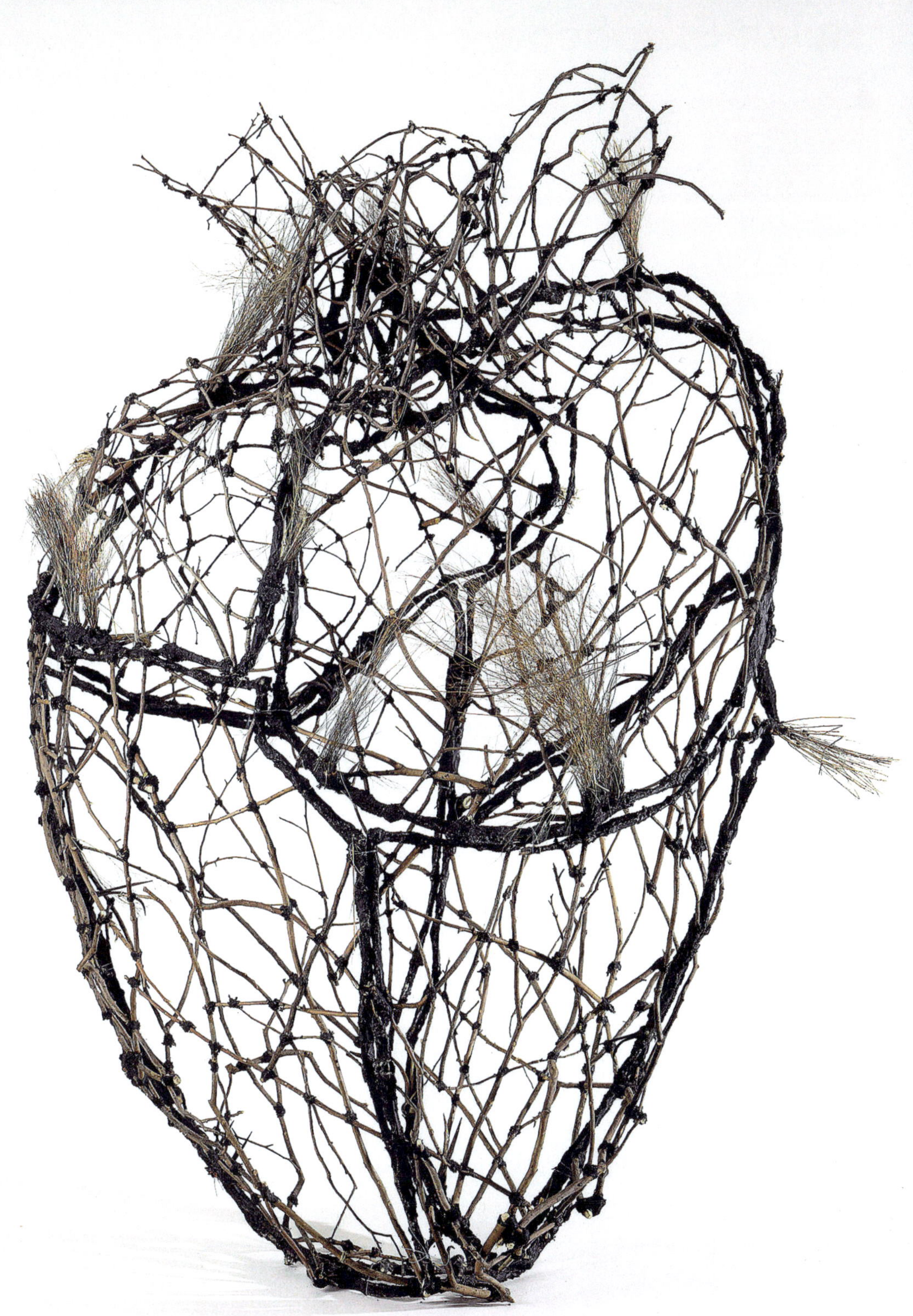

Helen Escobedo

Mexico City, Mexico, 1934–2010

Ambiente gráfico [*Graphic Atmosphere*], 1971

Lacquered iron
180 × 400 × 200 cm
Gift of the artist, 1990

In June 1971, Helen Escobedo was invited to participate in the XI Sculpture Biennale organized by the Middelheim Museum in Antwerp. In response, she designed a piece based on the *Ambiente gráfico* she had presented at the *III Salón Independiente,* held at the Museo Universitario de Ciencias y Arte in 1970. The artist built, *in situ,* an ephemeral piece out of cardboard and newspaper (as was required), not only as a material platform but also as a means of criticizing the media. She assembled a series of large-scale letters that showed a clean, decorative typeface on the front. On the back were three examples of good, bad, and ugly journalism: cartoons by Rius and interesting articles, color-printed clippings from the society pages, and tabloid headlines. For the open-air Sculpture Biennale in Antwerp, Escobedo decided to use lacquered iron to render letters as signs that would be recognizable to various social groups, as structural elements, and as aesthetic forms.

In 1967, Helen Escobedo abandoned the classic training she had received in the 1950s at London's Royal College of Art (a style based on small-format, figurative bronze sculptures) and became interested in creating ephemeral environments and assemblages: inhabitable, urban-scale works that addressed her desire to combine art forms associated with design, architecture, and nature. This piece inaugurated the prominence of typeface in Escobedo's work, a form of homage to the printed advertising materials that were prevalent at the time.

P. G.

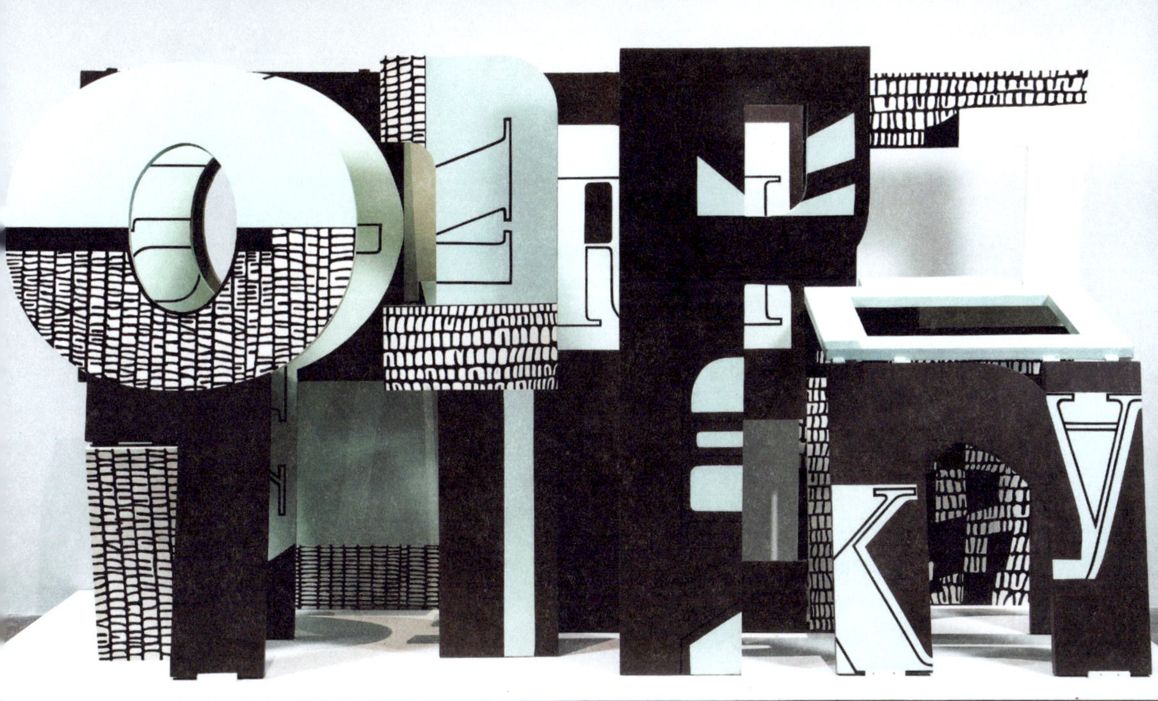

Manuel Felguérez

Valparaíso, Mexico, 1928–Mexico City, Mexico, 2020

Canto al océano. **Mural Deportivo Bahía**
[*Song to the Ocean*: **Bahía Sports Club Mural**], 1963

Oyster shell, abalone, mother-of-pearl and
wire rod on reinforcing concrete (fragment)
500 × 800 cm
Gift of Ángel and Mario Sánchez y Gas, 2016
This piece was restored with support from FEMSA

In April 1963, Felguérez inaugurated this majestic hundred-
meter-long mural at the Deportivo Bahía: a community pool
located in the Peñón de los Baños area, near the Mexico City
airport. At the suggestion of Gelsen Gas, the owner of the facil-
ities and a friend of the artist, Felguérez paid artistic homage to
the book *Chants de Maldoror* by the Comte of Lautréamont. The
project consisted of two works: *Canto al océano* and the sculpture set *Muro de las formas mecánicas* [*Wall of Mechanical
Forms*]. For the former, Felguérez turned to discarded materials
once again: oyster, and abalone shells combined with metal and
stonework to cover the upper part of the changing rooms, forming
shapes evocative of Jean Arp.

Alejandro Jodorowsky participated in the inauguration of
the mural with a sophisticated ephemeral "panic" that included
a helicopter, film screenings, and over 40 dancers, actors, and
mimes, in addition to the sound and light crew. During the show,
Jodorowsky, dressed as a blue demon with feathered wings,
recited an episodic poem, its stanzas linked together by oceanic
sound effects. In the changing rooms, located beneath the mural,
human scenes portraying partnership and solitude were performed.

During the last rehearsal, just hours before the inauguration,
the helicopter from which Jodorowsky was supposed to descend
fell into the pool. The product of chance and improvisation, the
artifact became an unwitting participant in a highly unusual and
now-legendary performance.

P. G.

Detail

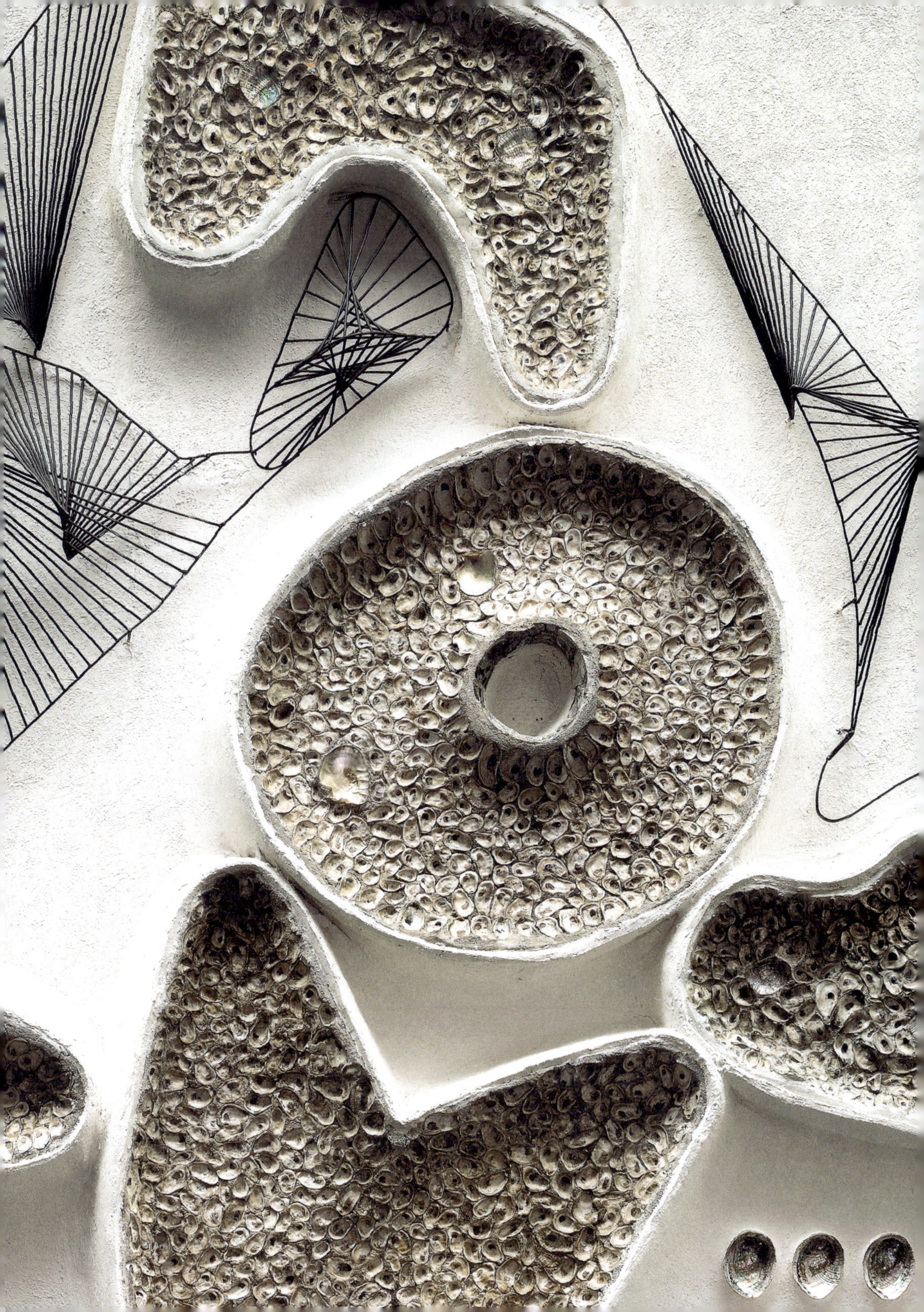

Claudia Fernández

Mexico City, Mexico, 1965

Interior, 1998

Installation. Oil on canvas and wood
Variable dimensions
Acquisition, 1999

The creation of playful visual universes is a constant presence
in the paintings, installations, videos, and photographs of Claudia
Fernández. In tune with the abstract tradition in modern art
history, this polyptych, composed of hundreds of paintings displayed in constellated montage, depicts stars suspended in a blue
void. Each piece delves, both individually and collectively, into the
possibilities of painting as a poetic space that convokes sub-
jective experiences, shot through with wonder at the totality of
space and time. The work also explores the infinite relationships
between the cosmic universe and the intimate one.

M. A.

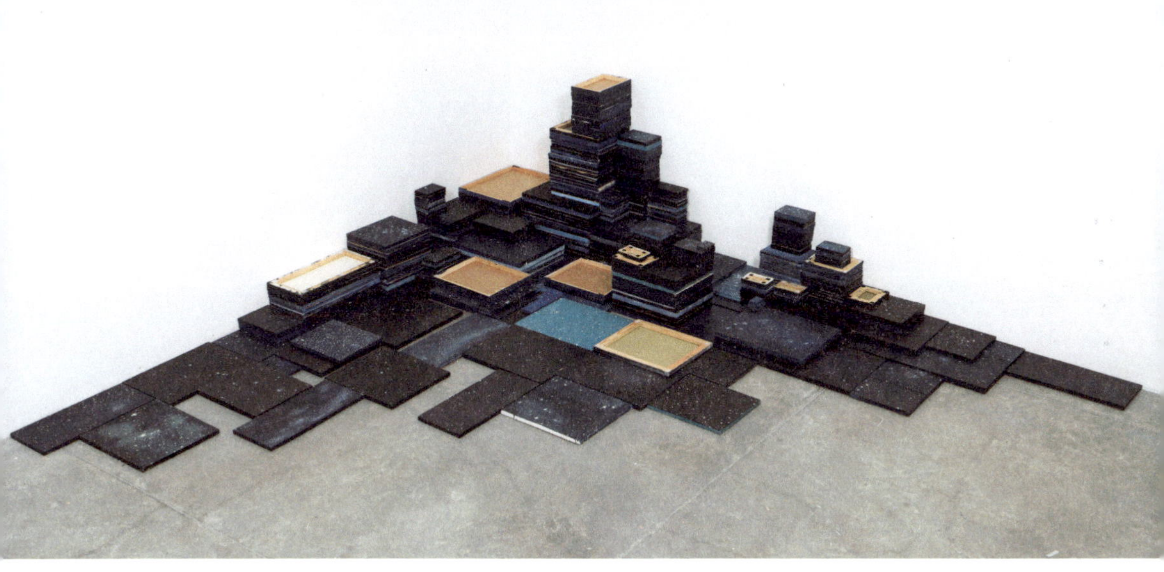

Julio Galán

Múzquiz, Mexico, 1958–Zacatecas, Mexico, 2006

Niño elefante tomando Ele-rat 7
[*Elephant Child Drinking Ele-Rat 7*], 1985

Oil and acrylic on canvas
117 × 188 cm
Acquisition, 2005

Galán's work is often distinguished by cryptic tales encoded in quotes, visual vocabularies inherited from popular tradition, and the avant-garde of 1920s Mexico. These references allow him to combine self-referential images with interrogations of identity. In this painting, the depiction of an animal transmutation expresses a discomfort with personal history and intimate imagery. In this way, the piece exceeds the bounds of so-called *neomexicanismo*—the category so often used to constrain the work of artists like Galán—and proves his ability to analyze a time of crisis marked by complex social and emotional challenges.

J. G. S.

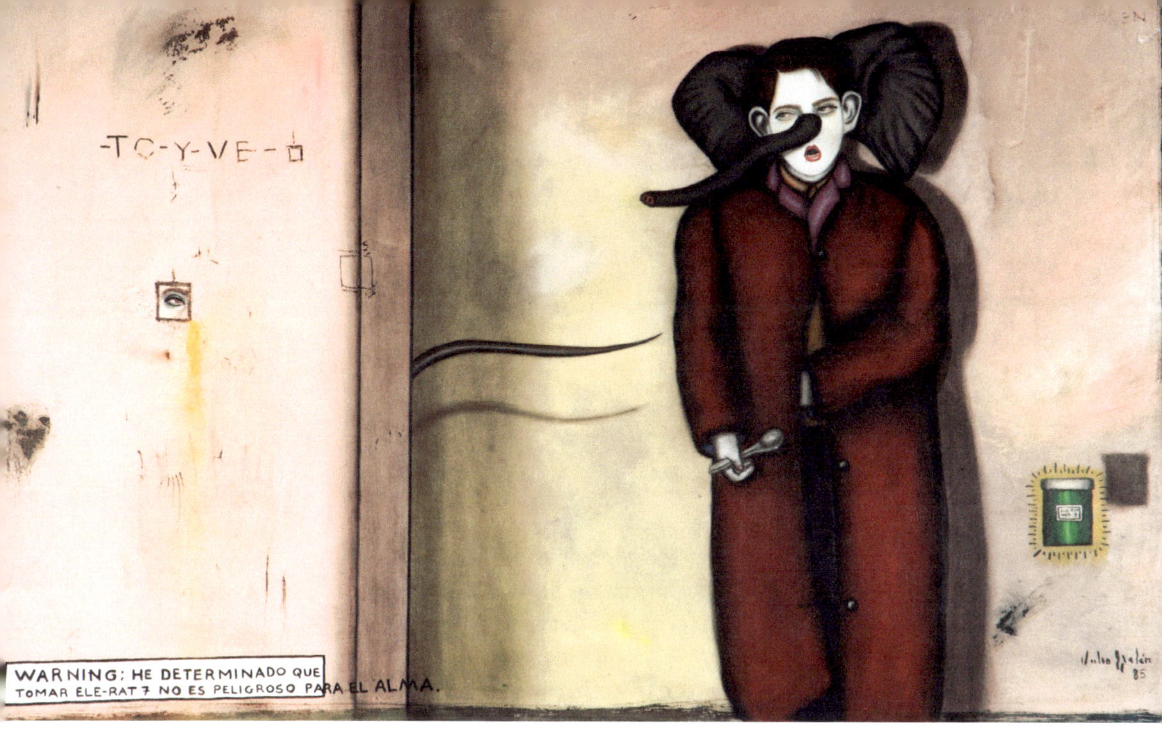
-TO-Y-VE-
WARNING: HE DETERMINADO QUE
TOMAR ELE-RAT 7 NO ES PELIGROSO PARA EL ALMA.

Fernando García Ponce

Mérida, Mexico, 1933–Mexico City, Mexico, 1987

G.P. 33, 1981

Collage and acrylic on wood
170 × 150 cm
Gift of Sara Sierra, 1990

The title of this collage, and the printed text at the center of the composition, allude to the two surnames and birth year of the artist in 1933. This is a placard of expressive modernity, made with a bold-face sans serif font and minimal spacing between characters. Around this inner signature, García Ponce orchestrates something like a spiral of painted planes that evoke spaces framed, in turn, by other pictorial gestures. These inner paintings, which open like slits and split off into gashes and dry brushstrokes, culminate in the plump drops and red accents that blot the wood at broad intervals. Together, these elements suggest a curious self-portrait—less of the artist as a physical presence than of his craft and the joy that Fernando García Ponce found in what his brother, the writer Juan García Ponce, called "the allure of the void and the artist's natural tendency to fight it."

C. M.

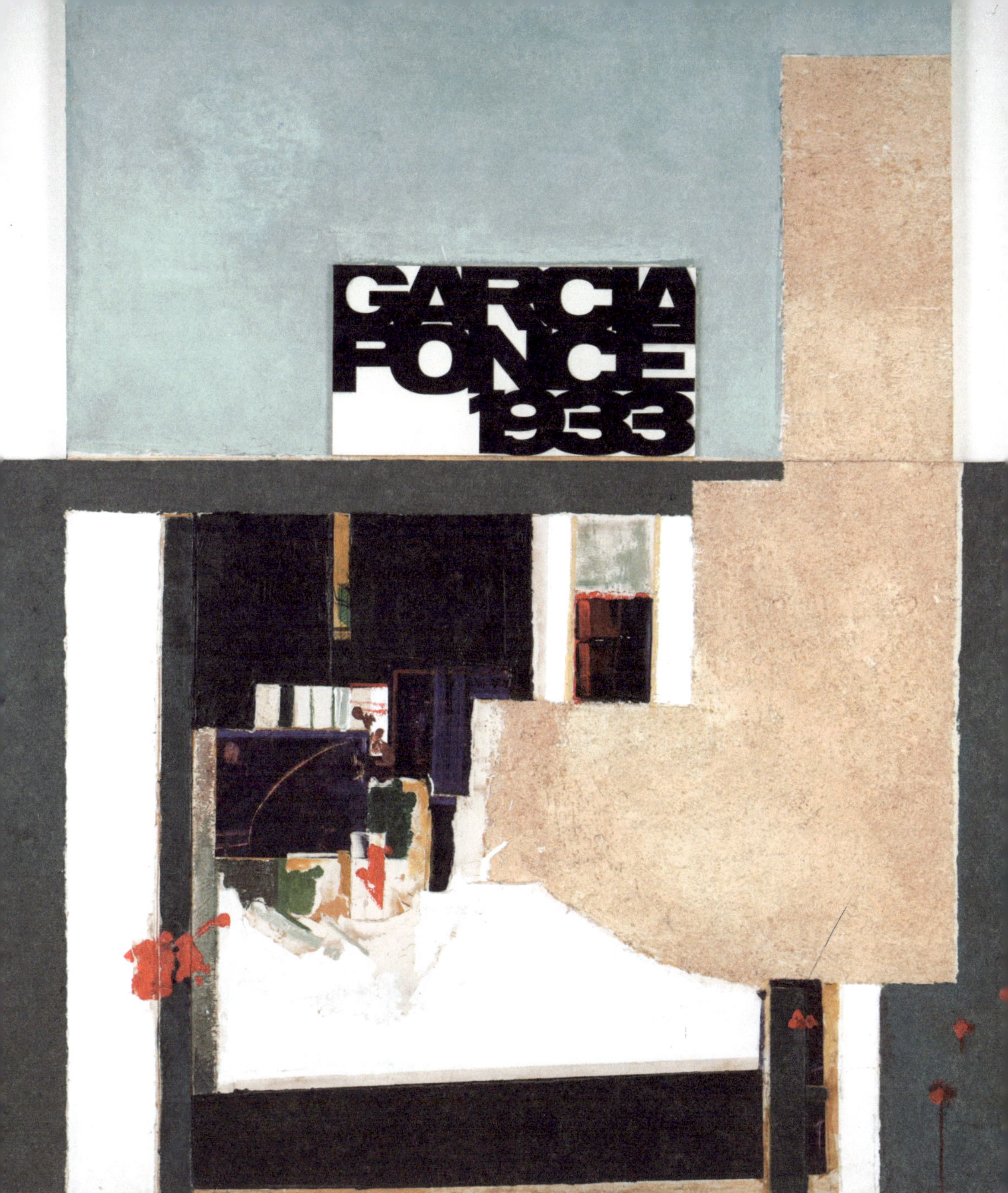

GARCIA
PONCE
1933

Mario García Torres

Monclova, Mexico, 1975

Carta abierta al Dr. Atl
[***Open Letter to Dr. Atl***], 2005

Color Super 8 film transferred
to DVD, silent
5' 40"
Acquisition, 2007

Through his conceptual production, Mario García Torres's work questions the artistic practice itself, employing modern and contemporary art history as a resource to establish a relationship between past, present, and future.

Following the strategy of imaginary correspondence employed in several of his works, García Torres mixes real and fictitious elements. In this case, the artist writes an imaginary letter to the painter Gerardo Murillo, known as Dr. Atl. The background of the piece shows Barranca de Oblatos, a canyon in Guadalajara that recurs in Atl's paintings. In the audio, however, he tells the dead painter about a plan to build a franchise of the Guggenheim Museum in this space. In his missive, García Torres addresses the connections between tourism, the market, the landscape, and art—and how art can disrupt a territory charged with cultural meaning.

V. R. L.

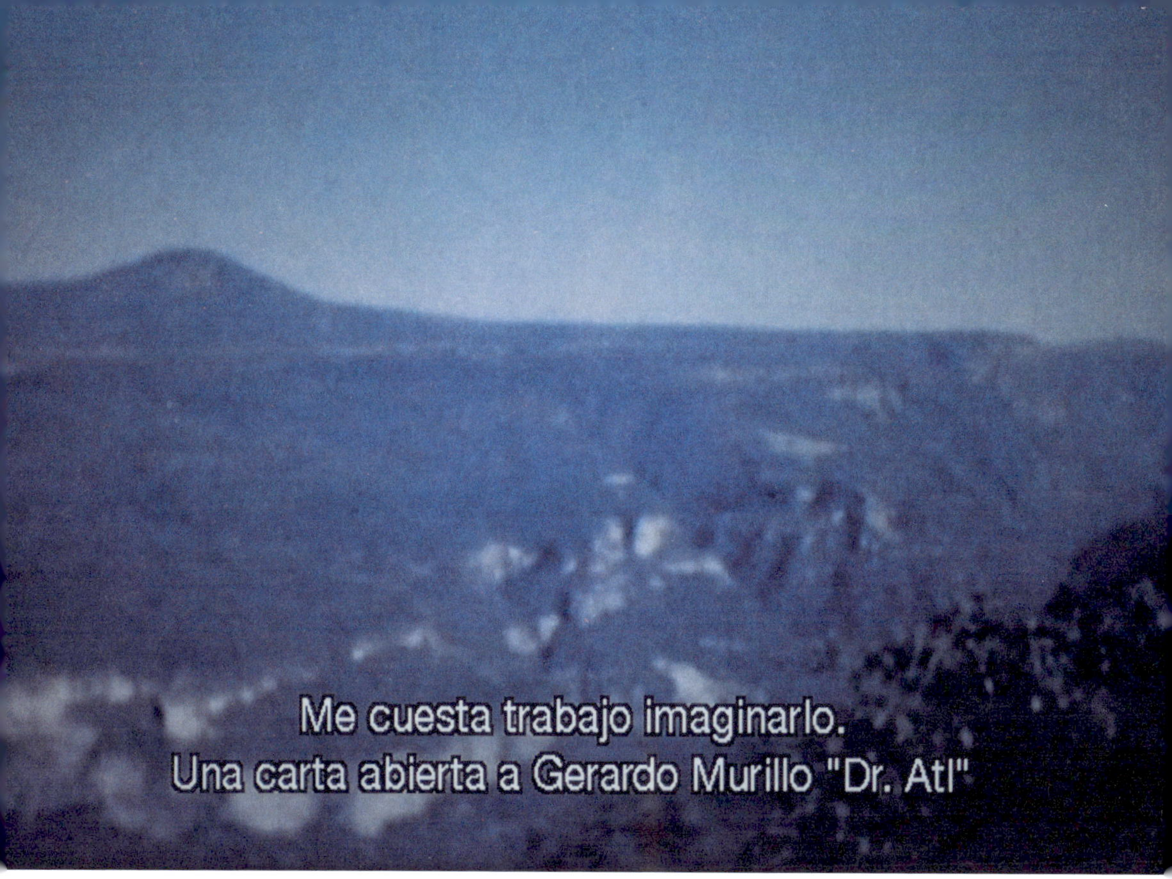

Me cuesta trabajo imaginarlo.
Una carta abierta a Gerardo Murillo "Dr. Atl"

Javier de la Garza

—

Tampico, Mexico, 1954

Cuauhtémoc (Captura de Cuauhtémoc.
"Toma tu puñal, hábreme [sic] *las venas,*
déjame desangrar, etc. etc.") [The Capture
of Cuauhtémoc: "Take your dagger, open
my veins, let me bleed, etc. etc."], 1986

Acrylic and oil on canvas, velvet, and paper flowers
222 × 155.5 cm
Acquisition with funds from the Presupuesto
de Egresos de la Federación, 2014

In his paintings on Mexico's indigenous mythology from the mid-
1980s, Javier de la Garza subverts the racial and sexual codes of
patriotic lore in a way that challenges the national archetypes
produced by the Mexican state. This depiction of Cuauhtémoc,
the last Aztec ruler, emphasizes how the mythification of the
national hero (as depicted by artists such as Jesús Contreras,
Saturnino Herrán, and Jorge Enciso) created an idealization of
the pre-Hispanic past by exhibiting largely androgynous, sexualized indigenous bodies. In critiquing the subliminal eroticism
of patriotic Mexican images, De la Garza incorporates kitsch elements from the commercial Aztec iconography that appeared in
Jesús Helguera's almanacs of the 1940s, school monographs, and
mythical scenes exalted by the Golden Age of Mexican Cinema.
This scene's camp aesthetic is bolstered by the velvet frame and
lace and plastic flowers. At the bottom of the canvas, the artist
has inscribed a quote from the song "Amor gitano" [Gypsy
Love] by José Feliciano—"Toma este puñal, hábreme [*sic*] las
venas, déjame sangrar" [Take this dagger, open my veins, let me
bleed]—as a melodramatic scene of spite.

Cuauhtémoc is portrayed ironically, and on an almost human
scale, as a trim, muscular, effeminate hero with darkly outlined
lips and eyebrows and clad in a small loincloth dyed the colors
of the Mexican flag. This attire is, in itself, blasphemous: it both
covers and accentuates the hero's genitals, depicting them on
the verge of erection, an intimation of a largely narcissistic drive.

P. G.

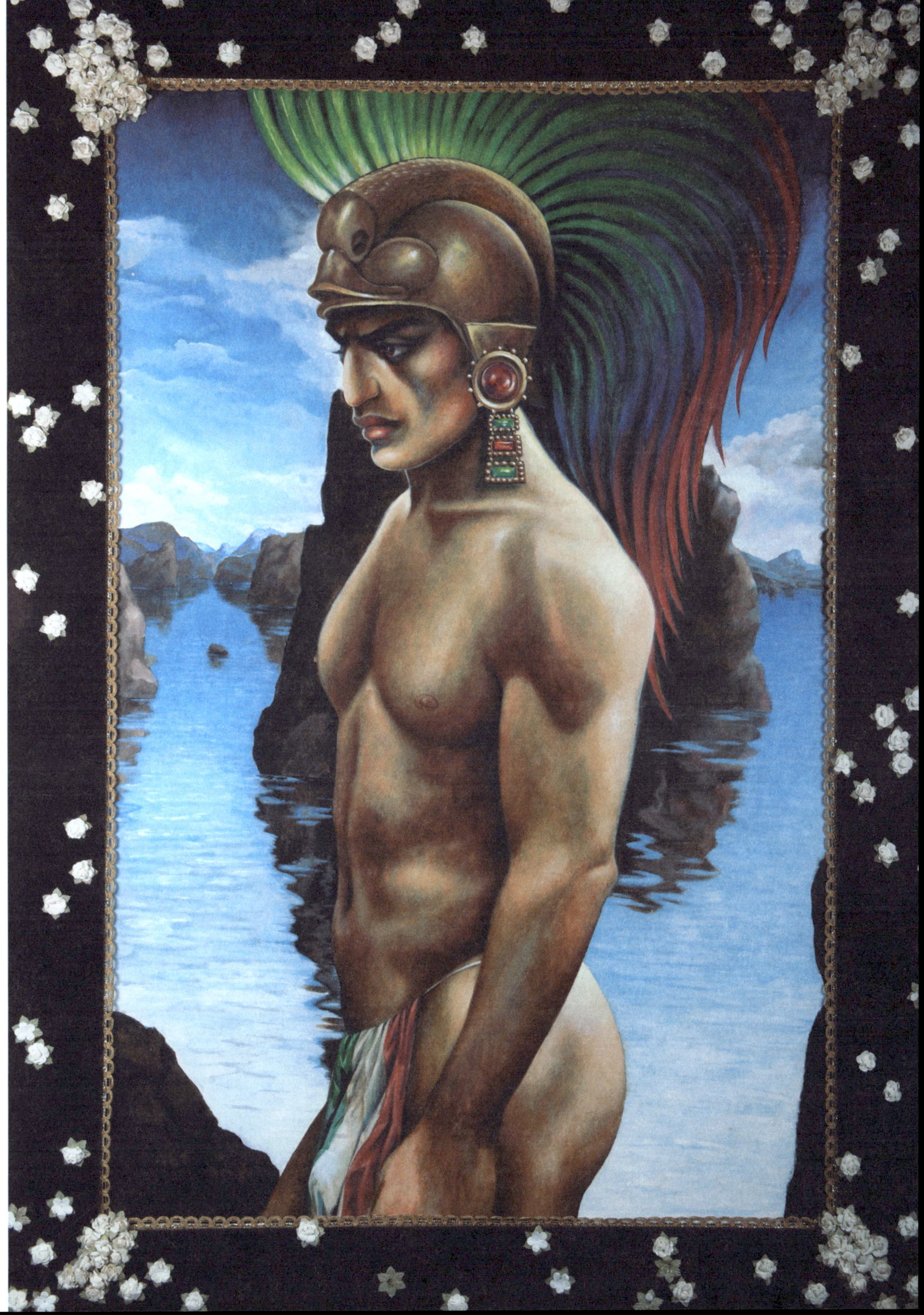

Gelsen Gas
(Ángel Sánchez Gas)

Mexico City, Mexico, 1933–2005

AutoGelsen, 1971

Installation. Oil on canvas, chair,
and embroidered denim jacket
Variable dimensions
Gift of the artist, 2008

During the early 1970s, Gelsen Gas produced experimental films,
paintings, collages, and logic puzzles, in addition to practicing a
genre of painting that prefigured elements of late-twentieth-
century postmodern appropriationism. *AutoGelsen* moves beyond
the plane of the painting to contradict the traditional terms of
self-portraiture. The piece is part of a series based on overlap-
ping modern pictorial compositions (in this case, a reference to
Homage to the Square [1964] by the German artist Josef Albers)
with images rendered in different styles: for example, a realist
landscape, a hyper-realist artist raising his fist, and a character
sketched as a pop-art-style cartoon. Unlike a traditional self-
portrait, this depiction of the artist has his back turned to the
viewer, a gesture reinforced by placing a chair in front of the
painting as if to suggest the painter's position. A double set of
signatures, in a font that parodies Walt Disney's, is repeated in
both mediums.

J. G. M.

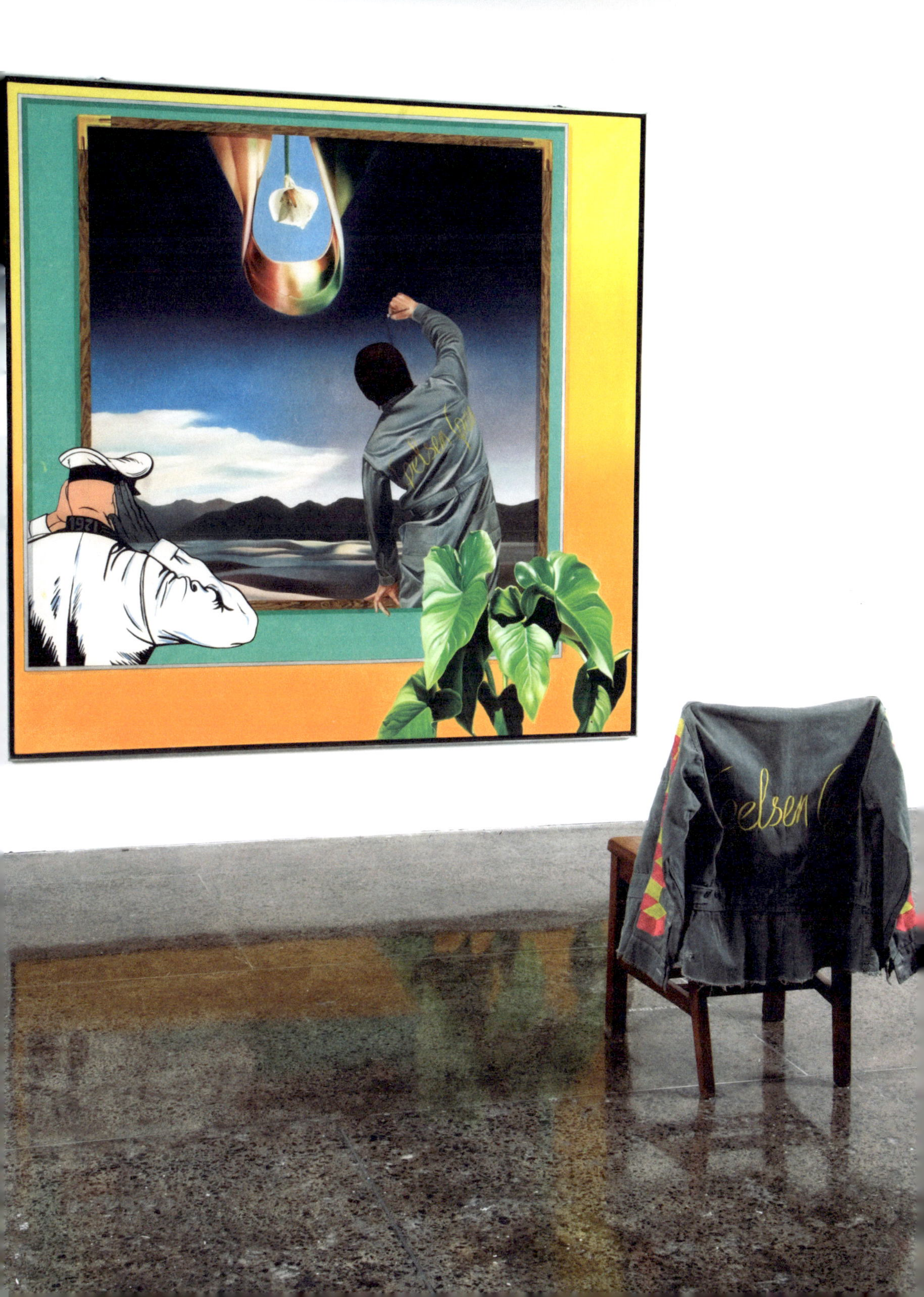

Gunther Gerzso

——

Mexico City, Mexico, 1915–2000

Boceto [*Sketch*], 1965

Oil on chipboard
36.5 × 80 cm
Acquisition, 2018

Following the artistic and existential torment (splendor notwith-
standing) that afflicted Gunther Gerzso in his so-called "Greek
period" of the late 1950s and mid-1960s, he began to deploy
his classical vocabulary as a rigorous abstract painter. With its
linguistic economy, discreet size, and elongated format, empha-
sizing the phenomenology of the landscape, *Boceto* can serve
as a benchmark for his mature language. The piece's modest
dimensions contain key discoveries from at least the previous
quarter-century of his painting: the allusion to a confined space
submerged in the dark background, with large geometric shapes
enclosing the forms in the foreground, alluding to the roundness
of the body and traversing cracked surfaces that evoke, in turn,
antiquity and violence.

The deep red and green iridescence of the masses and walls
—colors representing the ghosts of jungles and blood—would
become one of the painter's most frequently recurring palettes.
He went on to refine them in several series in 1967, all acrylic
and pencil on paper: *Paisaje* [*Landscape*], *Huracán* [*Hurricane*],
Paisaje en azul [*Landscape in Blue*], and *Sin título (paisaje verde)*
[*Untitled (Green Landscape)*]. These culminated in different versions of one of his finest paintings from the 1970s: *La mujer de la
jungla* [*The Woman of the Jungle*]. It is ironic that Gerzso chose
a term alluding to a preparatory work, a study: in retrospect,
this painting synthesizes some of the finest painted work in the
second half of the twentieth century.

C. M.

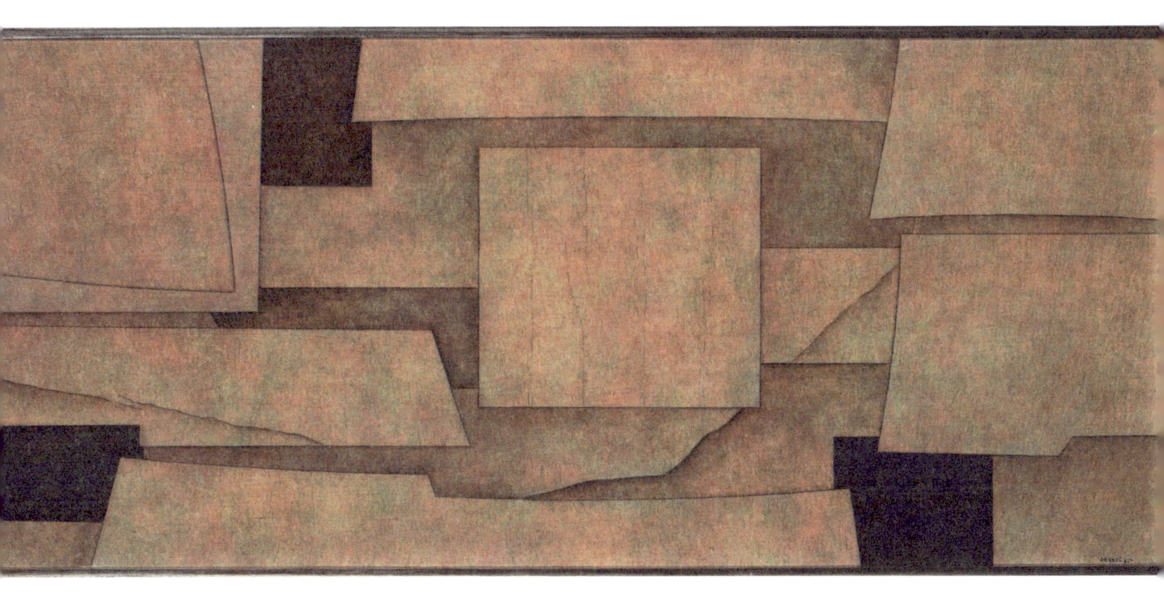

Alberto Gironella

—

Mexico City, Mexico, 1929–1999

Homenaje a Buñuel [*Homage to Buñuel*], 1962

Assemblage. Wooden box, oil on canvas, metal
trumpet, wooden sculpture, oil, and chrome
168 × 148 × 40 cm
Acquisition with funds from the Presupuesto
Egresos de la Federación, 2014

This is one of several tributes made by Alberto Gironella to the
Spanish filmmaker Luis Buñuel, his friend and one of the direc-
tors he most admired. The piece also exemplifies the intersections between painting and sculpture that distinguish Gironella's
work, as well as his strategy of incorporating objects and images
by chance. In this assemblage—which evokes both a surrealist
attitude toward objects and Gironella's penchant for baroque
retables—we find a clear criticism to the church in the piece's
context of production. The depth of his paintings reflects his fascination with the "España Negra" school of the writer and painter
José Gutiérrez Solana.

The assemblage was originally part of a complex set design he
co-created with his colleagues Manuel Felguérez, Lilia Carrillo,
and Vicente Rojo for the play *La ópera del orden* [*The Opera of
Order*] by Alejandro Jodorowsky. This collaborative exercise was
consistent with these artists' spirit of renovation; the group was
drawn to abstraction, neo-avant-garde currents, and different
kinds of formal experimentation that showed an affinity with
Jodorowsky's bold theater projects. In fact, Gironella appeared
as an actor in one scene—dressed as a Franciscan, chalice in
hand—before his section of the set design. *La ópera del orden,*
with an original script by Jodorowsky and starring himself and
Beatriz Sheridan, turned out to be so scandalous in its portrayal
of traditional institutions, such as the family and the church, that it
was censored before its official premiere in 1962 by Mexico City's
Departamento de Espectáculos.

E. P.

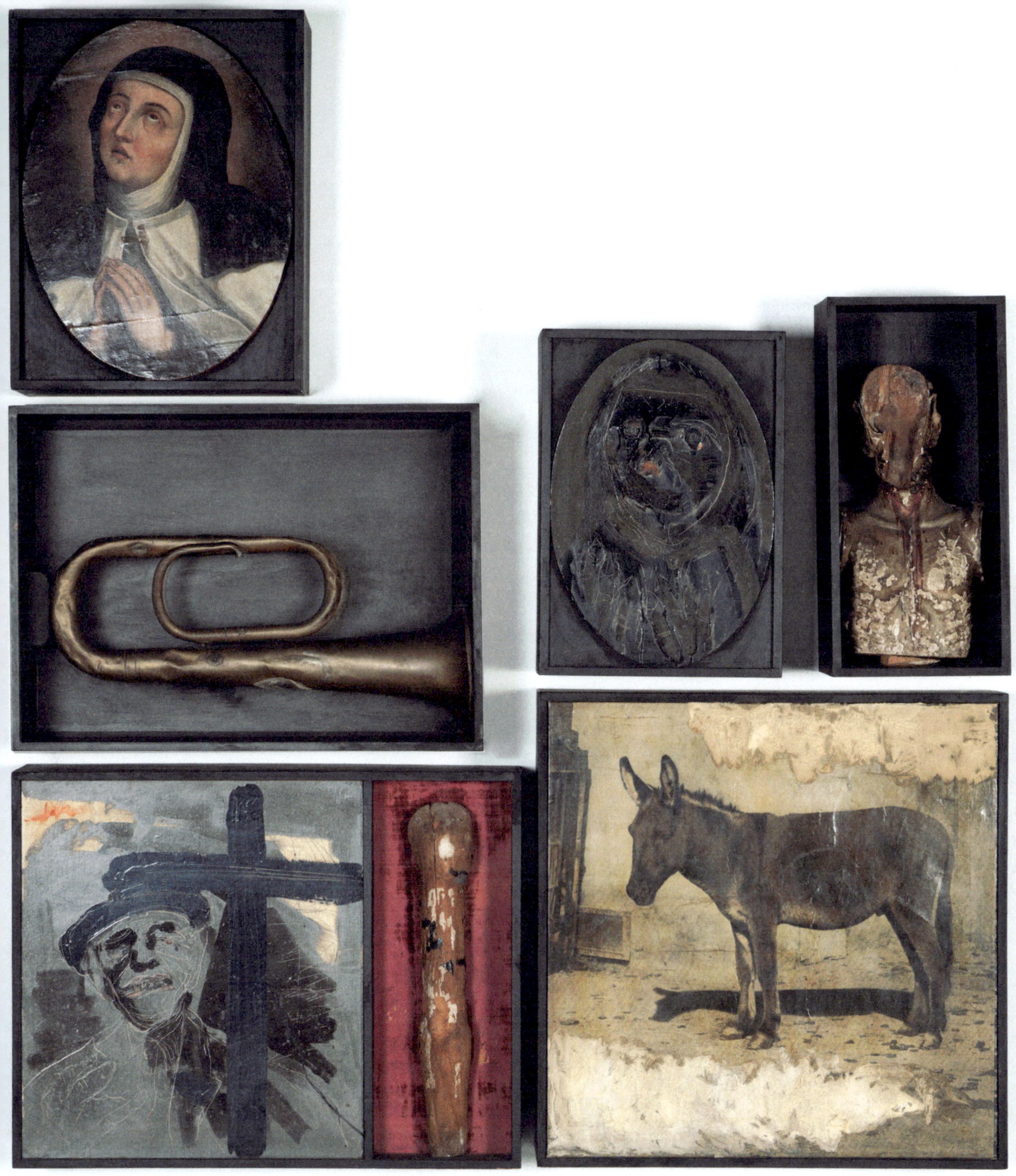

Thomas Glassford

—

Laredo, United States, 1963

Alluvium: Pipe Dreams, 1991

Gourds and nickel-plated brass
38 × 455 × 35 cm
Acquisition, 2005

During the 1990s, Thomas Glassford made a series of pieces exploring the cultural meaning and materiality of the gourd, an object of natural origins that is representative of Mexican folk culture. Glassford's gourd-interventions yielded artifacts that evoke their use as receptacles and flasks in ancient civilizations, and which emphasize their ambiguous resemblance—with shapes both phallic and voluptuous—to aspects of the human body. In *Alluvium: Pipe Dreams*, the gourd is depicted as detrital matter, or dreamlike residue, of its profound cultural and visual references, expressed by the contrast between metal and the gourd's organic origins.

J. G. S.

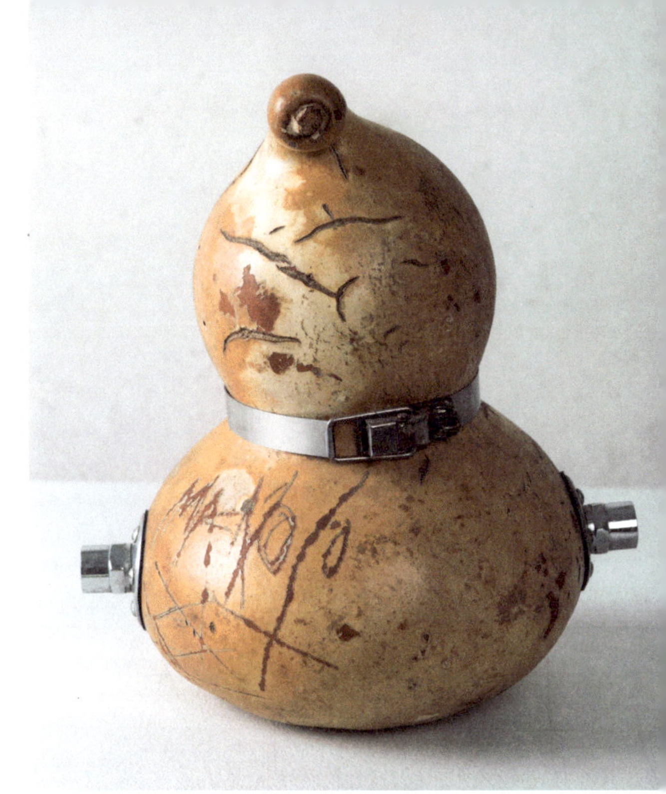

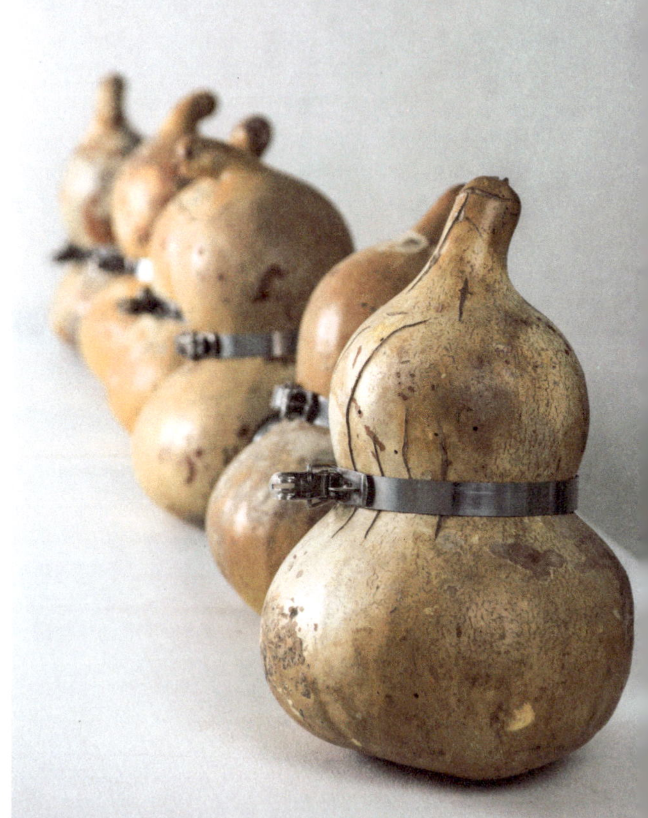

Mathias Goeritz

Danzig, Prussia, 1915–Mexico City, Mexico, 1990

Oro [*Gold*], *ca.* 1960

Gold leaf on wood
120 × 120 cm
Acquisition, 2005

This piece is part of the series known as *Mensajes* [*Messages*]
or *Dorados* [*Gold Finishes*], in which the artist sought to incorporate spiritual or religious concepts into modern art. Goeritz used
the radiance and luminosity in these works as an allusion
to the sacred, employing monochrome to negotiate the ancient
Judeo-Christian debate on the prohibition against representing
the divine. The *Mensajes* are associated with Goeritz's own
spiritual quests from the early 1950s onward. In the following
decade, these quests became openly religious, using manifestos,
texts, and declarations to speak of God as a "stable" value in
confronting the humanitarian crisis and general confusion of the
post-war years. The luminous nature of these works was accentuated by their exhibition in dark spaces, lit only with candles, as
in the Galería Antonio Souza in 1960.

In opposition to New Realism and abstraction, modes to which
he referred in explicitly negative terms, Goeritz sought to develop
a form of transcendental, metaphysical art, absorbing a spiritual
function into his artistic practice. In his ties to European art, these
works engage in dialogue with the monochromes of Yves Klein
and Heinz Mack, which were practically unknown in Mexico at the
time. This series participates in the international phenomenon
of "updating" religious art in the 1950s and '60s. Goeritz was
a key actor in this liturgical aesthetic renewal in the Mexican
context: in addition to *Mensajes,* he designed stained glass
windows for churches and created medium-format crucifixes
and sculptures to decorate both private and ritual spaces.

E. P.

José Miguel González Casanova

Mexico City, Mexico, 1964

La escuela de Atenas
[***The School of Athens***], 1997

Cantera blocks engraved with words
260 × 200 cm Ø
Acquisition, 1999

This installation—composed of an incomplete tower of cantera stone blocks, engraved with words from Aristotelian definitions of substance, and arranged in a spiral formation until they gradually reach the word NADA [nothing]—offers an aesthetic model to explain the political operation of the appearance and disappearance of essences and accidents. The effect is a back-and-forth of cognitive categories and sensitive initiations. Combining concepts and the entropic deployment of symbolic forms in a precarious state, this work questions the aesthetic processes used to study and explain our relationship with the world, as in the eponymous fresco painted at the Vatican by Raphael in 1509.

M. A.

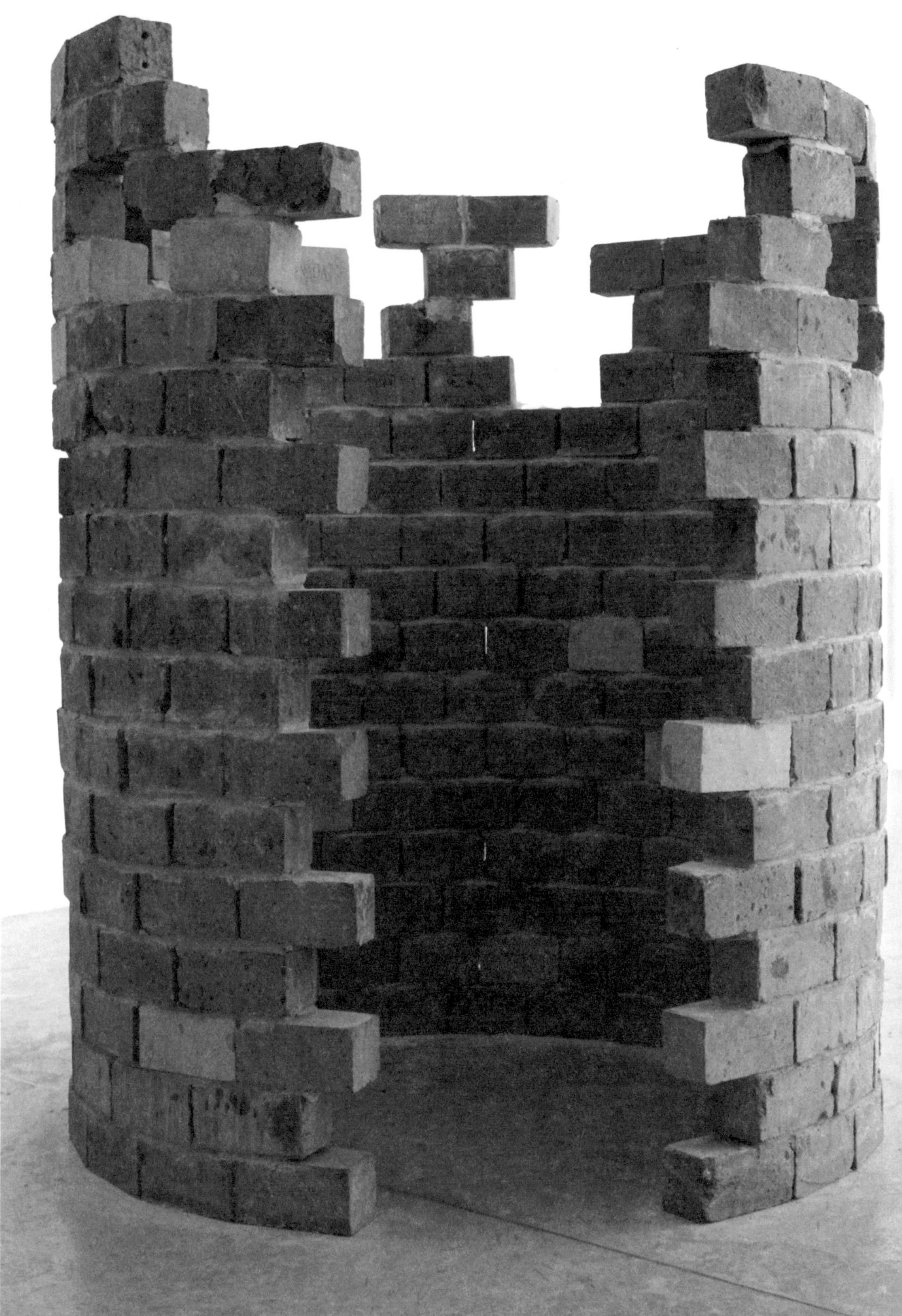

Graphics of 68

—

Jesús Martínez (Los Sauces, Mexico, 1942)
Untitled [Dove of Peace Wounded by a Bayonet], 1968
Banner. Stencil, gouache on cardboard
48.5 ×71 cm

Jorge Pérez Vega (Mexico City, Mexico, 1946)
1968 año de la prensa vendida [*1968 Year of the Sold Press*], 1968
Poster. Linoleum embossing on paper
39.3 × 23 cm

Desaparición del cuerpo de granaderos
[*Disappearance of the Grenadier Corps*], 1968
Poster. Silkscreen on paper
61.5 × 69.7 cm

Gift of Arnulfo Aquino, 2002

These flyers, posters, stickers, and banners constitute a set of
visual testimonies produced during the 1968 student movement
to share information on the demands, arrests, and government repression of the popular movement. They often feature
the re-smantization of imagery from the XIX Olympics or figures
such as Che Guevara, Demetrio Vallejo, and (antagonistically)
then-President Gustavo Díaz Ordaz. These works, rather than
responding to an artistic ambition, seek visual effectiveness in
communicating slogans and demands in the midst of collective and anonymous actions. Their stylistic diversity reveals the
technical and iconographic influence of many different sources:
the Taller de Gráfica Popular, Cuban poster art, pop art, and the
iconography of May '68 in France. Most of these pieces were
produced in the studios of the UNAM's Escuela Nacional de Artes
Plásticas (Antigua Academia de San Carlos, now Facultad de
Artes y Diseño), the Escuela Nacional de Pintura, Escultura y
Grabado "La Esmeralda", and, to a lesser extent, the Instituto
Politécnico Nacional. The graphics were fixed on the sides of
buses, hung on walls in the street, and carried by protesters'
bodies at demonstrations.

S. H.

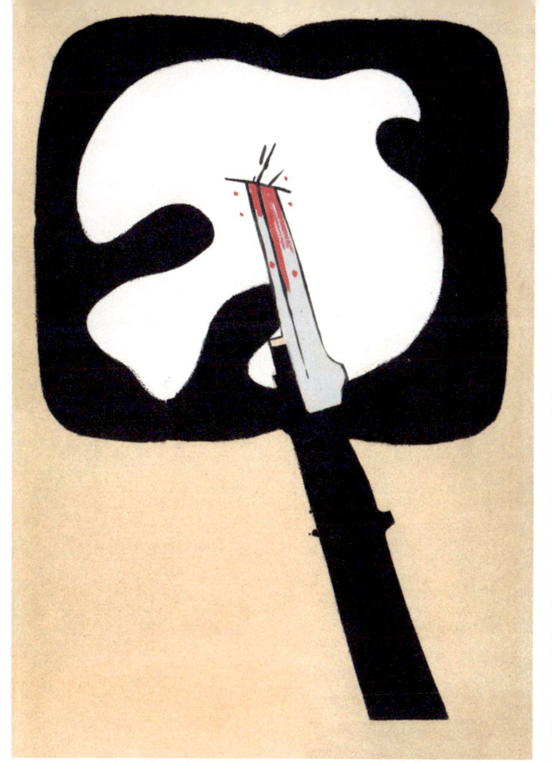

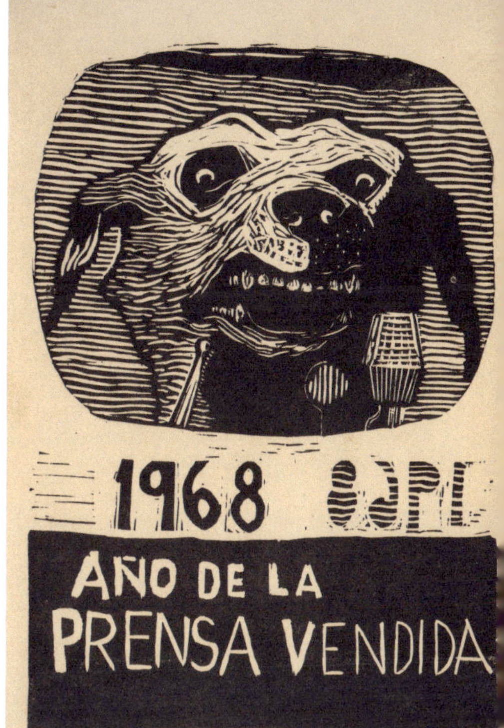

1968
AÑO DE LA
PRENSA VENDIDA

DESAPARICION
DEL CUERPO
DE GRANADEROS

Lourdes Grobet

Mexico City, Mexico, 1940

La India Sioux en su casa
[*India Sioux at Home*], *ca.* 1983

From the series *La doble lucha* [*Double Fight*]
Vintage gelatin silver print
40 × 50 cm
Acquisition with funds from the Presupuesto
de Egresos de la Federación, 2014

India Sioux (Hidalgo, 1954) made her debut as a wrestler in 1977
and remained a major presence in the ring throughout the 1980s.
From 1979 to 2003, Grobet documented the world of *lucha libre*
through its varied elements: the spectacle itself and the chore-
ographies in the ring, the reactions of the audience, the wrestlers'
own lives, and their jobs beyond the arena. This image is part of
the series *La doble lucha*, a set of photographs focused on the
everyday lives of female wrestlers (in this case, an entire family
in the same line of work). As if adhering to a principle of ethical
anthropology, Grobet's shots insist on always depicting their subjects with their masks on.

J. G. M.

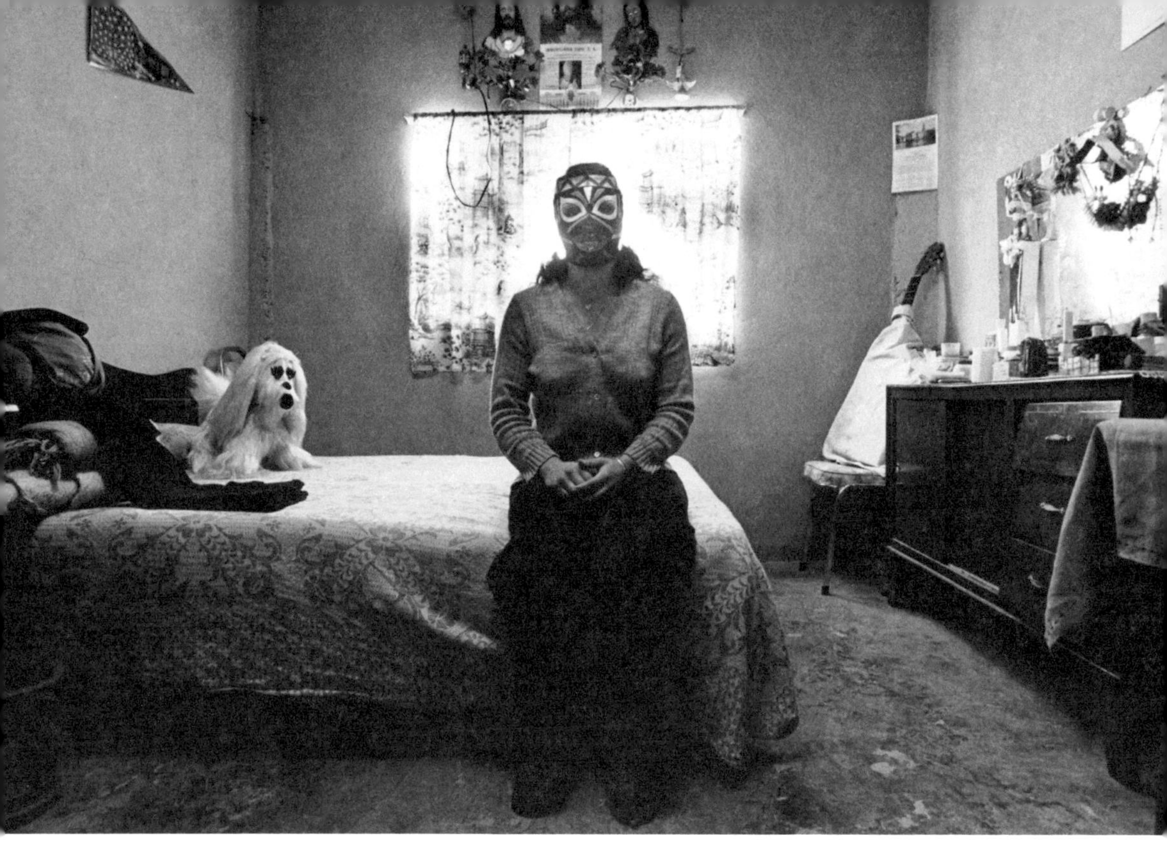

Silvia Gruner

Mexico City, Mexico, 1959

La expulsión del paraíso
[*Expulsion from Paradise*], 1993

Installation. Soap, pottery shards,
crystal, sugar, cloth, wood, and hair
Variable dimensions
Acquisition, 2005

Silvia Gruner's work is framed by her critique of identity-based positions and the use of symbols in historical processes.

Initially designed to cover the windows of the convent in Tepoztlán, Morelos, the installation comprises yellow bars of Tepeyac-brand laundry soap, which have been carved to accommodate small pre-Colombian figurines. The piece revisits the artist's recurring language by associating ideas of cleanliness and bodily hygiene with signs of identity crisis and cultural erasure. The title is a clear reference to the Book of Genesis, and the brand of soap alludes to popular religiosity—yet Gruner reinvents these references with materials belonging to the feminine and domestic realms, in tension with idolatry, the power of relics, and a historical perspective.

V. R. L.

Detail

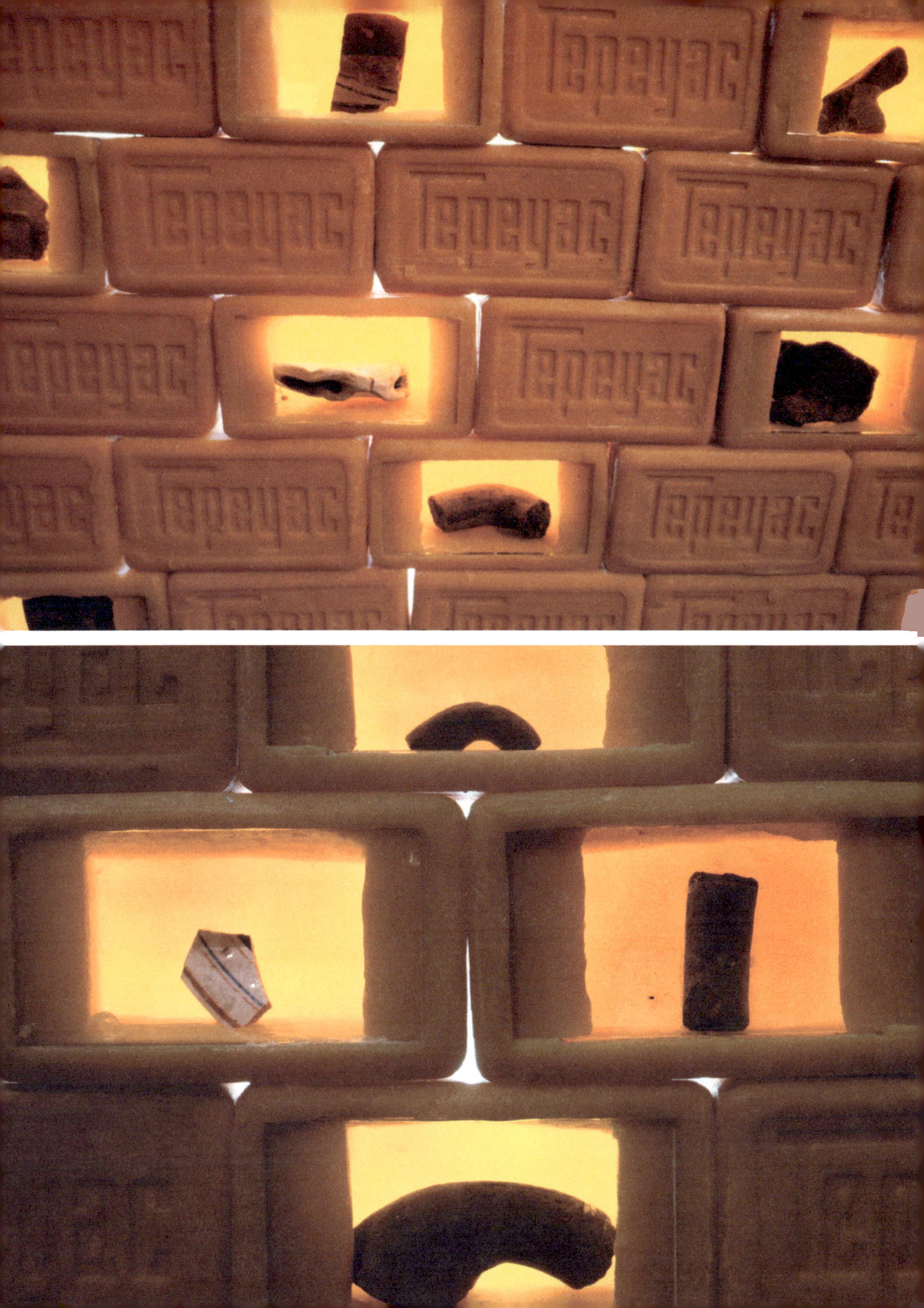
Tepeyac
Tepeyac
Tepeyac
Tepeyac
Tepeyac
Tepeyac
Tepeyac
Tepeyac
Tepeyac
Tepeyac

Yolanda Gutiérrez

—

Mexico City, Mexico, 1970

La corriente [*The Current*], 1997

Installation. Palm tree pods
wood, and animal ashes
Variable dimensions
Acquisition, 1999

Yolanda Gutiérrez's installations combine an ecological sensibility, experiments with materials of natural origin, and a defiance
of the convention that deposits sculptures on a base or on the
ground. Gutiérrez has often located her interventions in bodies
of water or in open space, hanging them from the ceiling of an
architectural structure. *La corriente* is one of her hanging installations. This evocation of a fleet of rustic palm tree pods boats
was made expressly so that they would be reflected in the illuminated drop ceiling of the UNAM's Museo Universitario de Ciencias
y Arte, in which the boats appear to be floating on a lake, viewed
from below. This combination of lyricism and material creativity is
characteristic of Gutiérrez's work as a sculptor.

C. M.

Detail

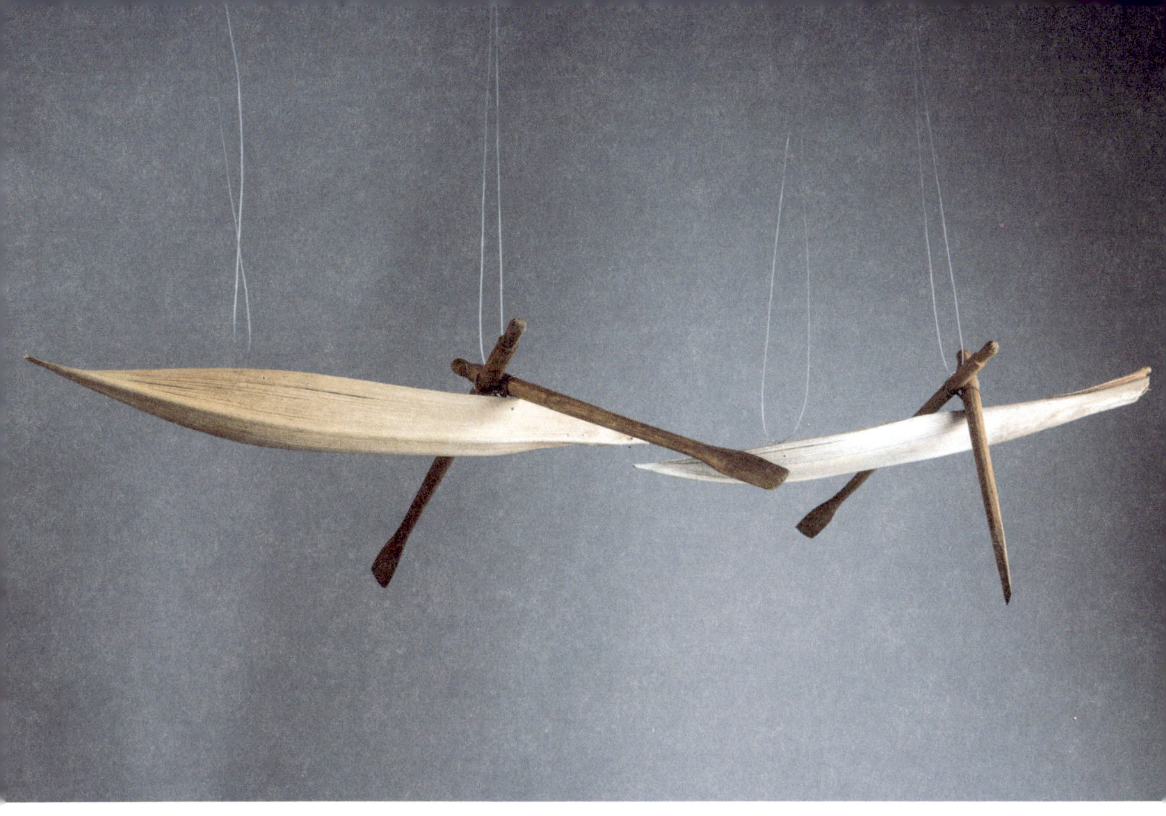

Enrique Guzmán

Guadalajara, Mexico, 1952–Aguascalientes, Mexico, 1986

Vértigo [*Vertigo*], 1975

Oil on canvas
60.5 × 80.8 cm
Acquisition, 2007

By age 30, Enrique Guzmán had achieved a certain stylistic solidity as a painter, as well as the attention of local gallery owners and critics. His style combined appropriations of Surrealism and Dadaism in his use of references and techniques, in addition to a highly unusual version of pop art mixed with ironic references to religion and Mexican identity. Such elements were later described as *neomexicanismo*.

Olivier Debroise indicates the presence of "visualized verbal metaphors" in Guzmán's work, while Teresa del Conde alludes to a constant access to "his own labyrinth." *Vértigo* is a piece from the final phase of his career that contrasts with his earlier style, confronting us with intimate, impossible architectures. Carlos Blas Galindo describes this period of his work as "a series of tectonic sculptures in which he alludes, among other things, to perceptual modifications of space and time through drug use." These elements grant the work a certain sense of existential drama. His interest in erratic lifestyles and explosive behavior associates Guzmán with the generational concerns expressed in the *literatura de la Onda,* (a literary exploration of rock, generational rupture, and substance use), by authors like Parménides García Saldaña and José Agustín.

J. G. M.

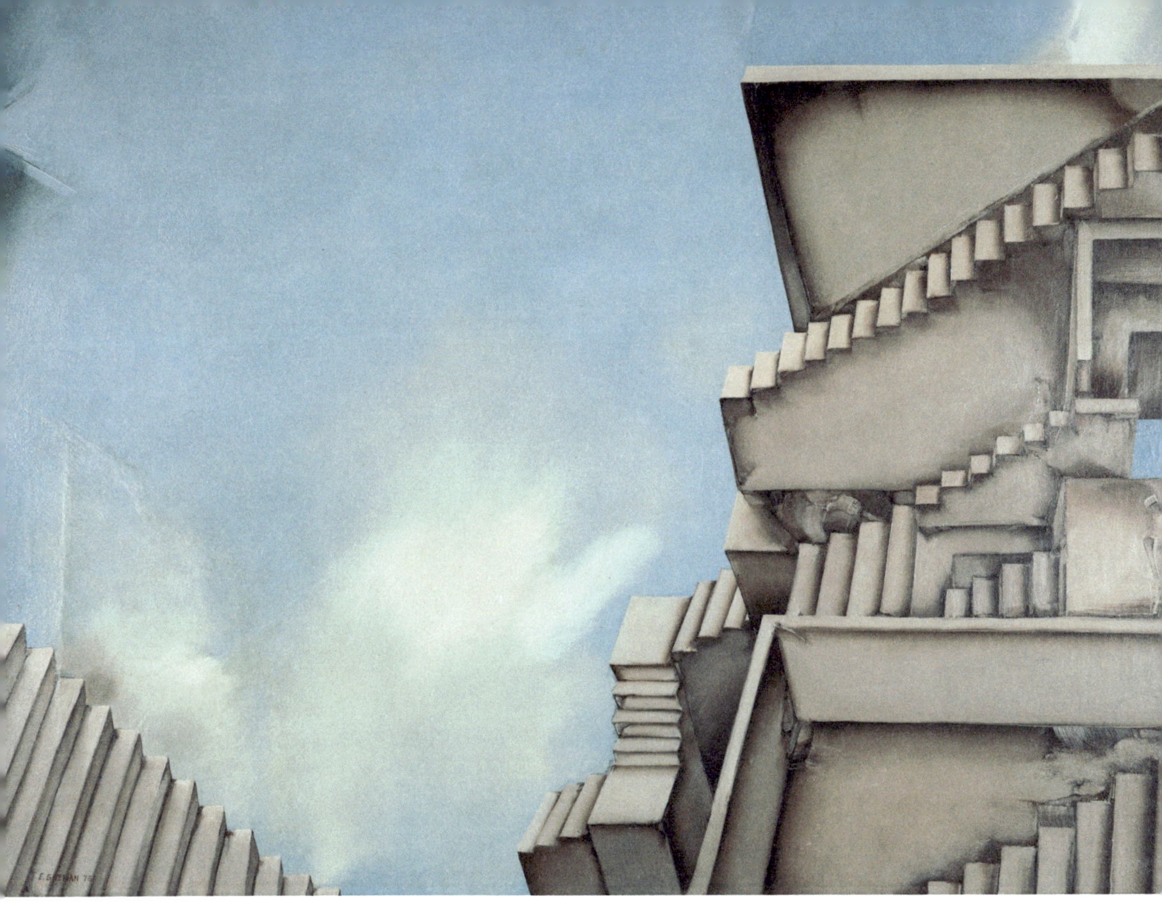

Jan Hendrix

Maasbree, Netherlands, 1949

Script, 1996–2002

2 000 serigraphs on Nepalese paper
Approx. 12 × 18 cm each
Acquisition, 1999
Donation by the artist, 2007

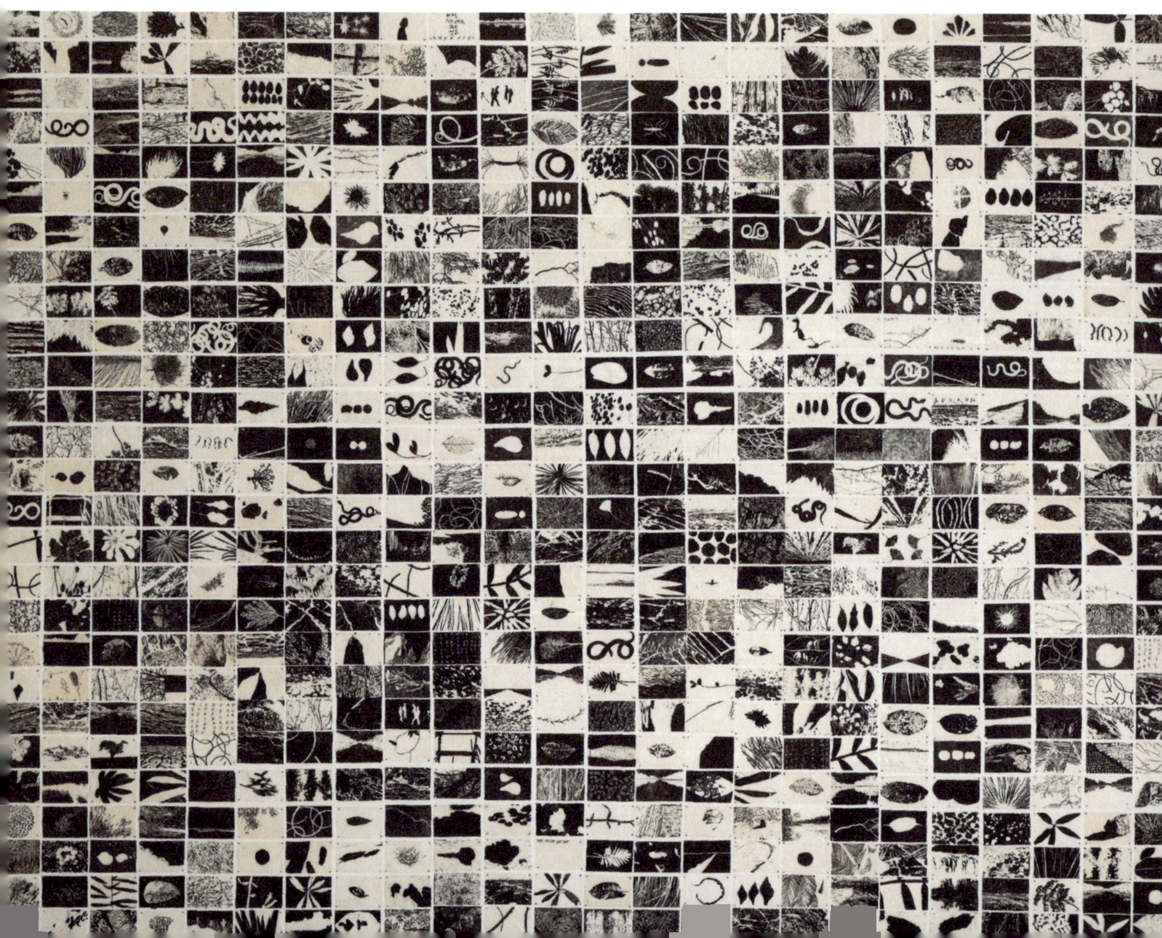

The 2000 serigraphs on Nepalese paper that make up *Script* also compose a catalog of Jan Hendrix's visual vocabulary over a fifteen-year period. They consist of images taken from notes and photographs obtained throughout his extensive travels: a visual archive to which the artist constantly turns and returns. The work is mounted in different ways to suit each space. The image-turned-icon plays with scale by drawing viewers closer to a particular fragment, a segment of the landscape, before pulling them away again and inviting them to explore the mosaic as a varied, boundless universe. By nature, *Script* is both instrument and œuvre, as well as Hendrix's attempt to define the universe of his own gaze in the transition between the twentieth and twenty-first centuries.

A. d. C.

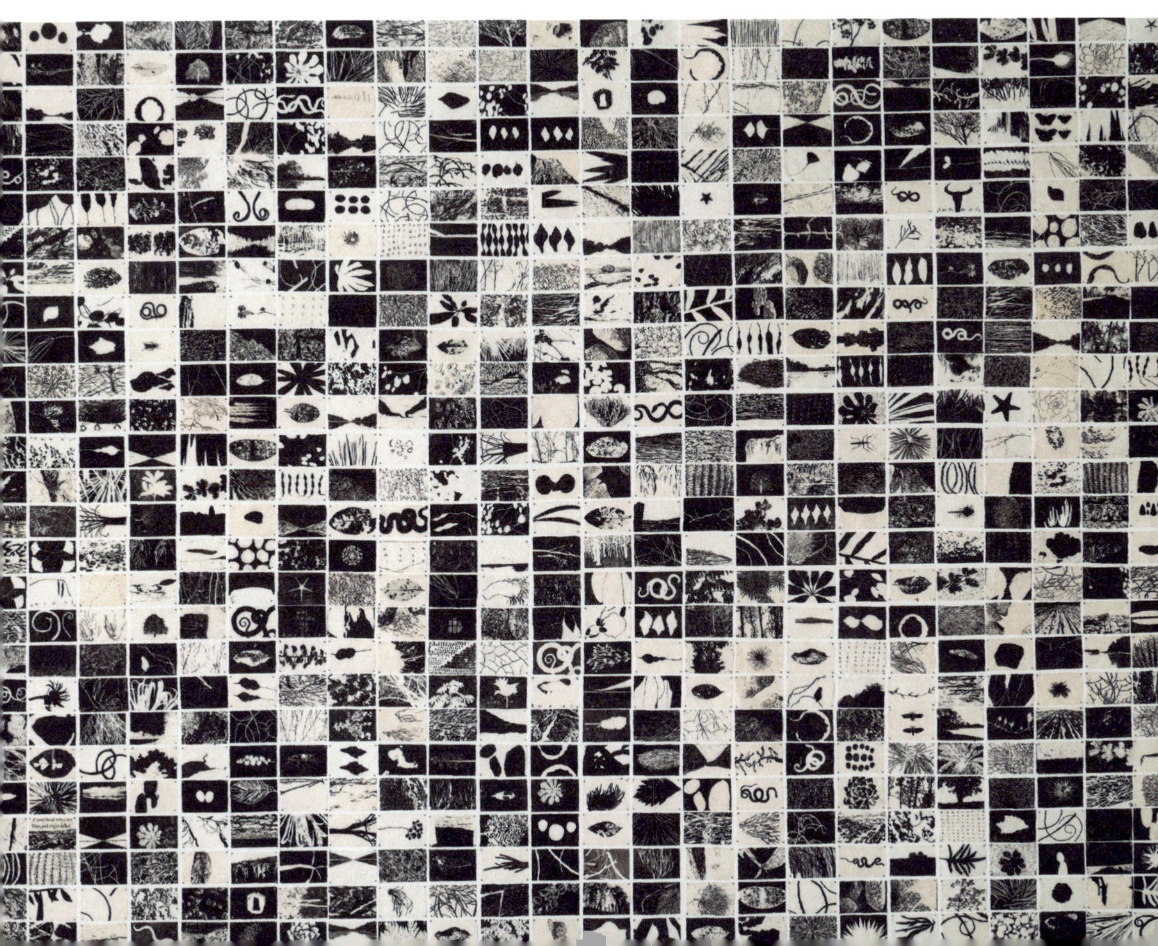

Melquiades Herrera

—

Mexico City, Mexico, 1949–2003

Untitled, 1979

La lonchera [*The Lunchbox*], action of the No-Grupo
at the Annual Experimentation Section, INBA
Coca-Cola glass bottle, landyard, and paper card
23.3 x 6.5 cm
Fondo Melquiades Herrera, Centro de
Documentación Arkheia, MUAC (DiGAV-UNAM)
Acquisition, 2013

In 1979, the Instituto Nacional de Bellas Artes held the first and
only Sección Anual de Experimentación of the Salón Nacional
de Artes Plásticas. The No-Grupo presented a *Montaje de
Momentos Plásticos* [*Exhibition of Visual Moments*]. With this
nomenclature, they proposed a kind of performance in which
each member of the collective would use an object, expressly
designed for the occasion, to produce actions and critical commentary. At the end of the event, they distributed *La lonchera,* a
multiple-item kit with printed matter and objects alluding to the
intervention. Herrera added a bottle of Coca-Cola—a constant
conceptual presence in his work—to the kit, with remarks printed
on labels much like the cards that once described pieces in
museum collections.

The allusion to art's "rescue" of reality (and, therefore, its
prior kidnapping) and the determining factor of transforming it,
if consumed, into an everyday object, should be interpreted as
Herrera's highly personal notion of the ready-made: a brutal wink
to Duchampian tradition.

J. G. M.

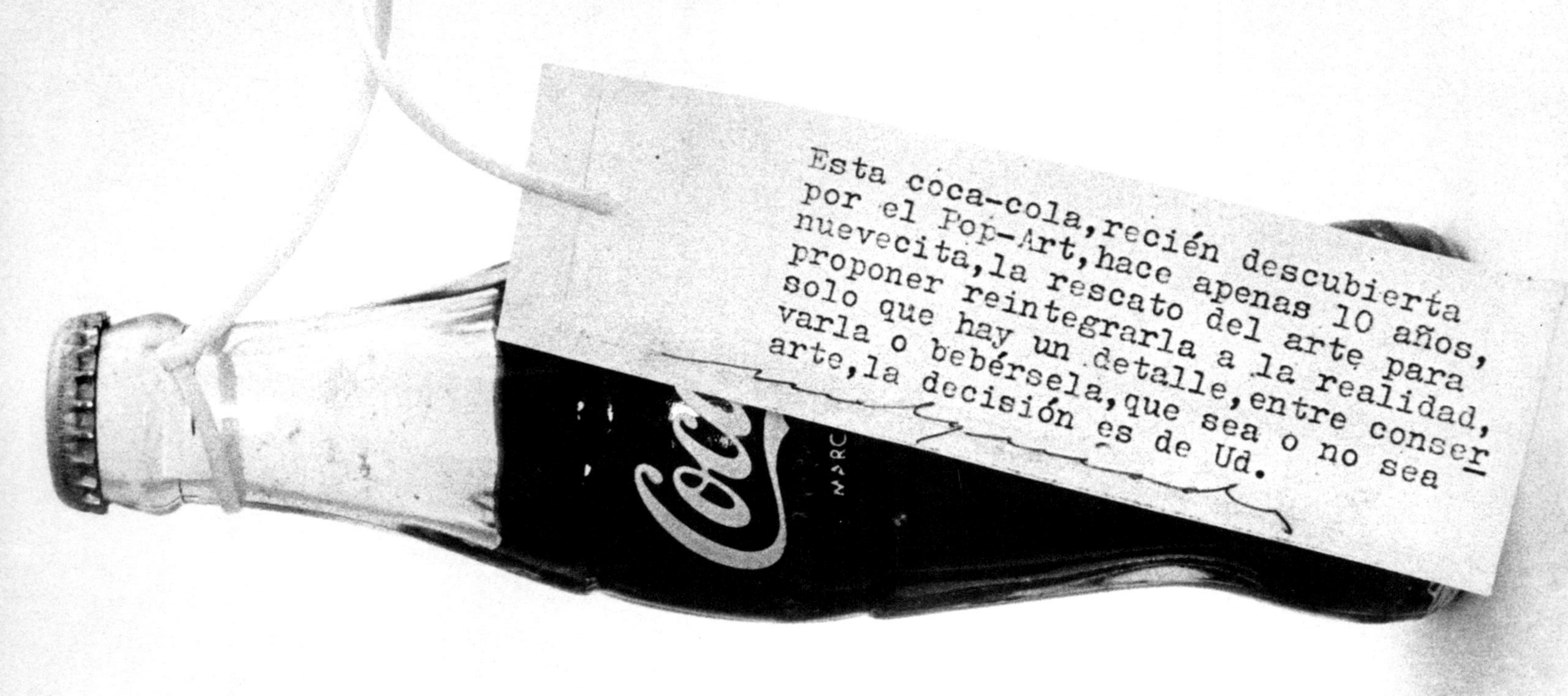

Esta coca-cola, recién descubierta
por el Pop-Art, hace apenas 10 años,
nuevecita, la rescato del arte para
proponer reintegrarla a la realidad,
solo que hay un detalle, entre conser
varla o bebérsela, que sea o no sea
arte, la decisión es de Ud.

Hersúa
(Manuel de Jesús Hernández Suárez)
—

Ciudad Obregón, Mexico, 1940

Ambiente circular [*Circular Environment*], 1974

Replica, 2007, with the collaboration of the artist
2 modules. Metal structure, aluminum
sheet, and automotive paint
366 × 330 × 450 cm
Acquisition, 2006

Originally conceived as an ephemeral piece for the exhibition *Ambientes urbanos* [*Urban Environments,* 1973–1974] at the Palacio de Bellas Artes, *Ambiente circular* seeks to trigger profound bodily sensations with its formal and chromatic characteristics. The piece is an example of the artist's effort to design traversable sculptural/architectural experiments that could only be completed through audience participation; in this case, the public has to move the sculpture's parts, which are equipped with wheels at the bottom. The piece was destroyed at the end of the exhibition, but a replica was produced in 2007 under the artist's supervision for the show *The Age of Discrepancy*.

J. G. S.

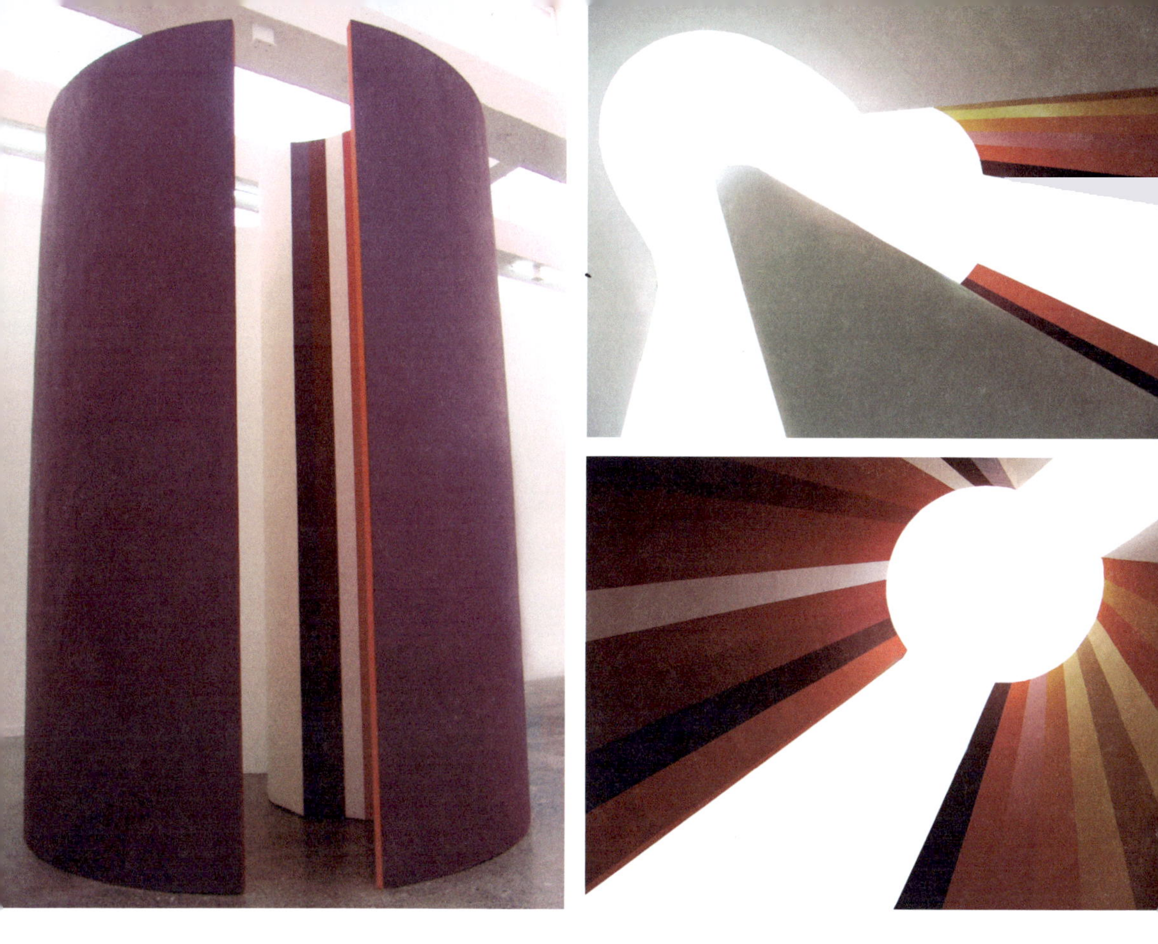

Roberto Huarcaya

Lima, Peru, 1959

Amazonagrama n.3
[*Amazongram No. 3*], 2014

Ilford multigrade RC paper
108 × 3000 cm
Gift of Fundación Espacio V,
in process, 2020

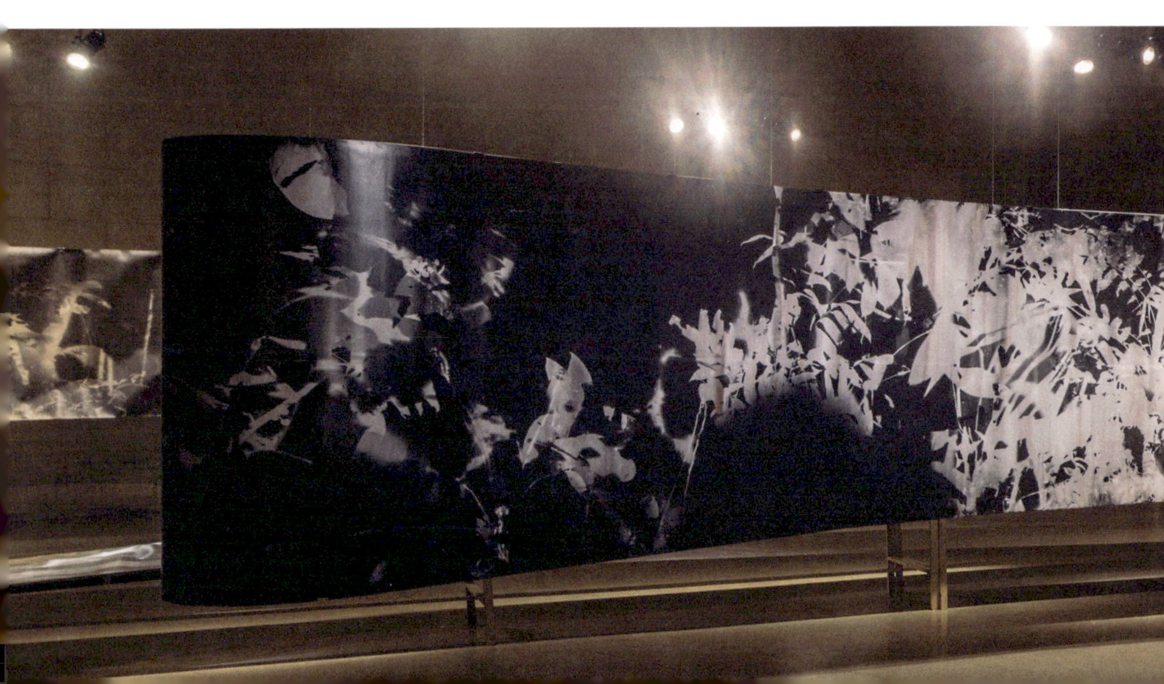

In 2014, the Wildlife Conservation Society invited various artists to develop work inspired by the Parque Nacional Bahuaja
Sonene in Tambopata, Peru. Roberto Huarcaya, interested in
experimenting with photographic processes, brought a roll of
photosensitive paper into the jungle, measuring 1.08 by 30 m,
and with the help of a small flash, he captured the surrounding
environment. The rain, humidity, moonlight, and lush vegetation
all played a part in creating a map of light and shadow, one that
treats chance and error as expressions of the power of nature.

A. d. C.

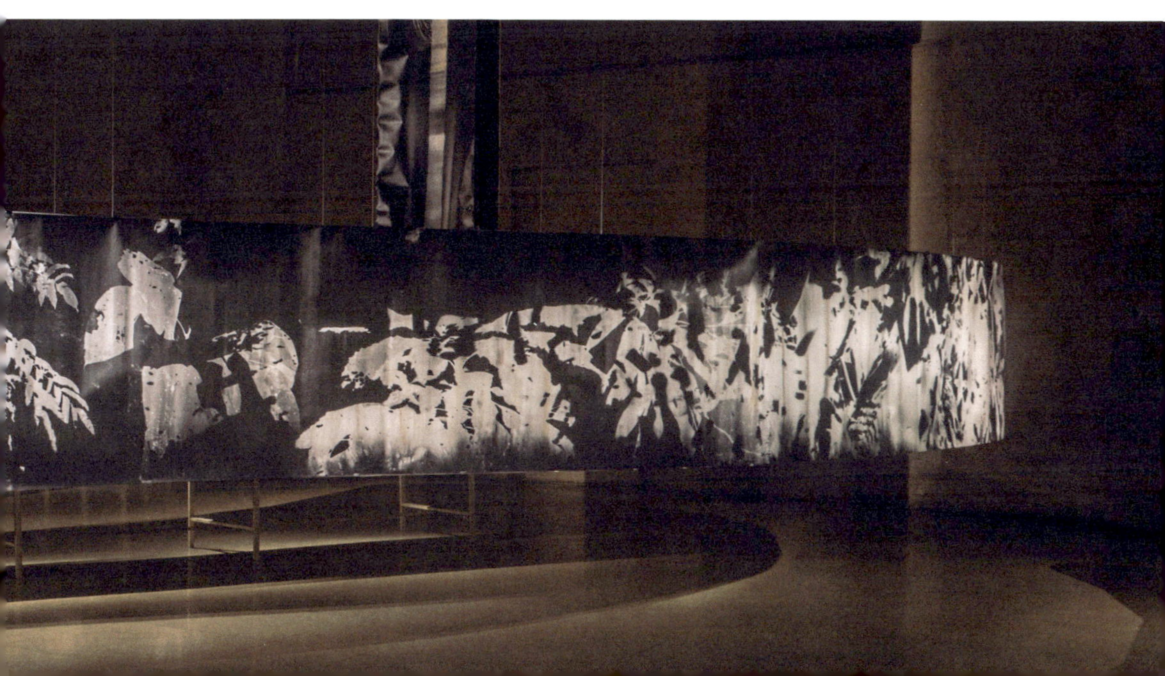

Graciela Iturbide

Mexico City, Mexico, 1942

Cayó del cielo
[*Fallen from Heaven*], 1990

Gelatin silver print
29.5 × 43.5 cm
Acquisition, 2005

The feast of Saint Michael is celebrated on September 26 in Chalma, Mexico State. During the day, festivities, fairs, and processions are held as part of this tradition devoted to the town's patron saint. The holiday is also an excuse for some people to dress up—like the woman in the photograph who, in the middle of the celebration, walks neatly over the bare earth in her plastic sandals and white wings. Iturbide has chosen not to show us her face, a recurring decision in her work; instead, she lets the truncated wings and the gesture of her hand, gathering up her skirts, express the subject's identity and attitude as she walks. The image reveals the photographer's obsession with masks and disguises as a means of creating fiction and reality in everyday life.

In Graciela Iturbide's work, we can see a striking degree of personal involvement, the construction of intimate bonds with the communities documented therein. Her camera approaches people in such a way that the final image defies a merely anthropological interpretation.

A. d. C.

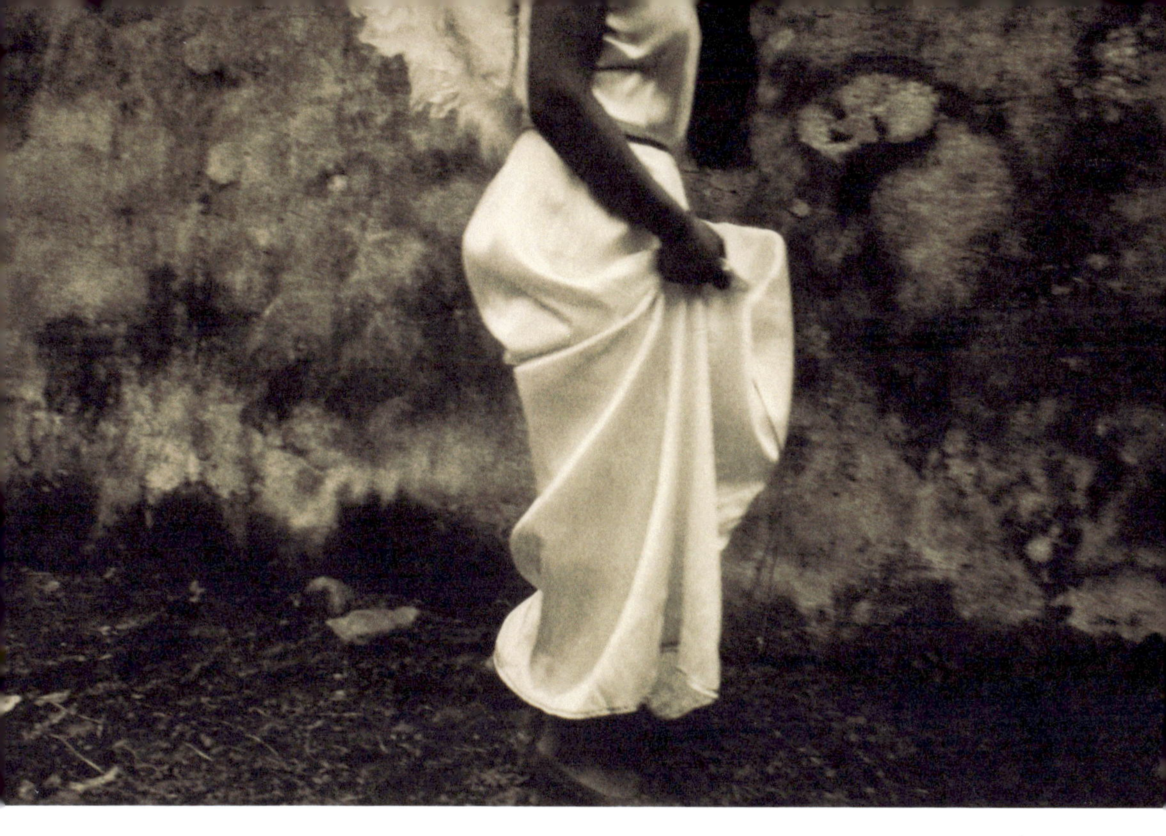

Enrique Ježik

Córdoba, Argentina, 1961

Ejercicio de percusión
[*Percussion Exercise*], 2006

Video
3' 52"
Ed. 1/5
Acquisition of Amigos del MUAC, 2019

Some meters away from Mexico City's Palacio Nacional [National Palace], the headquarters of the executive branch, a squad of riot police burst into a museum: the Ex Teresa Arte Actual. The startling soundtrack produced by the clatter of their shields and clubs sparked tension and unease among the spectators, who shrank back as they passed. Sowing doubt as to whether the police charge was an artistic action an actual repressive strike, the piece alludes to suppression and intimidation tactics, as well as to the violence and imposition of power so often faced by dissent and protest. The formation of the security elements and the sound of their armored bodies activates the social memory of a choreography of terror, one we associate with the dissolution or dispersion of demonstrations through the abuse of force and the argument of "restoring public order."

Ježik produces a diverse range of artistic registers that are generally formalized in photography or video. As records, they tend to seek direct images to express the state of acts involving confrontation and force. In this case, sound is a crucial protagonist in the action.

S. H.

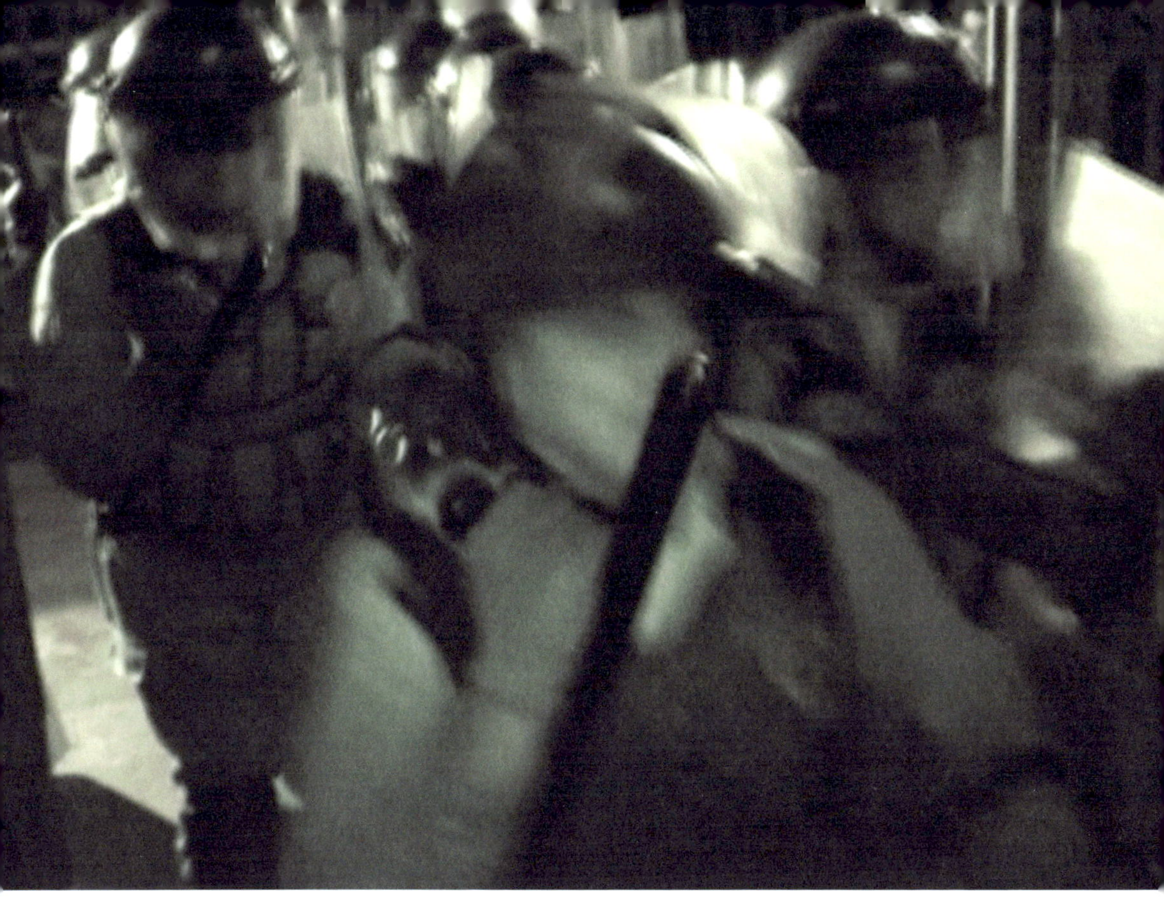

Yishai Jusidman

Mexico City, Mexico, 1963

Astrónomo XXV
[***Astronomer XXV***], 1990

From the series *Astrónomo*
Encaustic on wood
182 × 65 cm Ø
Acquisition, 2005

Jusidman's work has consistently reaffirmed the possibilities
and importance of painting amid the prevailing skepticism of
the contemporary art world. His work questions the limits of the
pictorial medium and revises the two-dimensionality of the disci-
pline and its spatial explorations, resisting the modernist zeal
to treat it as a mere platform.

The series *Astrónomo*, which borrows its title from the eponymous painting by Johannes Vermeer of 1668, is one of his first
works to defy the convention of the pictorial "plane." Jusidman
paints naturalist landscapes on wooden spheres, alluding to the
mapamundi, while also inverting the logic of deformation in
representation in flat media. He thus evokes the visual perception
of the human gaze and the depiction of the visual field, a clear
allusion to the artificial perspective of historical references.

V. R. L.

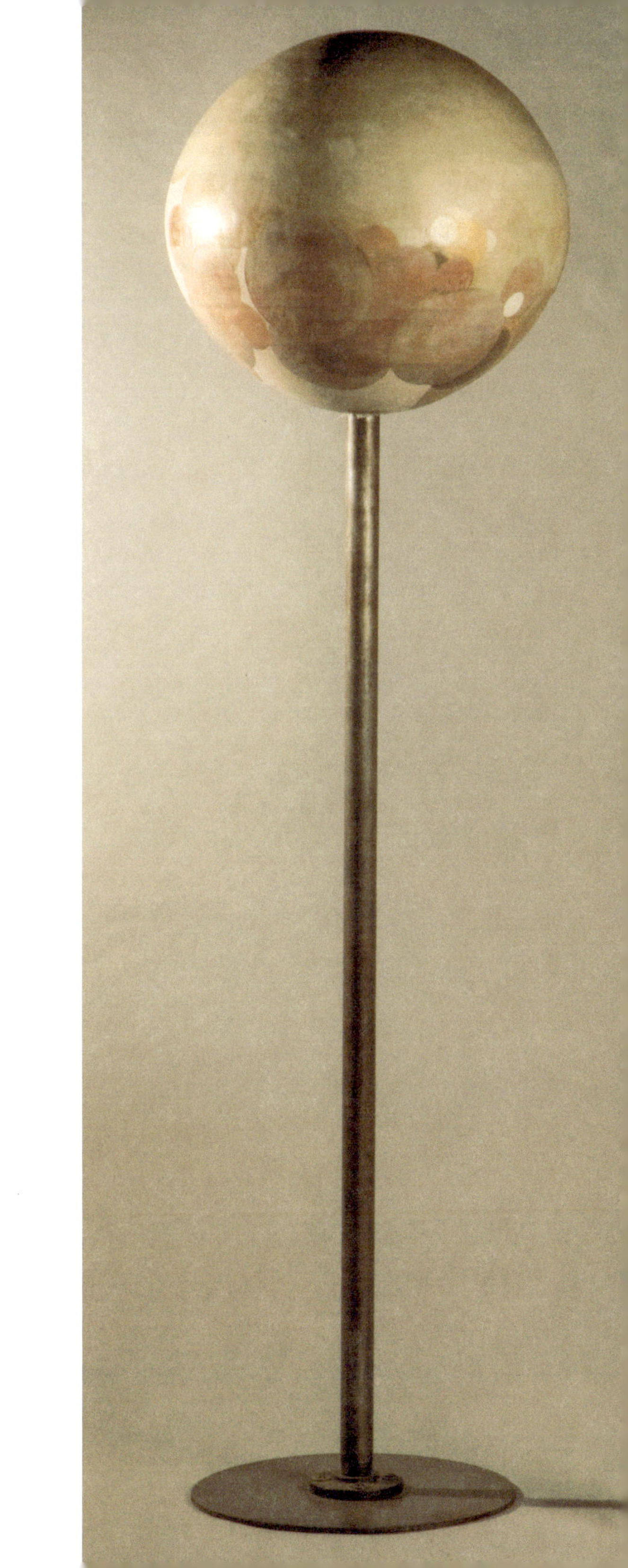

Leandro Katz

Buenos Aires, Argentina, 1938

La huella de Viernes
[*Friday's Footprint*], 1984

Installation. Illuminated photographic
transparency, sandbox, and human footprint
Light box: 153 × 195 × 22.5 cm
Sandbox: 22 × 195 × 50 cm
Ed. 1/5
Gift of the artist, in process, 2018

There is no more dramatic moment in Daniel Defoe's *Robinson Crusoe* (1719) than the shipwrecked man's discovery of a footprint in the sand: a declaration of the presence of an indigenous person that disrupts his illusion of inhabiting a deserted island. Leandro Katz recalls this figure of the colonial imaginary to name an installation that involves a footprint in sand beneath an illuminated box: the beautiful image of a Maya nobleman's foot, found in a nearly destroyed fragment of the Temple of the Inscriptions at Tikal. This transhistorical assemblage is characteristic of Katz's explorations, which evoke the enigma of these images with the sensitivity of a poet and a photographer.

C. M.

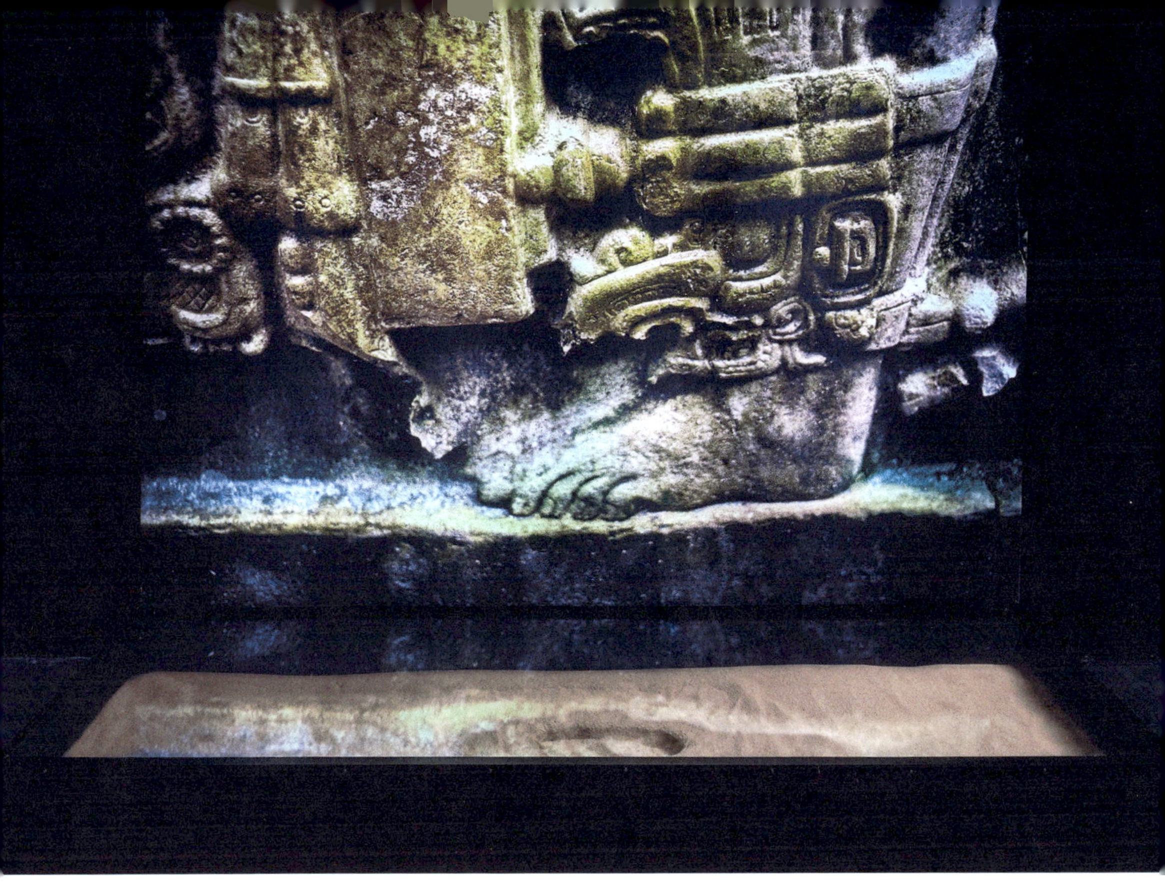

Perla Krauze

—

Mexico City, Mexico, 1953

Construcción #4
[*Construction #4*], 2018

Installation. Graphite imprints on canvas, water,
lead sheet, cement, wood, gold leaf, and oil
Variable dimensions
Acquisition through the SHCP
Pago en Especie program, 2017

Perla Krauze visited scores of stone workshops, quarries, brick-
works, fossil deposits, salt flats, natural springs, and other spaces
in the Mexican state of Puebla, researching the artistic possibilities of the region's stone-extraction industry. She was particularly
fascinated by the rock slabs used in workshops as a base to cut
marble and fine stone; these slabs end up etched by the blade
of the diamond saw, suggesting a random drawing. Based on
these marks, Krauze produces "imprints" in the form of frottages
on those surfaces, capturing the memory of artisanal labor. The
series *Construcción* is among the hybrid pieces—sculpture meets
painting meets collector's-cabinet—with which Krauze archives
her explorations and compilations.

C. M.

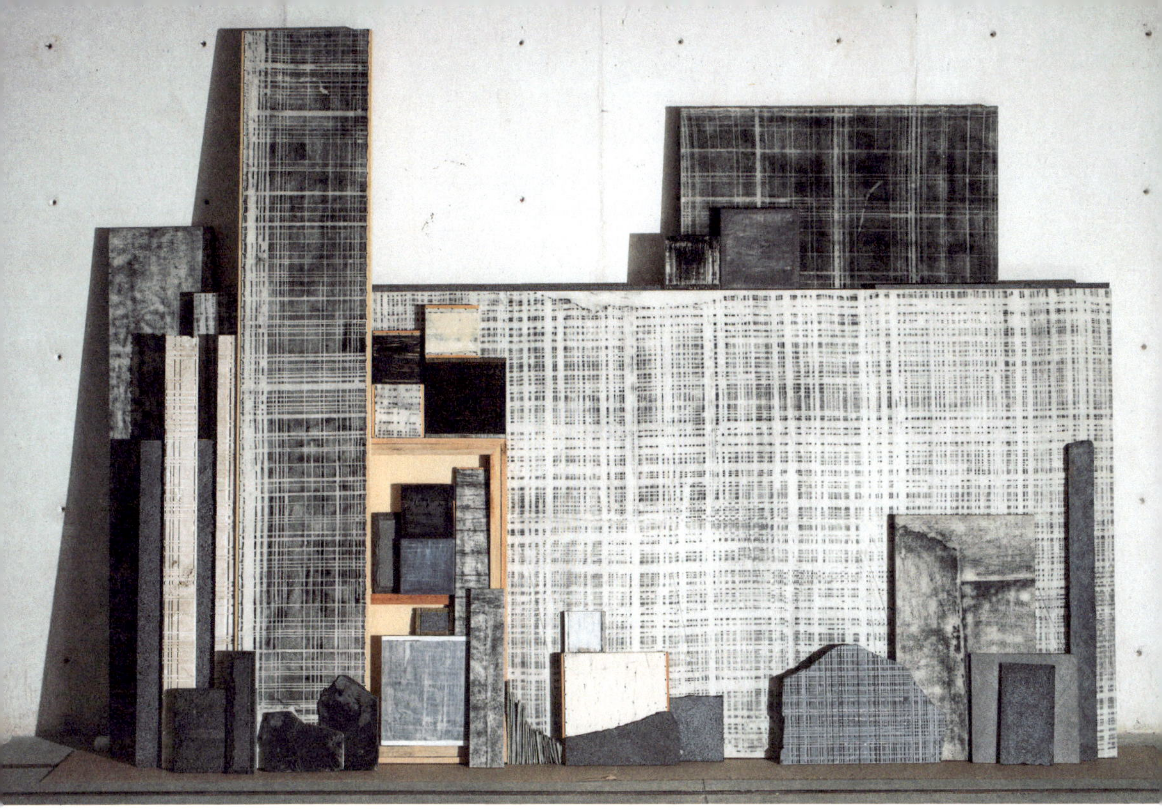

Myra Landau

Bucharest, Romania, 1926–Alkmaar, Netherlands, 2018

Ritmo paranoico
[*Paranoid Rhythm*], 1975

Pastel on linen
130 × 130 cm
Gift of the artist, 1990

After living for some time in Brazil, Myra Landau came to Mexico at a key moment for the solidification of abstract art. Her work from the mid-1960s into the late '70s is characterized by free-hand drawings of concentric rectangles and flat colors applied in pastel onto unprepared linen. She calls these pieces *Ritmos* [*Rhythms*], and they reveal the influence of op art and Brazilian geometrism, as well as Landau's interest in creating work with an expressive essence more than a formalist one.

With "stripes" (as she called them) that break concentrically or intertwine, Landau weaves patterns that evoke textiles, pentagrams, or labyrinths. In this painting, as the title suggests, the artist explores concepts of rhythm, repetition, and contrast to depict a paranoid mental state on the canvas.

A. d. C.

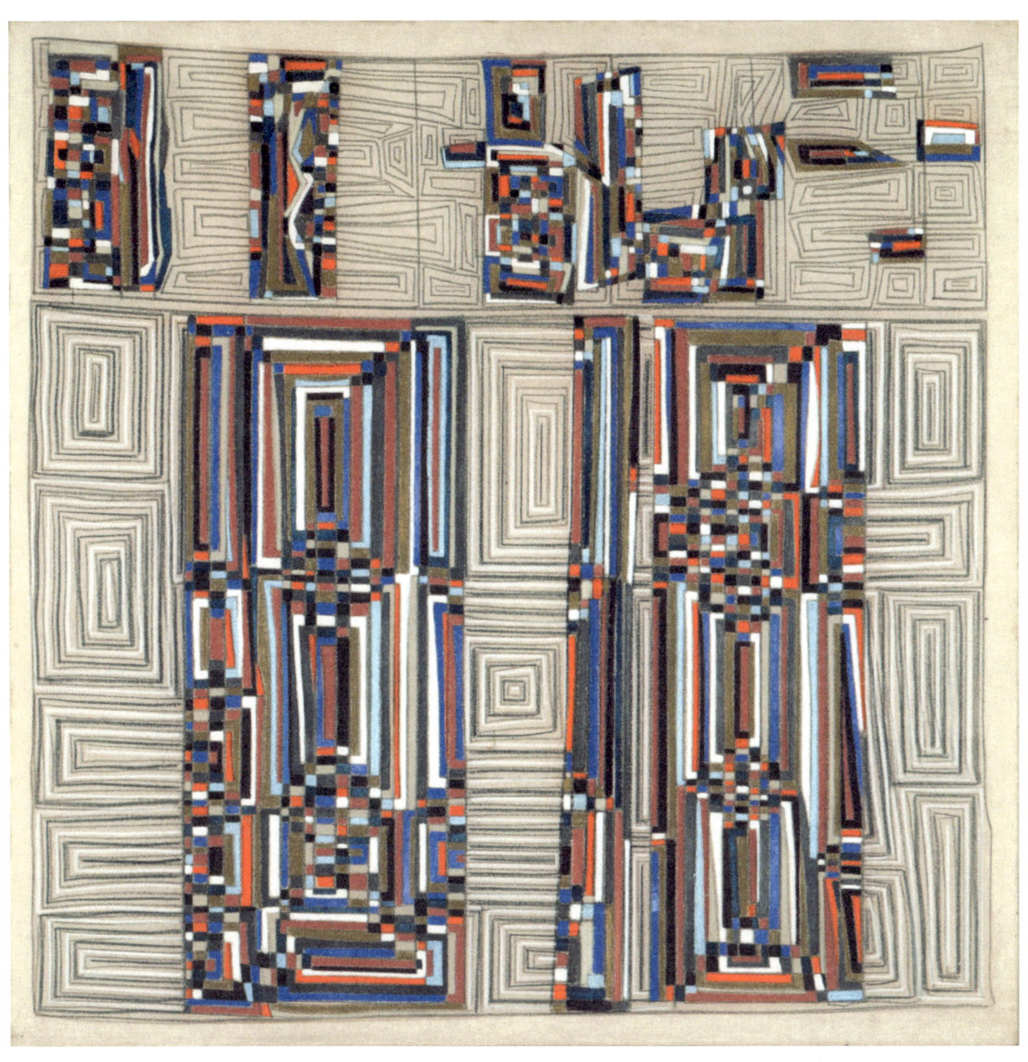

Magali Lara

Mexico City, Mexico, 1956

Cae [*Falls*], 1999

Embroidery on high-wrap wool tapestry,
dyed with mineral anilines and woven
by hand, mattress, and vinyl text
300 × 400 cm
Acquisition with funds from the Presupuesto
de Egresos de la Federación, 2014

In 1999, Magali Lara tested the technical capacities of the Taller Mexicano de Gobelinos in Guadalajara by commissioning a series of textiles based on her subtle drawings made in pencil and India ink on Albanene paper. This drawing, dated 1997, was particularly difficult: the barely recognizable likeness of a fallen tree trunk that the artist found evocative of loss. For this association, Lara decided to exhibit the tapestry by using it to cover a futon that still conserved the shape of her body—and, implicitly, the loss of her husband, the artist Juan Francisco Elso. A line by Silvio Rodríguez, displayed on the wall, completed the scene: "And the causes began to besiege him / Ordinary, invisible / And fate began to entangle him / Powerful, invincible."

The traces don't register an object-cadaver so much as a field of possibilities and forces. In fact, the tapestry was damaged during an exhibition, and the artist incorporated her repair work as yet another layer of meaning. As is typical of Lara, her imprint and images don't simply document appearances; rather, they undertake the transcription of the body's sensations. Despite its sorrowful nature, this work crackles with vital energy.

C. M.

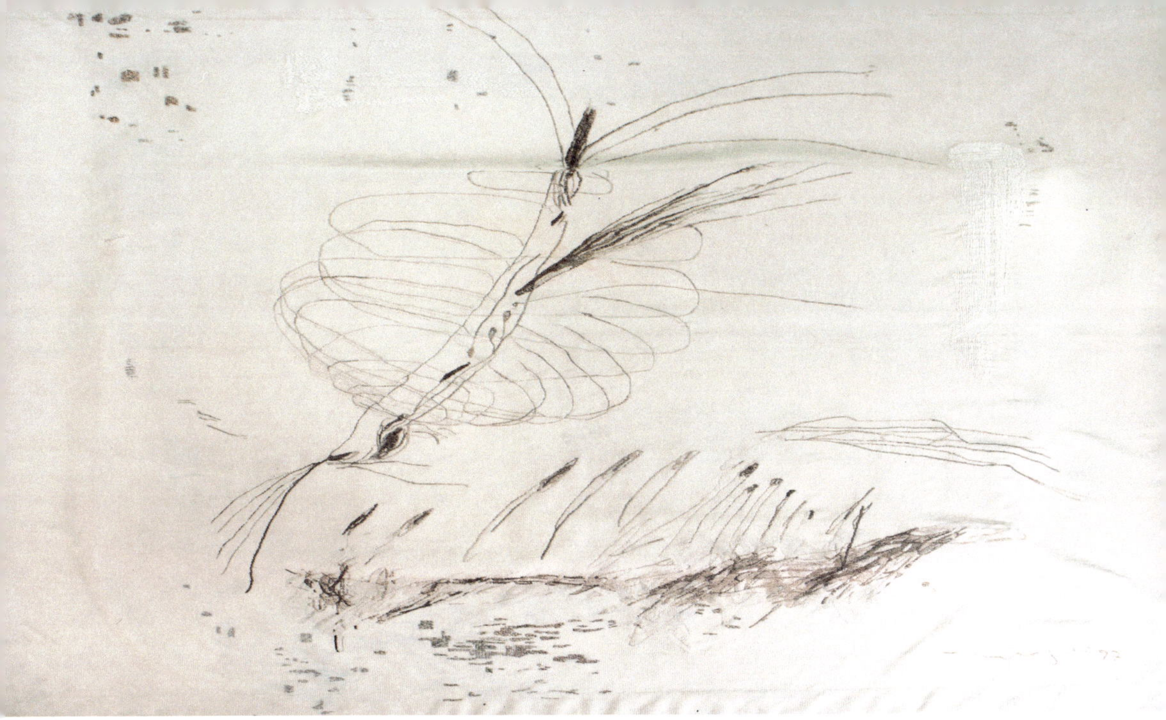

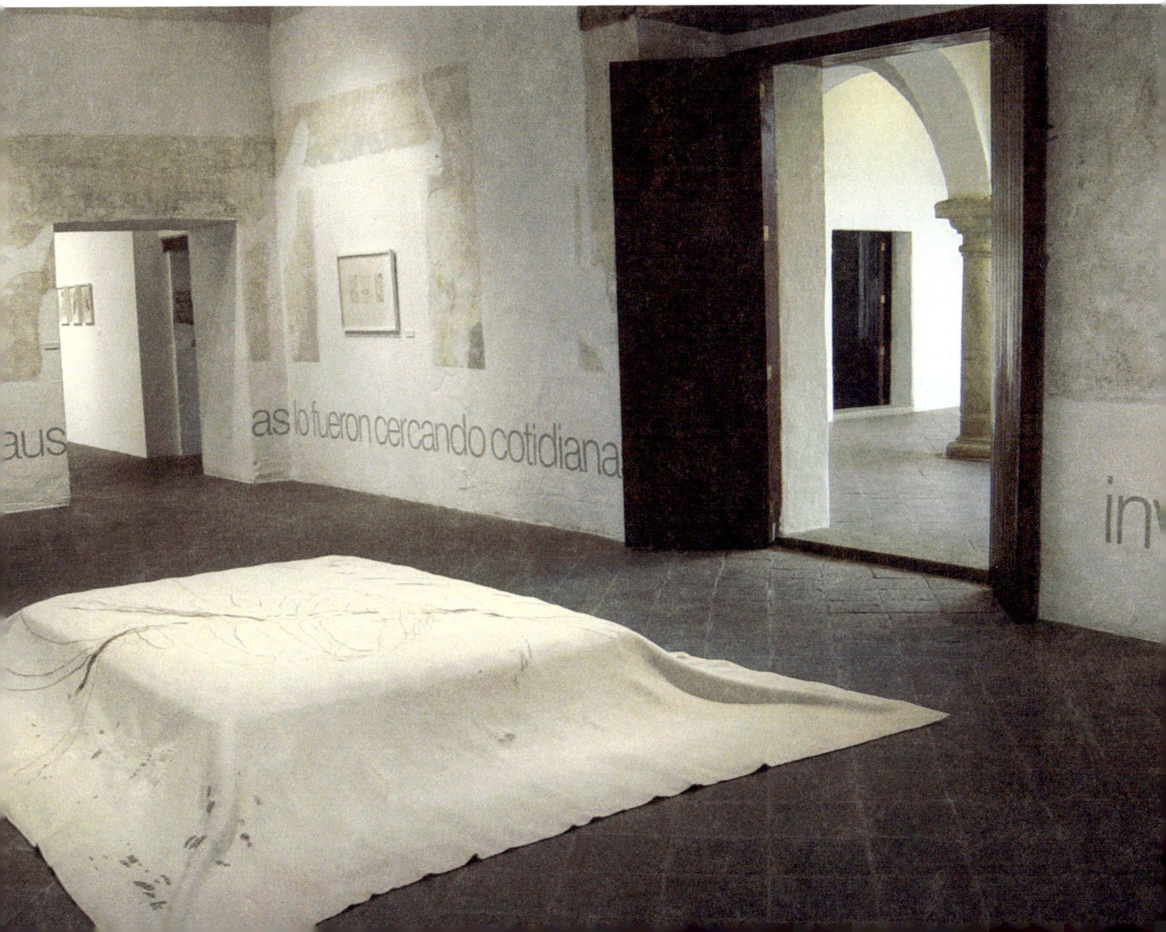

aus

as lo fueron cercando cotidiana

inv

Magali Lara

—

Mexico City, 1956

Tener/Desear [*To Have/To Desire*], 1998

Acrylic on canvas
150 × 240 cm
Acquisition, 1999

Lara has used painting to assemble a repertoire of forms that associate femininity with nature. A constant theme in her work is botanical observation as a poetics of the psychic and emotional imaginary. This painting is an aesthetic essay on the intimacy of the body and the natural world that both permeates and accompanies it. The composition traces the interior of female genitals and organic shapes that offer glimpses of flowers, birds, rhizomes, and fluids. Revealing this unconscious landscape, the work channels repressed impulses inside an undefined other.

M. A.

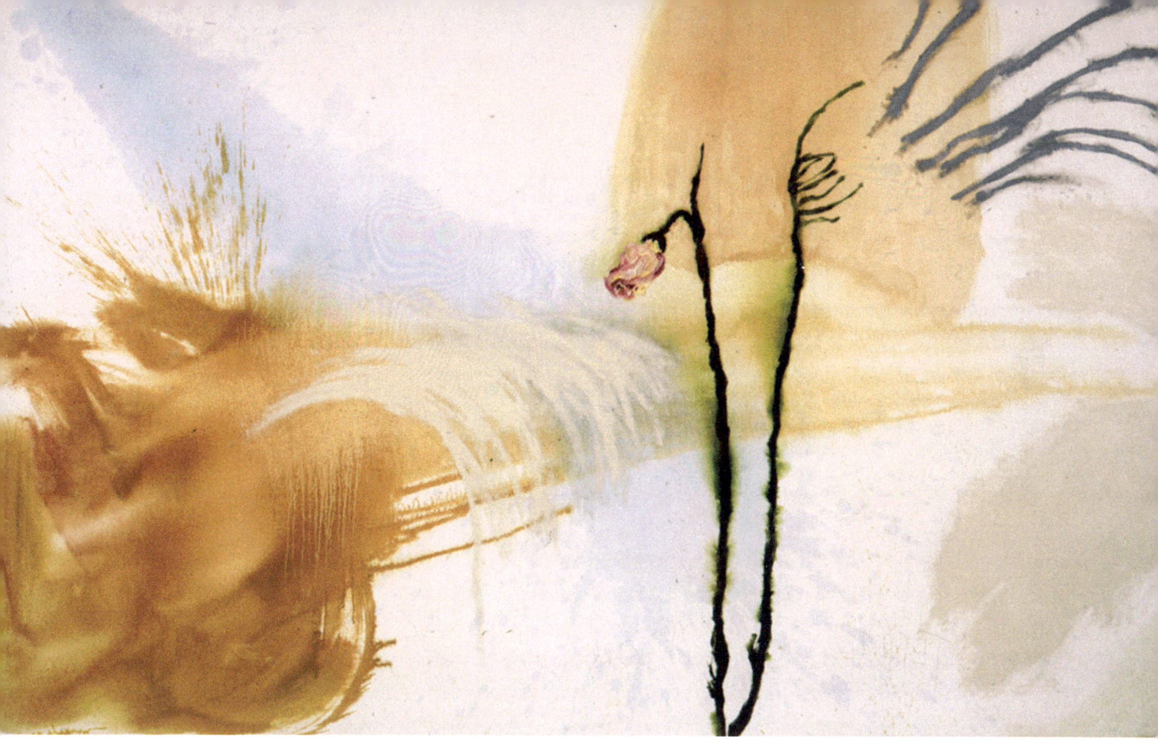

Pedro Lasch

—

Mexico City, Mexico, 1975

Espectro indígena: espejo negro 13 a 21
[*Indigenous Spectrum: Black Mirror 13 to 21*], 2014

Installation. Photographic prints behind
tinted glass and pre-Hispanic figures on
metal structures and wooden bases
Variable dimensions
Gift of the artist, 2016

This piece is part of a series of site-specific installations, titled
Black Mirror/Espejo negro, in which Lasch explores representations of coloniality through physically and psychologically
intersecting reflections that bring different historical moments
into the present. The piece is composed of "black mirrors" that
combine representations of "Indianness," drawn from Mexico's
postcolonial cultural repertoire, with pre-Hispanic masks placed
at the viewer's eye-level. By incorporating the viewer's body into
the interplay between these portraits and reflections, Lasch puts
pressure on the cultural associations and racial constructions
that constitute the split identity of the post-colonial spectator.

A. L.

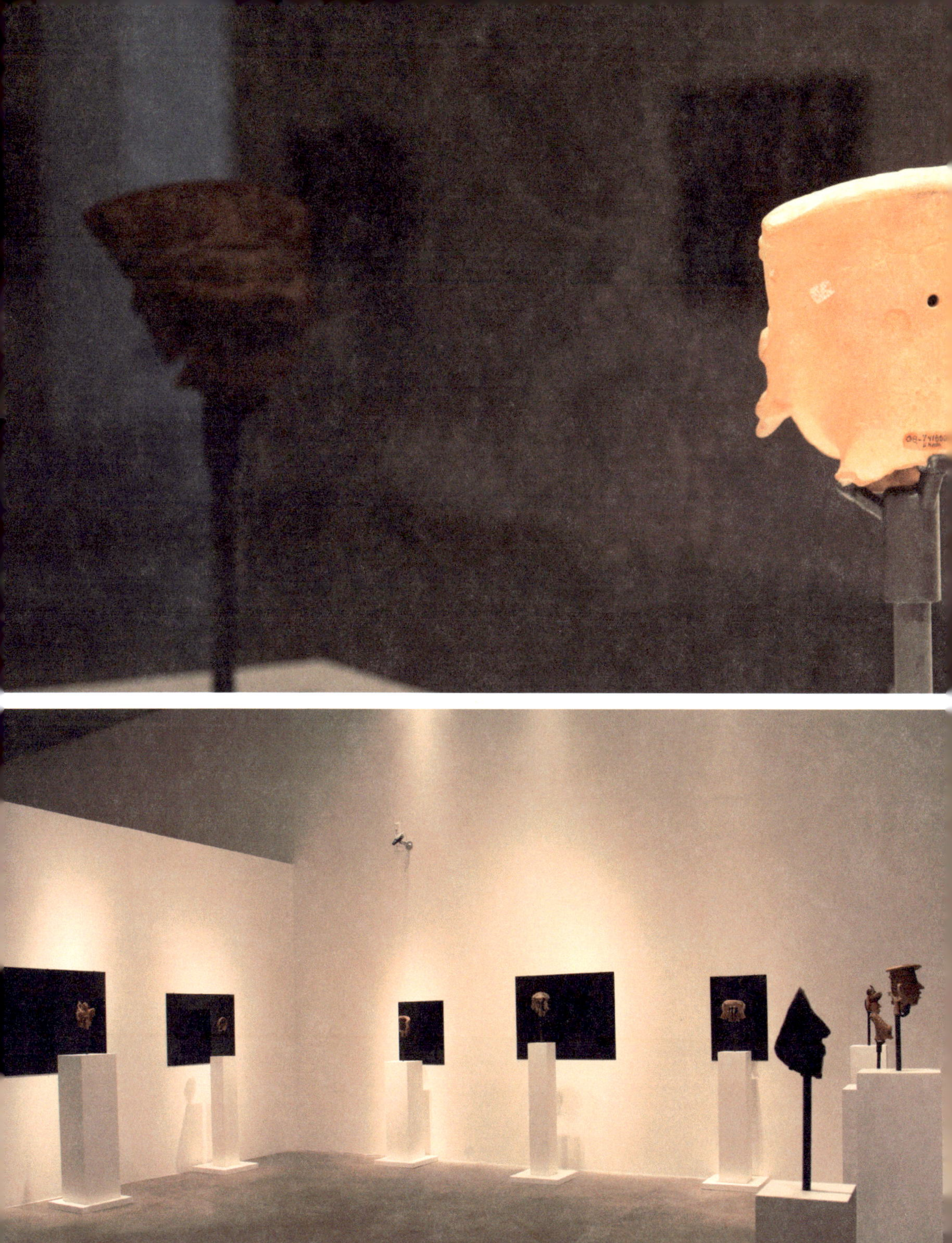

Daniel Lezama

Mexico City, Mexico, 1968

Carta para Agnes Egerton por E. Pingret
[*Letter to Agnes Egerton by E. Pingret*], 2010

From the series *Cartas de viaje* [*Travel Letters*]
Oil on canvas
180 × 140 cm
Acquisition with funds from the Presupuesto
de Egresos de la Federación, 2012

In this painting, Lezama alludes to the murder of Agnes Egerton
and her couple, the English painter Daniel Thomas Egerton, which
took place in 1842 in the neighborhood of Tacubaya, then on the
outskirts of Mexico City. Lezama's fictional interpretation depicts
an indigenous couple—portrayed in the style of Édouard Pingret's
costumbrista images—who have discovered the corpse of the
young woman, pregnant and assaulted. With the Valley of Mexico
in the background, the two naked youths hold open the body's
legs; in a secondary plane, a maguey flower seems to bloom from
the sex of the dead woman. The series *Cartas de viaje* explores
chronicles of Mexican territory—and their symbolic implications
—from the perspective of foreign travelers.

J. G. S.

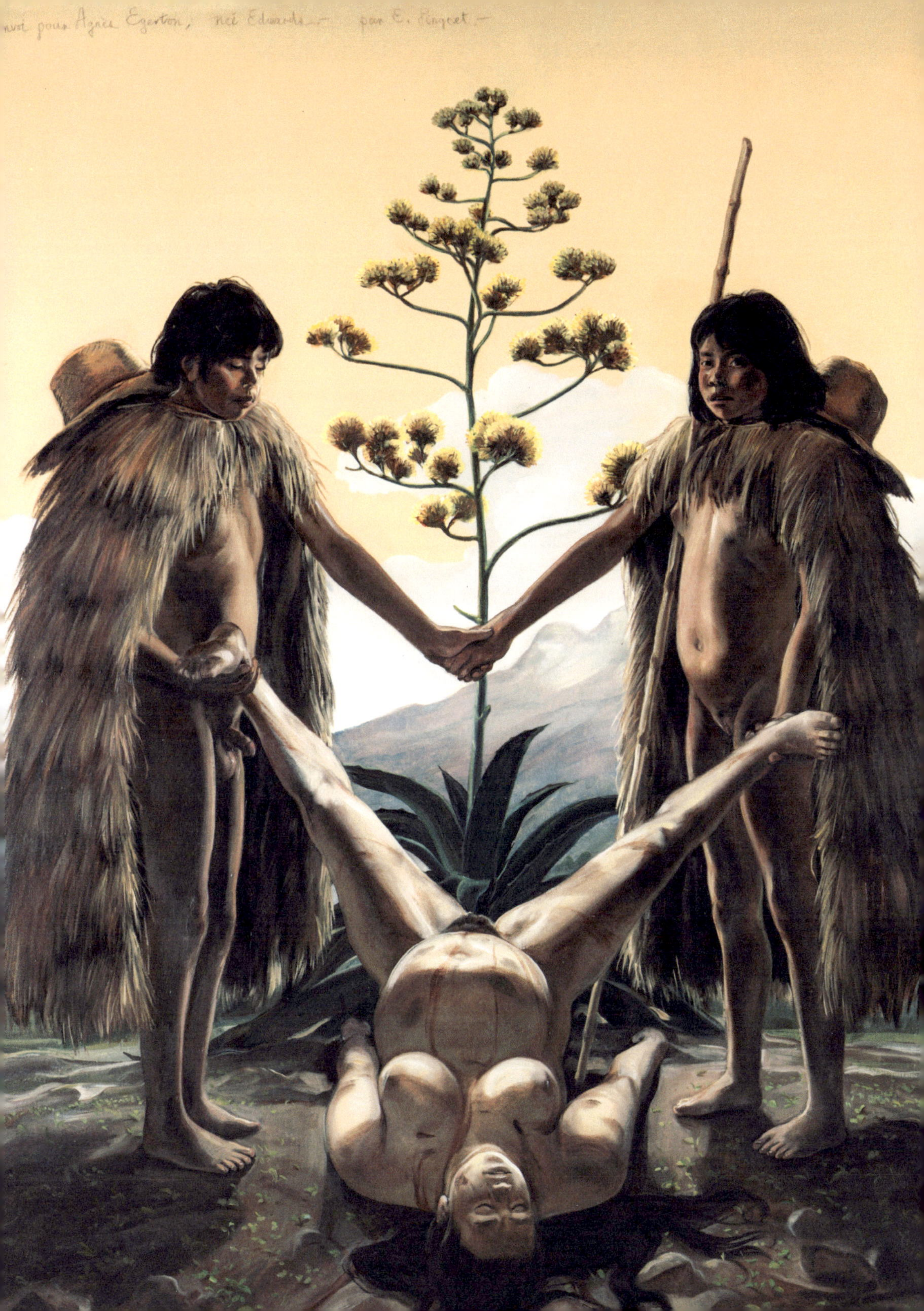
...voi pour Agnès Egerton, née Edwards — par E. Pinguet —

Rafael Lozano-Hemmer

—

Mexico City, Mexico, 1967

Level of Confidence, 2015

Facial recognition algorithms,
computer, screen, webcam
Ed. 2/12 + 1 AP
Gift of the artist, in process, 2020

Lozano-Hemmer's critical approach to systems of control and
subjectivity-production through technology has always sought
to understand their complexity. His objective is to take over or
"hack" them from the inside, often including the viewer's body
in the equation. To mark the six months since the forced disappearance of 43 students from the Ayotzinapa teachers' college,
Lozano-Hemmer reprogrammed a facial recognition system—
normally used to locate criminal suspects—to search for the
missing students. Once a person is registered by the camera, the
system seeks biometrical overlaps with the students' faces and
selects whomever shares the greatest number of features before
determining a percentage of certainty in its discovery. This experience questions our condition as subjects of new technologies
of control, as well as our ethical and personal relationship with
victims of state violence.

A. L.

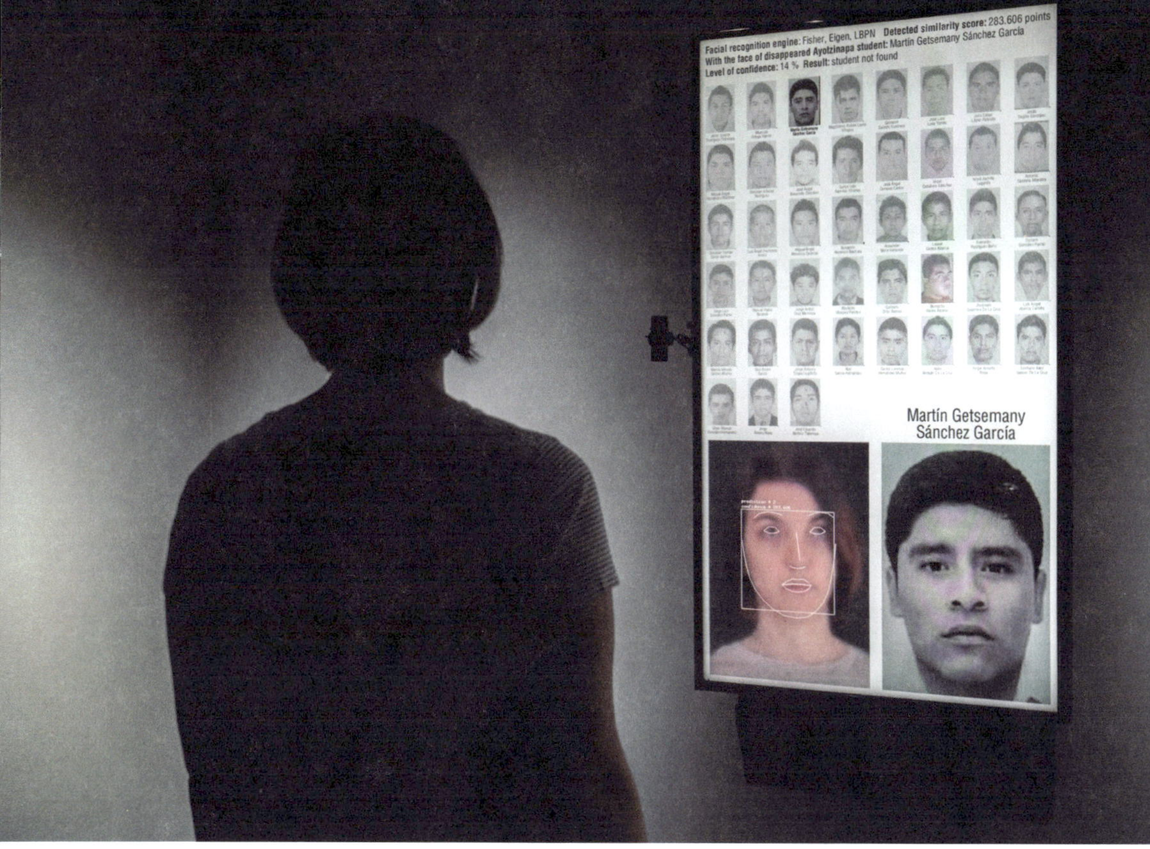

Facial recognition engine: Fisher, Eigen, LBPN   Detected similarity score: 283.606 points
With the face of disappeared Ayotzinapa student: Martín Getsemany Sánchez García
Level of confidence: 14 % Result: student not found
Martín Getsemany
Sánchez García

Ernesto Mallard

Cozamaloapan, Mexico, 1932

Doble visión [*Double Vision*], ca. 1968

From the series *Naturacosas* [*Naturethings*]
Acrylic, vinyl, and metal
110 × 80.5 × 14 cm
Acquisition with funds from the Presupuesto
de Egresos de la Federación, 2013

In pursuit of experimentation and innovation, avant-garde artists in mid-1960s Mexico sought to incorporate materials from outside the artistic tradition into their work.

This often resulted in pieces that defied the established categories of volume, sculpture, or painting. Such is the case with *Naturacosas,* which was Carlos Pellicer's term for the pieces Ernesto Mallard made out of plastic, metal tubes, and lacquer, oscillating between natural forms and human structures.

Mallard's work prioritized the dynamic possibilities of the line and the relevance of the viewer's own movement in completing the aesthetic perception of the piece—ideas in close alignment with kinetic and op art, which were gaining traction in Mexico at the time.

A. d. C.

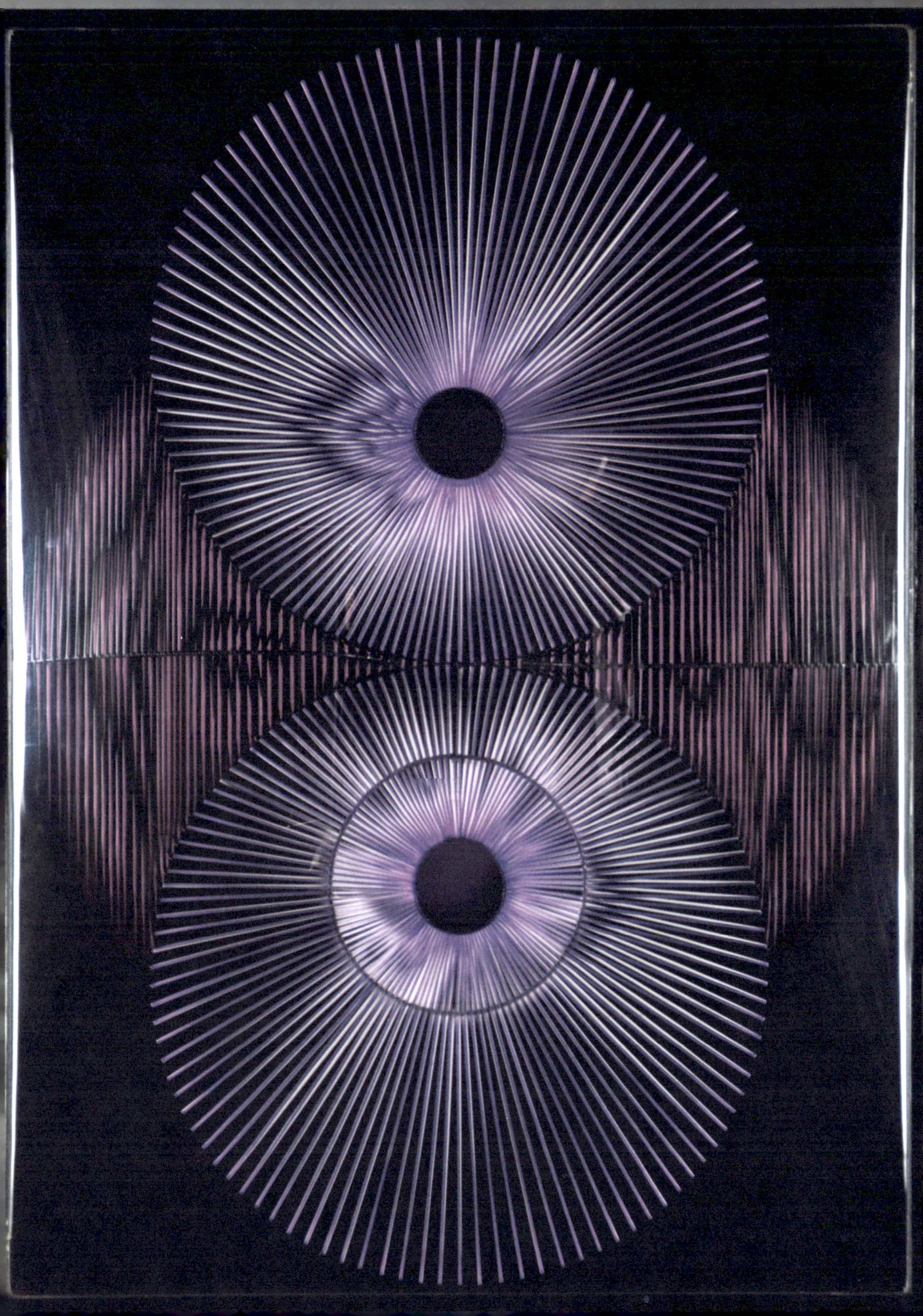

Teresa Margolles

Culiacán, Mexico, 1963

La promesa [*The Promise*], 2012

Demolition and pulverization of an abandoned house in Ciudad
Juárez to create a wall to be intervened each day, one hour
before the exhibition period. The sculpture is activated through a
performance by participants who had registered beforehand and
is complemented by a newspaper and documentary archive
Variable dimensions
Acquisition with funds from the Presupuesto
de Egresos de la Federación, 2015

In the early twenty-first century, Teresa Margolles focused her
practice on exploring the crisis of violence along the northern
Mexican border. Earlier work had focused on the bodies of victims of violence and social precariousness; now, she turned her
attention to people living in conditions of marginalization and
risk. Ciudad Juárez, Chihuahua became the heart of her œuvre.
In the 1980s and 1990s, with the arrival of the large maquiladoras,
this border crossing was transformed into a place of social
opportunity and promise. However, the wave of violence in recent
decades has forcibly displaced many of the migrants who came
to Ciudad Juárez from other parts of Mexico.

In her installation *La promesa*, Margolles questions that
horizon of unfulfilled aspirations, conjuring the presence of thousands of displaced people. The piece, following a procedure that
the artist carried out with meticulousness and care, comprises
the remnants of an abandoned home—one of thousands of such
houses in Ciudad Juárez—after its demolition.

In order to shed light on the city's troubles, the plot of land
was donated to a nonprofit organization for the creation of a
public space: precisely the kind of space that the violent environment has denied the city's residents.

Finally, the installation is presented with a participatory performance activated by volunteers, who rearrange the debris with their
own hands in order to gradually cover the surface of the exhibition
hall. The piece is accompanied by an archive containing videos,
texts, and articles on the issues explored by this project.

A. L.

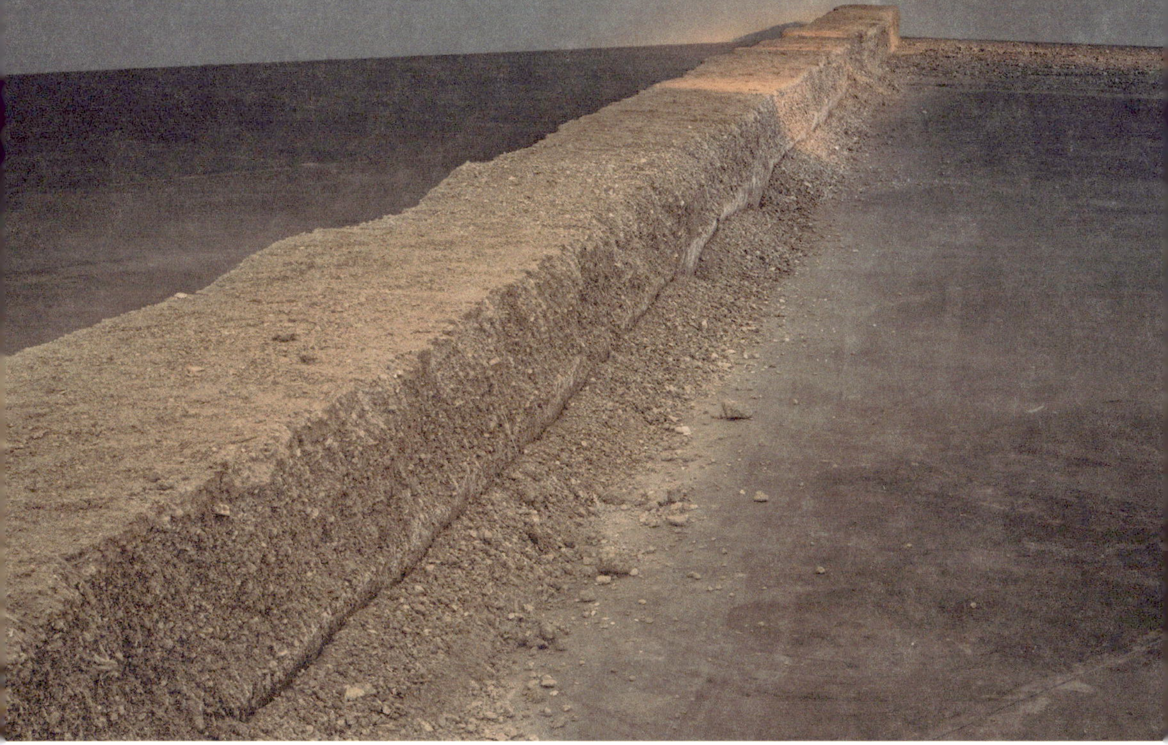

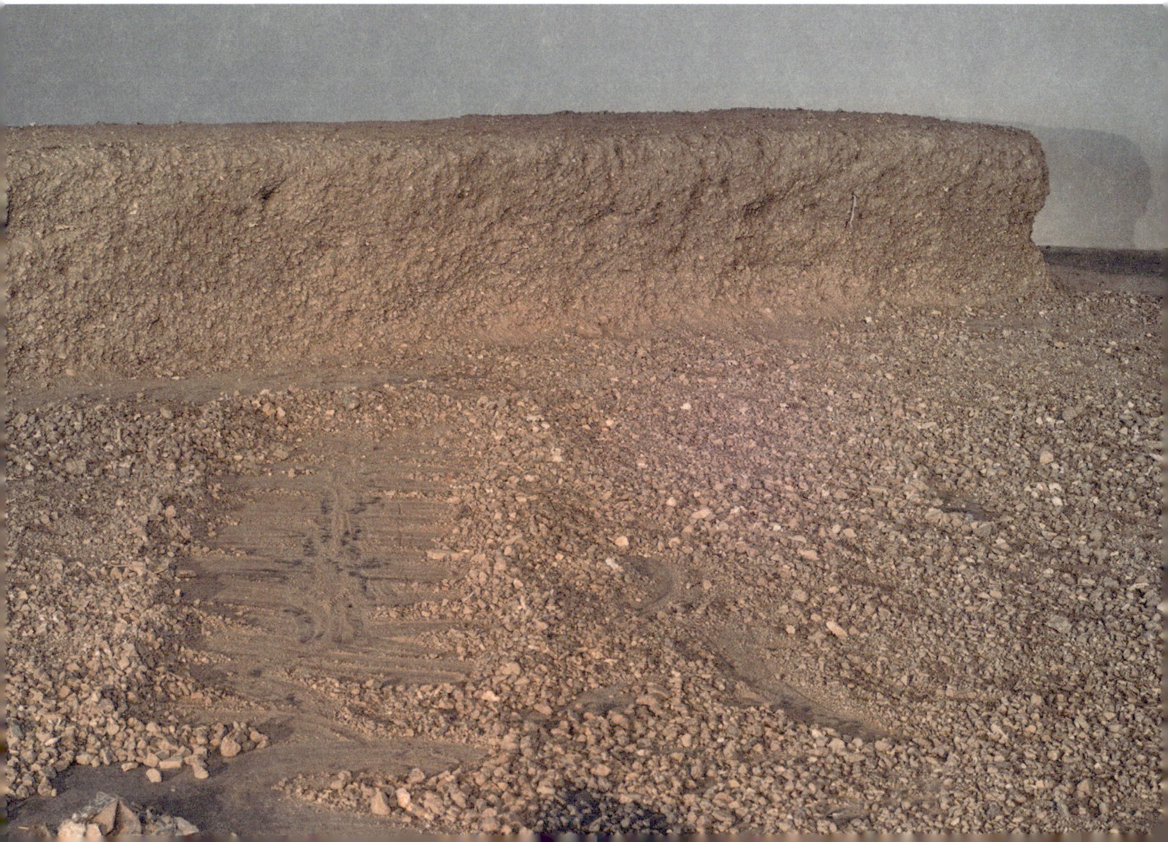

César Martínez

Mexico City, Mexico, 1962

El desgaste de la clase media en México o Geografía de la devaluación transpirada [*The Attrition of the Middle Class in Mexico or Geography of Transpired Devaluation*], 1999

Dynamic sculptures. Rubber latex, hoses, and hair dryers
Variable dimensions
Acquisition, 1999

Three human figures inflate and deflate through a mechanism activated by motion sensors. These "sculptural happenings," as the artist has called them, thus take on an ephemeral existence, functioning only when the viewer is present. As in his other anthropomorphic works, Martínez sheds light on the fragility of the body, which is also accentuated by his choice of materials: latex, for instance, or even edible elements. By mechanizing and protracting a process as automatic and imperceptible as breath, the artist emphasizes both the role of air as the basis of life and its biological and economic costs.

E. P.

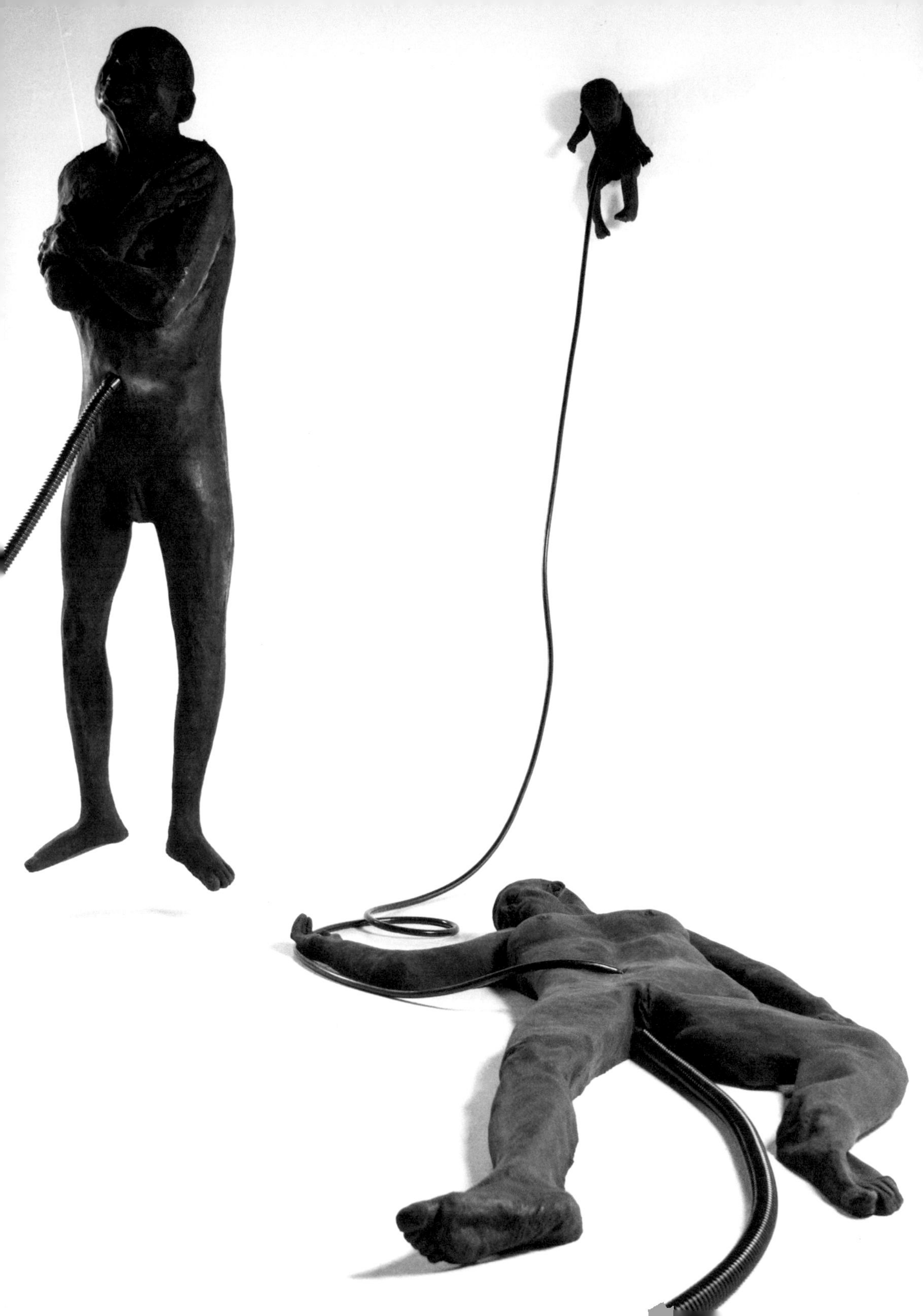

Daniel Joseph Martínez

Los Angeles, United States, 1957

*Self Portrait 4a: Fifth Attempt to Clone Mental Disorder or How
One Philosophizes with a Hammer. After Mary Shelley, 1816,* 1999

*Self Portrait 4b: Fifth Attempt to Clone Mental Disorder or How
One Philosophizes with a Hammer. After Mary Shelley, 1816,* 1999

*Self Portrait 5: Fifth Attempt to Clone Mental Disorder or How
One Philosophizes with a Hammer. After Edgar Allan Poe, 1842,* 1999

Digital inkjet print on plexiglass
122 × 152.4 cm each
Acquisition, 2007

True to form for Daniel Joseph Martínez, the radical Chicano artist
who personifies the role of the artist as agent provocateur, these
images cause an uproar. Their technical perfection is obscene
as they emerged from the factory of illusion of the film industry,
so-called "special effects." so-called "special effects." These
Nietzschean/Artaudian self-portraits express an inclination for
"soft, sweet madness" in their raw perfectionism. With the violent
marks of the serrated knife or scalpel on his skin, he alludes to a
meditation on the post-human utopia we have inherited from Mary
Shelley's *Frankenstein.* As is always the case in Martínez's work,
we have to suspect a hidden agenda: to persevere in an art that
assumes the risk of being unforgettable and misunderstood.

C. M.

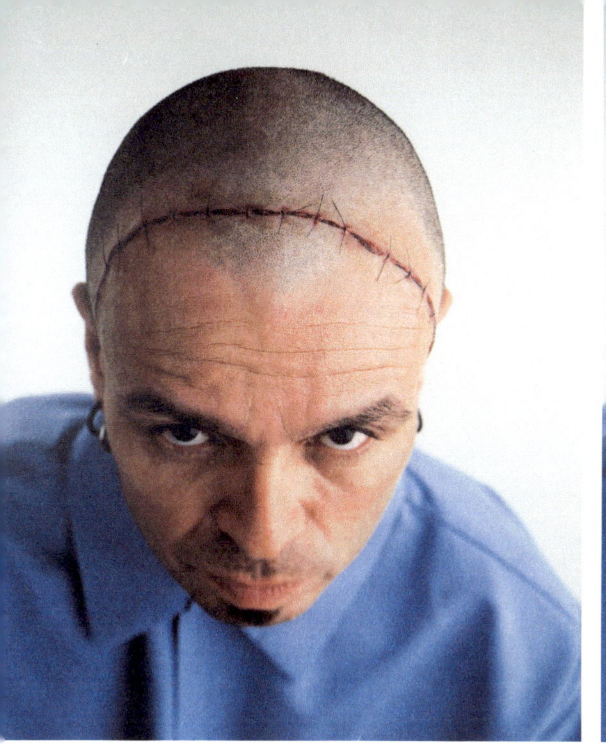
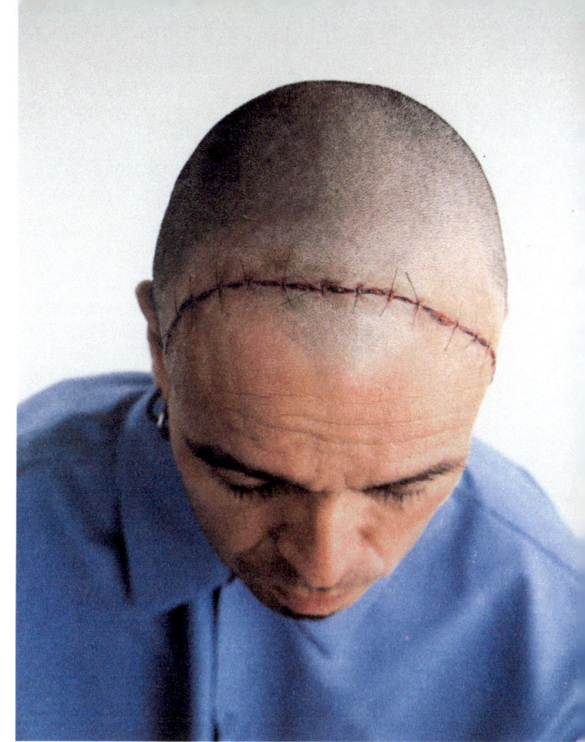
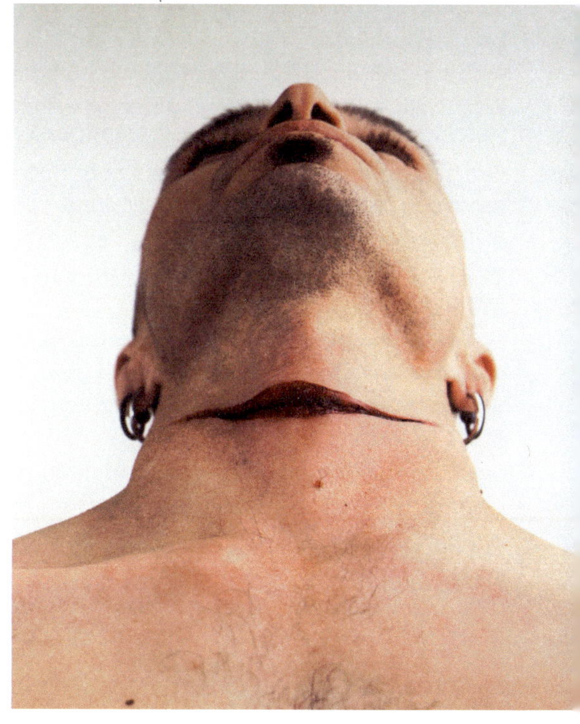

Mónica Mayer

Mexico City, Mexico, 1954

El tendedero MUAC [*The* MUAC *Clothesline*], 2016

Participatory installation. Metal and wooden structure,
cords, clothespins, 6 464 response cards, photocopies,
and photographic and hemerographic records in different
versions at the Museo de Arte Moderno (1978), Los Angeles
(1979), Universidad Iberoamericana (2009), and MUAC (2016)
Variable dimensions
Gift of the artist, 2017

This piece, carried out for the first time in 1978, is now considered a feminist landmark in Mexico. Presented as part of the *Salón 77-78 Nuevas tendencias* [*Expo '77-'78: New Trends*] at Mexico City's Museo de Arte Moderno—and subsequently as part of the 1979 project *Making It Safe,* organized by Suzanne Lacy in Los Angeles—the piece involves a structure that simulates a clothesline. There, women are invited to hang confessions of their experiences of endurig violence, inscribing pink posters with the sentence "As a woman, what I hate most about my city is…." In line with post-conceptual experimentation during the same period, the piece shows how a modest number of elements can be assembled to articulate a scathing question—one that summons, in this case, a chorus of condemnations. The relevance of this participatory piece has yielded, in its many different reactivations, a wall packed with accusations that preceded the viral #MeToo movement, launched in 2017.

Mayer's work critically movilized the personal and the domestic realms even before her experience in Los Angeles at the Feminist Studio Workshop and Woman Building. A pioneering feminist figure in Mexico, Mayer has upheld her position through many different forms of production and participation, both individual and collective; for example, in Tlacuilas y Retrateras, or as a member of Polvo de Gallina Negra.

S. H.

Detail

¿Qué has hecho o harí[as c]ontra el acoso?

Decirle a alguien q[ue pue]da
ayudarme

Alejarme inmediatamente

No quedarme callada.

¿Qué has hecho o ha[rías] contra el acoso?

Demostrar que no tengo miedo, mirándolos a los ojos, de conmigo no te metas.

¿Qué has hecho o [harí]as contra el [acoso]

Acosaría quien me acosa
(cambio de redes y de...

[¿Qué h]as hecho o harí[as c]ontra el acoso?

hace un tiempo [at]rás he comenzado a tomar
[...] ante el acoso [cu]ando me sucede en la
[...] es el más usual, enfrento al acosador. Me
[...] o miro a los ojos y cuestiono lo que me
[aca]ba decir o hacer, si responde a mi
[cuestiona]miento, le pido que no lo vuelva a hacer,
[aunque n]o lo conozco, que respete y que eso que
[hace] entre nosotros, se llama ACOSO
[...]ERO y es violento hacia mi persona.
[La mayo]ría de los acosadores no dicen nada,
[...] o dicen mucho la frase "YO NO FUI, YO NO
[FUE NA]DA, YO NO" y se van. Me ha tocado la
[ocasi]ón de ver su cobardía y huir con la
[...] o tomar distancia de mi o hasta han salido
[corriendo] como si mi enfrentamiento y sólo mi
[mirada fu]era un arma... "VAYA QUE LO ES".
Paty Rodríguez

¿Qué has hecho o harí[as c]ontra el acoso?

RECHAZO TODO TIPO DE ACOSO
QUE HE EXPERIMENTADO.
HABLANDO EXPLICO QUE ME MOLESTA
Y EXIJO QUE SE ALEJE DE MI.
AYUDARÍA A QUE EL TEMA TENGA
EXPOSICIÓN PORQUE PARECE ALTAMENTE
NECESARIO QUE SE HAGA VISIBLE Y
CONVERSANDO SIENDO QUE ES TAN COMÚN.
VISIBILIDAD, YA!!   HELSA RJ

¿Qué has hecho o harías contra el acoso?

Siempre he [cre]ído que
la clave es hacerl[o]
evidente, cuando se
hace en tiempo - espacio

[¿Qué h]as hecho o ha[ría]s contra el acoso?

Dejé de creer que
los hombres son
acosadores.

ERIKA KABEL.

¿Qué has hecho o harías [con]tra el acoso?

DENUNCIAR AL ACOSADOR,
ACTIVIDADES PARA INFORMAR LOS
DERECHOS Y LAS INSTANCIAS
A LAS QUE PODEMOS ACUDIR.

ERANDI FAJARDO

¿Qué has hecho o haría[s con]tra el acoso?

Pues siempre re[acciono], si el
acoso es físico r[...] resisto, me alej[o]
y no ha pasado na[da]. Lo he contado
a mis papás cuando era chica de
personas que me decían cosas
que me incomodaban. Ya de adult[a]
pues no lo cuento pero es constant[e]
y siempre el acoso o con palabras
o con intenciones y no llega a mas
en una ocasión si un hombre me
agarro por atrás [...] y me dijo cosas

Qué has hecho o harí[as c]ontra el acoso?

[pro]ducer junto a [las] niñas
[y tamp]oco a los niños d[...]

¿Qué has hecho o ha[rías] contra el acoso?

Aunque puede[ser] difícil y
se necesita valor para hacerlo,

¿Qué has hecho o harías [con]tra el acoso?

Acciones específicas n[ingun]a. Solamente he
hablado del tema con mis sobrinas para
que tomen sus precauciones y [...]

Enrique Metinides

Mexico City, Mexico, 1934

Primer plano de mujer rubia arrollada e impactada contra poste,
Av. Chapultepec y calle Monterrey, 29 de abril de 1979 [*Close-Up*
of Blonde Woman Run Over and Crushed Against a Pole at
Chapultepec Ave. and Monterrey Street, April 29, 1979], 1979

Photograph. Chromogenic print
50.8 × 60.7 cm
Gift of the artist, 2002

The journalist Adela Legarreta Rivas had gone to the beauty salon
in preparation for her latest book launch. On the way, she was
struck by a white Datsun that crushed her body between two
lampposts.

Starting in the 1940s and for nearly fifty years, Enrique
Metinides covered accidents, tragedies, urban chaos, and other
misfortunes afflicting Mexico City residents for the newspaper *La
Prensa*. This startling image puts the photojournalist's storytelling
prowess on full display, as well as his ability to light and compose
images that evoke film scenes.

E. P.

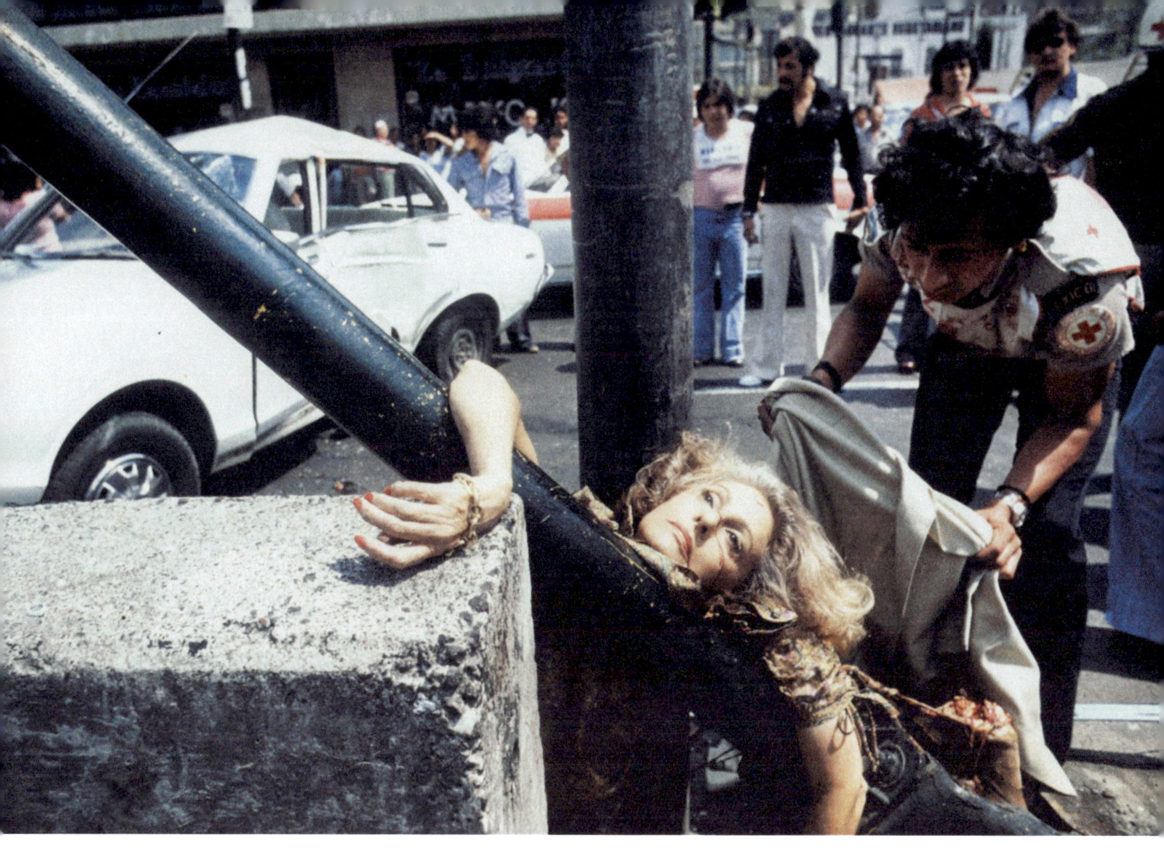

Erick Meyenberg

Mexico City, Mexico, 1980

24 FPS, 2015

Single-channel video, color, stereo sound
2' 55"
Ed. 1/3
Sound design: Félix Blume
Acquisition through the SHCP
Pago en Especie program, 2017

This video shows the interplay of lights and shadows projected onto the floor of the moving train Meyenberg took from Brittany to Normandy—the journey described by Marcel Proust in the first volume of *In Search of Lost Time* (1908–1922). Formally speaking, the image's behavior evokes the 24 frame-per-second speed of film projection, the technical principle that enables the human eye to perceive movement. This tribute to cinema—and to Proust—bears witness to the artist's experience of temporal fragility in relation to mortality and death.

J. G. S.

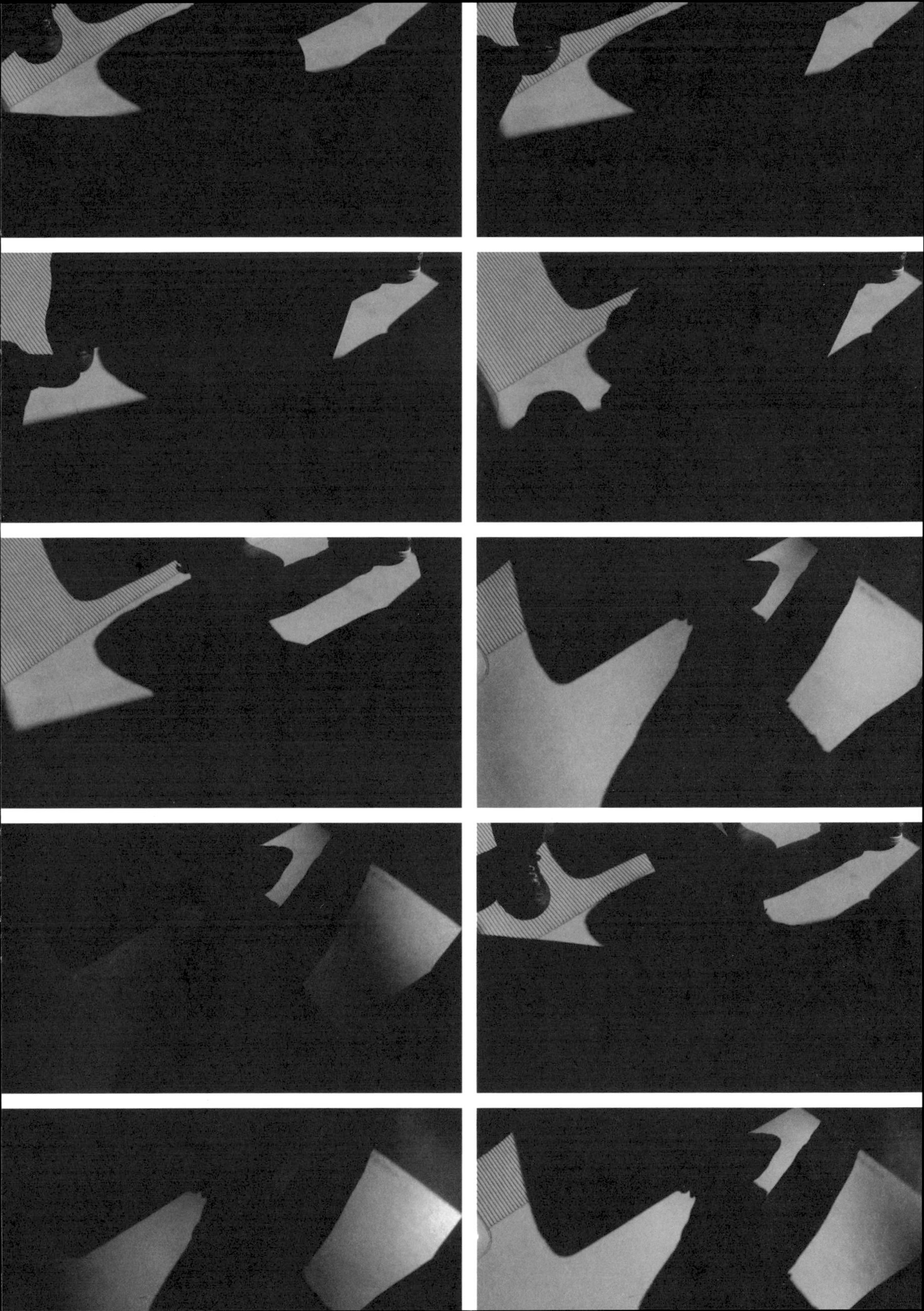

Sarah Minter

—

Puebla, Mexico, 1953–Mexico City, Mexico, 2016

Érase una vez un tren [*Once Upon
a Time There Was a Train*], 1985–2014

HD video, 4:3 format
12' 30"
Ed. 1∕3 + 2 AP
Acquisition with funds from the Presupuesto
de Egresos de la Federación, 2015

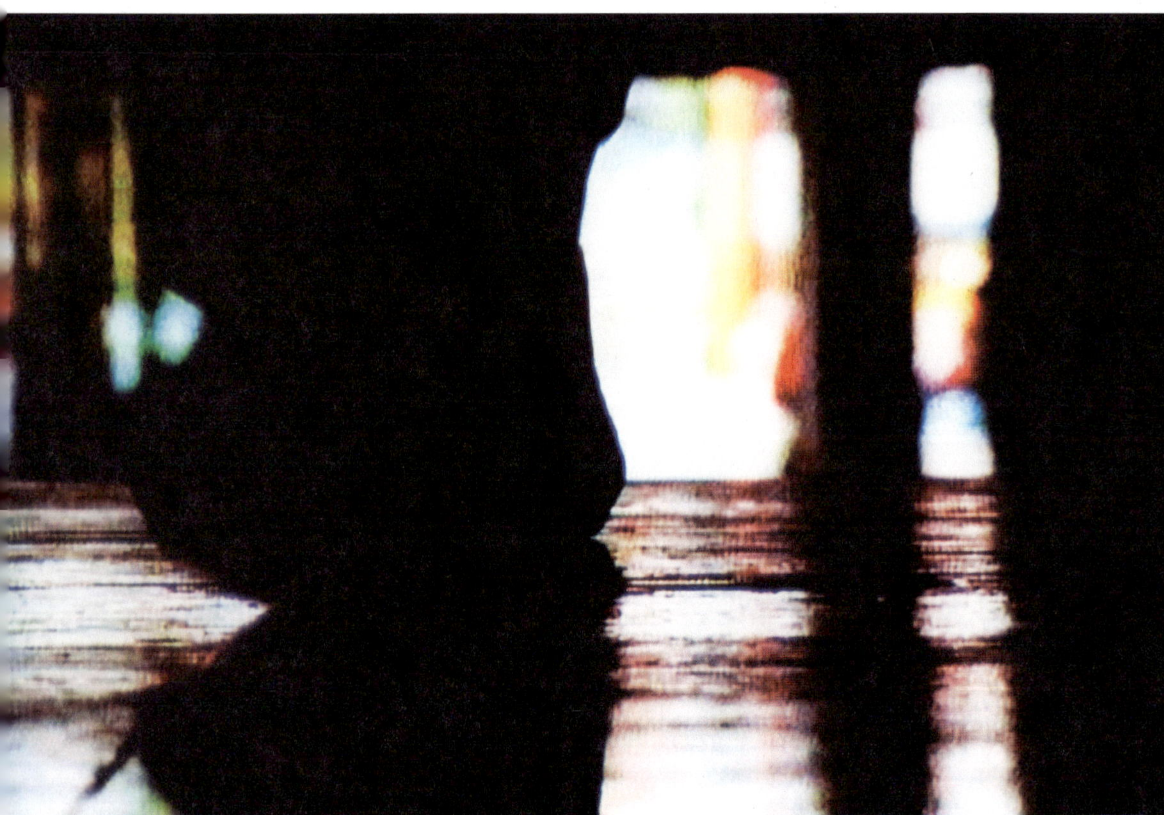

In the late 1980s and early '90s, Minter's work explored the Mexico City punk scene. Almost 30 years after making the films *Nadie es inocente* [*No One Is Innocent*, 1985–1987] and *Alma punk* [*Punk Soul*, 1991–1992], she uses scenes from earlier works to make a short film focused on train travel. This act of recycling, now presented in a two-channel format, follows two young people through both urban and natural landscapes. Edited to mimic the dizzying rhythm of the train itself, Minter creates bursts of experience emanating from marginal areas and agents of Mexican reality.

A. L.

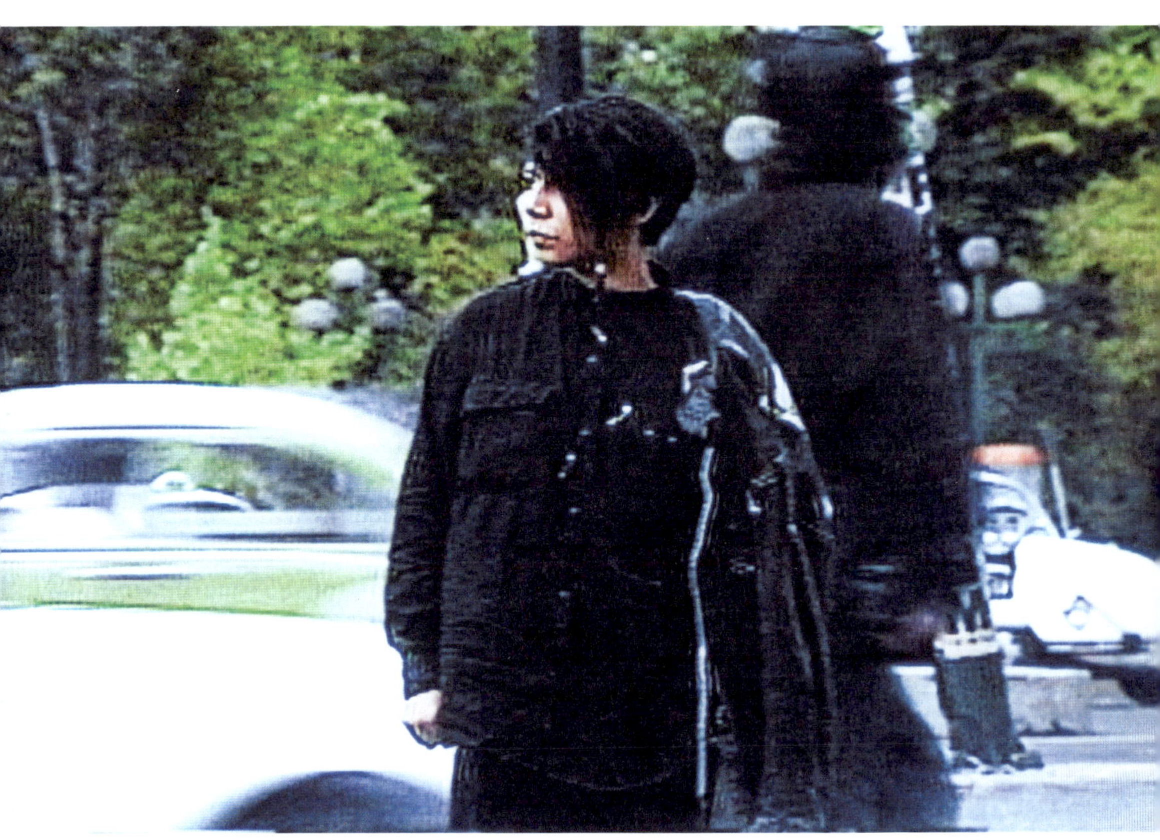

Grupo Mira

Active 1977–1982

Arnulfo Aquino, Nochixtlán, Mexico, 1942; Melecio Galván, San Rafael, Mexico, 1946–Mexico City, Mexico, 1982; Eduardo Garduño, Uruápan, Mexico, 1946; Rebeca Hidalgo, Nochixtlán, Mexico, 1950; Saúl Martínez, Mexico City, Mexico, 1943; Salvador Paleo, n.d.; Silvia Paz, Mexico City, Mexico, 1950; Jorge Perez Vega, Mexico City, Mexico, 1946

Comunicado gráfico No. 1 (La violencia en la Ciudad de México) [*Graphic Communiqué No. 1 (Violence in Mexico City)*], 1978

48 heliographic prints of drawings,
photo montages, and adhesive screens
60 × 60 cm each
Acquisition, 2007

The *Comunicado gráfico No. 1* was the first project of Grupo Mira, formed a decade after its members met at the Escuela Nacional de Artes Plásticas. The communiqué consists of a portable, duplicable mural designed for exhibition in spaces that would accommodate public discussion. Its 48 heliographic prints are organized into three topics: Problems Facing the City, Power Structures, and Social and Alternative Movements. It is among the most politically effective works of the so-called "los grupos" [the groups] movement of 1970s Mexico, offering a fusion of graphics and slogans that served as an alternative to "official" information.

E. P.

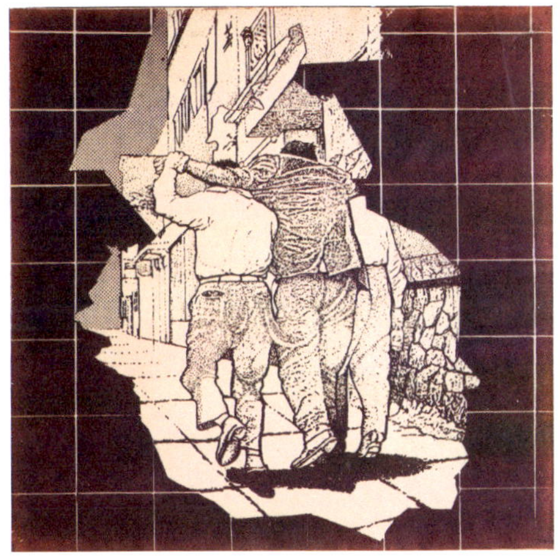

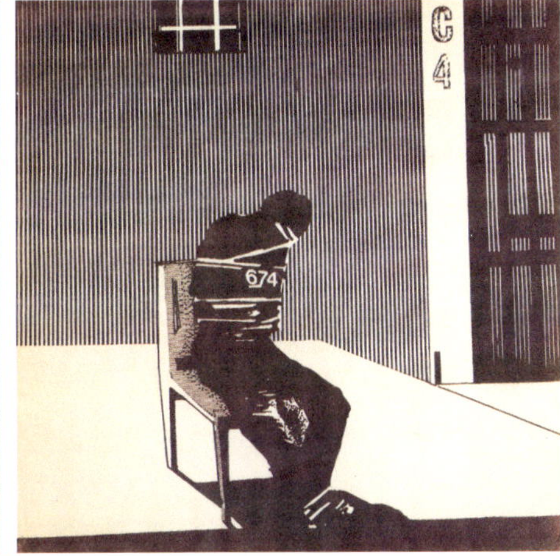
C4
674

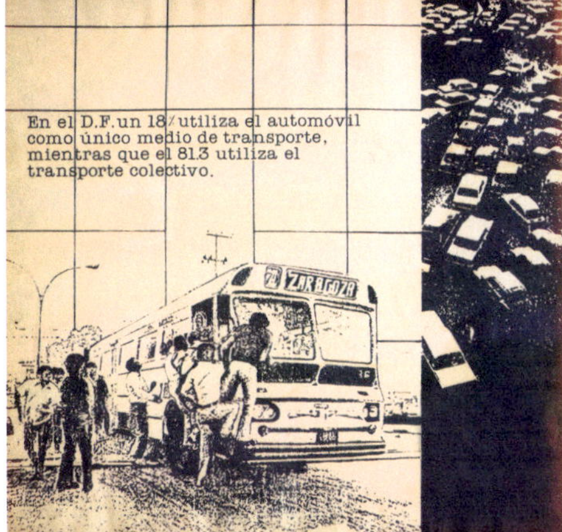
En el D.F. un 18% utiliza el automóvil
como único medio de transporte,
mientras que el 81.3 utiliza el
transporte colectivo.

ZARAGOZA

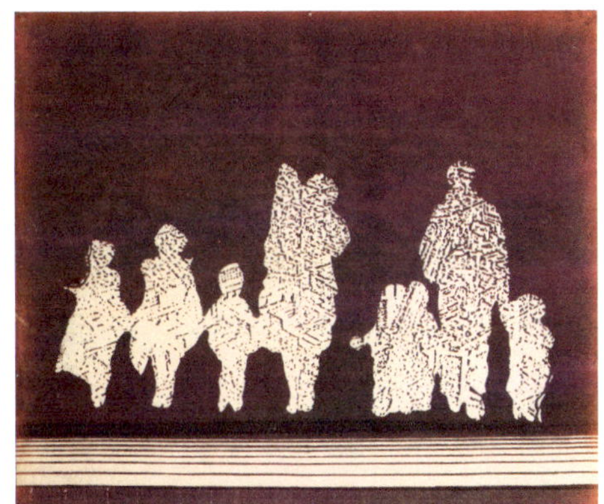
Pero llegan no por gusto ni por una elección libre,
sino impelidos por la miseria, el atraso, el desempleo
en sus lugares de origen..."

Gabriel Careaga.

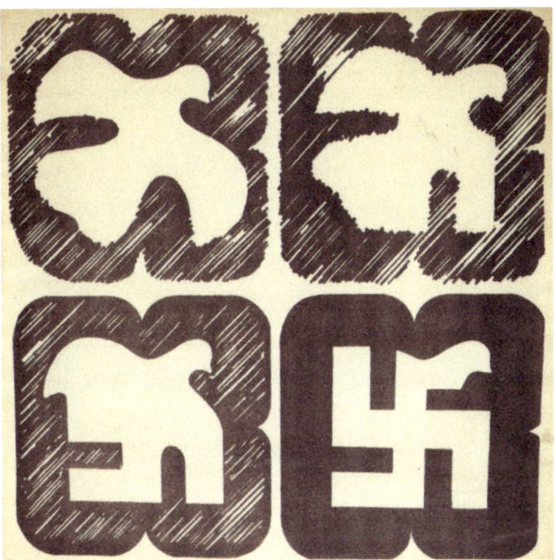

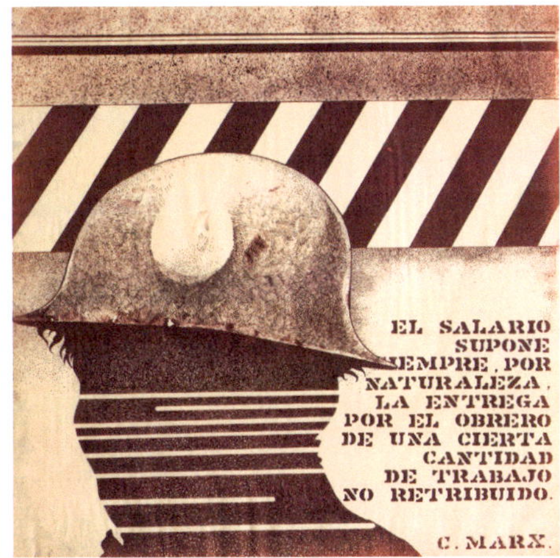
EL SALARIO
SUPONE
SIEMPRE, POR
NATURALEZA,
LA ENTREGA
POR EL OBRERO
DE UNA CIERTA
CANTIDAD
DE TRABAJO
NO RETRIBUIDO.

C. MARX.

Gabriel de la Mora

Mexico City, Mexico, 1968

Influences pág. 25 [*Influences p. 25*], 2003-2009

Influences pág. 26 [*Influences p. 26*], 2003-2009

Influences pág. 27 [*Influences p. 27*], 2003-2009

Influences pág. 28 [*Influences p. 28*], 2003-2009

Burned paper and acrylic box
Burned paper: 28 × 21.5 cm each
Acrylic box: 8.1 × 28.7 × 22.5 cm each
Acquisition through the SHCP
Pago en Especie program, 2016

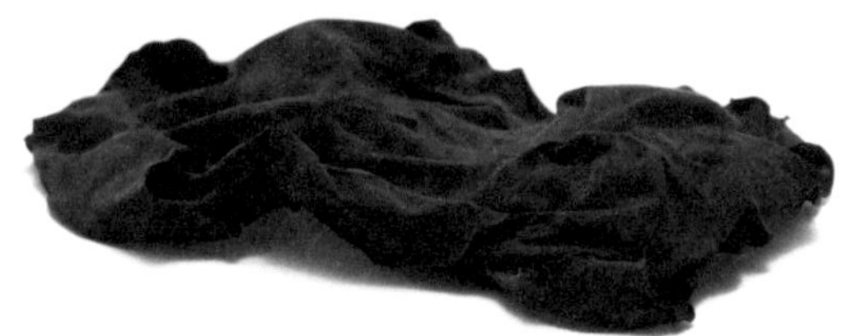
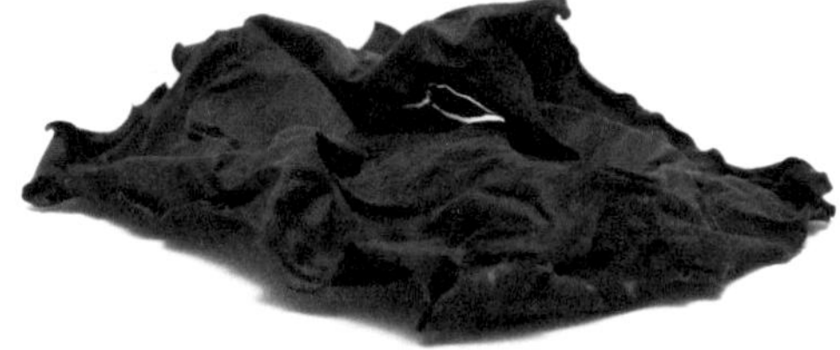

In 2007, De la Mora began the series *Papeles quemados* [*Burned Papers*] by setting his master's thesis on fire. *Influences* is part of this series. In a single entropic gesture of destruction as creation, De la Mora transforms the paper's two-dimensional surface into a three-dimensional sculptural object.

Gabriel de la Mora's artistic work involves practices based on the passing of time, meticulous material experimentation, and a constant dialogue with the history of post-minimalism and Latin American abstract art. Pieces like *Influences* mark a watershed in his career, inaugurating an exploration of the relationship between image and the monochrome that would permeate much of his later work.

M. A.

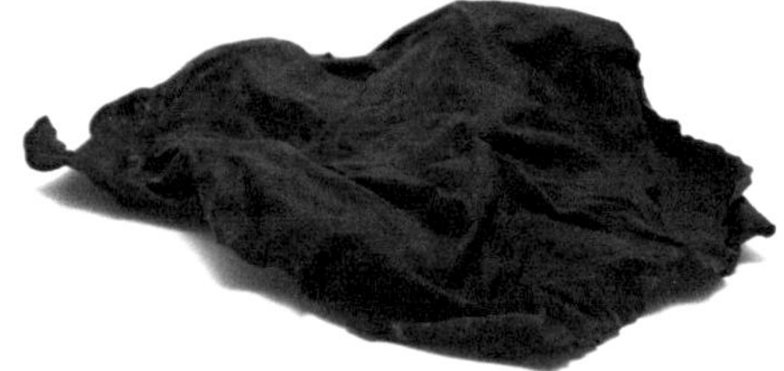 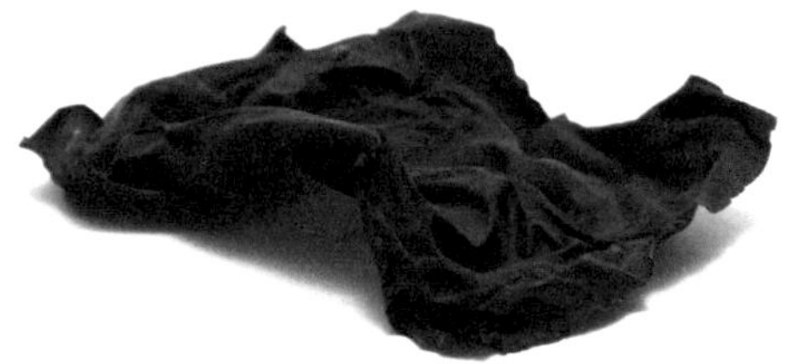

Rodrigo Moya

Medellín, Colombia, 1934

Hipotecados [*Mortgaged*], 1965

Gelatin silver print
40.6 × 50.8 cm
Acquisition with funds from the Presupuesto
de Egresos de la Federación, 2013

Hipotecados is a study in contrasts. The image itself emphasizes the monumental nature of the Conjunto Urbano Nonoalco–Tlatelolco, the most important urban housing project in modern Mexico. While official propaganda depicted the complex as a new housing model for the middle class, the title of Moya's photograph sheds light on the high price that such grandiose projects forced on the Mexican economy—and on the inhabitants themselves. This dialogue between text and image is characteristic of an artist like Rodrigo Moya, who worked as a photojournalist from 1955 and 1968 at magazines such as *Impacto* and *Sucesos para Todos*, in which his images and reporting maintained a critical view of state discourse.

E. P.

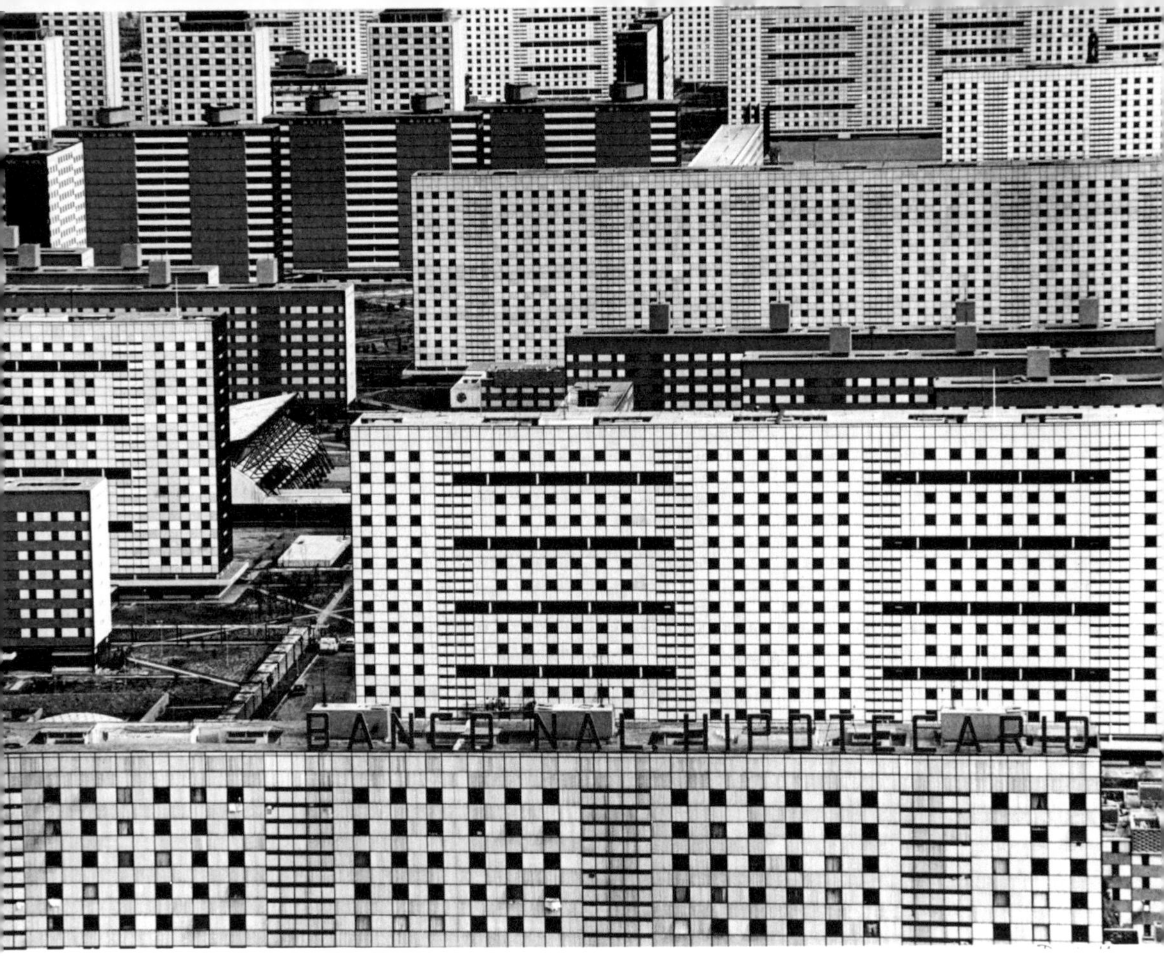
BANCO NAL. HIPOTECARIO

Ricardo Nicolayevsky

Mexico City, Mexico, 1961

Autorretrato 1 [Self-Portrait 1], 1982–1985

From the series *Lost Portraits*
Super 8 and 16 mm film transferred to video
6' 37"
Acquisition with funds from the Presupuesto
de Egresos de la Federación, 2013

Trained in film and working as a composer, Nicolayevsky captures the culture of personal bonds and his generational subculture in the series *Lost Portraits.* Produced in the 1980s in New York and Mexico City, the series gathers portraits of the artist and his friends in different contexts. *Autorretrato 1* is a snapshot of the artist's intimacy, a pagan ecology of pleasure and excess that led to experimentation with home-developed film. The ensuing "accidents" yield textures evocative of experimental cinema.

S. H.

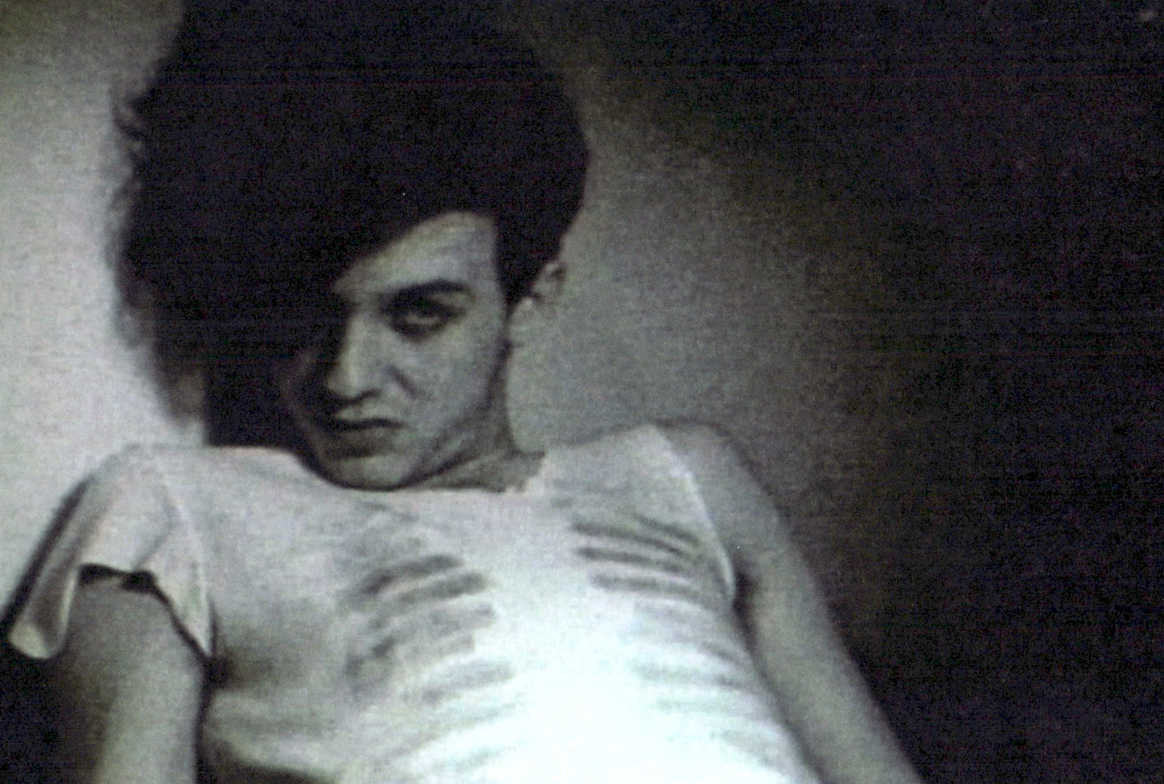

Yoshua Okón

Mexico City, Mexico, 1970

Oríllese a la orilla [*Pull Over to the Curb*], 1999–2000

Video installation
Variable dimensions
Ed. 3/3
Acquisition, 2012

The redundant phrase "oríllese a la orilla" is a pleonasm often used by the Mexican police in asking a driver to stop. Okón's video installation shows attempted interactions with the police that range from humane and humorous gestures to threats and insinuations of bribery.

Sometimes using a hidden camera, Okón hired police officers to carry out certain actions, revealing the degrees of negotiation that citizens frequently sustain with members of this institution. Okón's strategy produces a profound ambiguity between fiction and reality, a characteristic feature of his work. In the context of his output in the 1990s, when experimentation and the impact on public space carried significant weight, Okón's work criticizes neoliberal society while always winking to the viewer.

V. R. L.

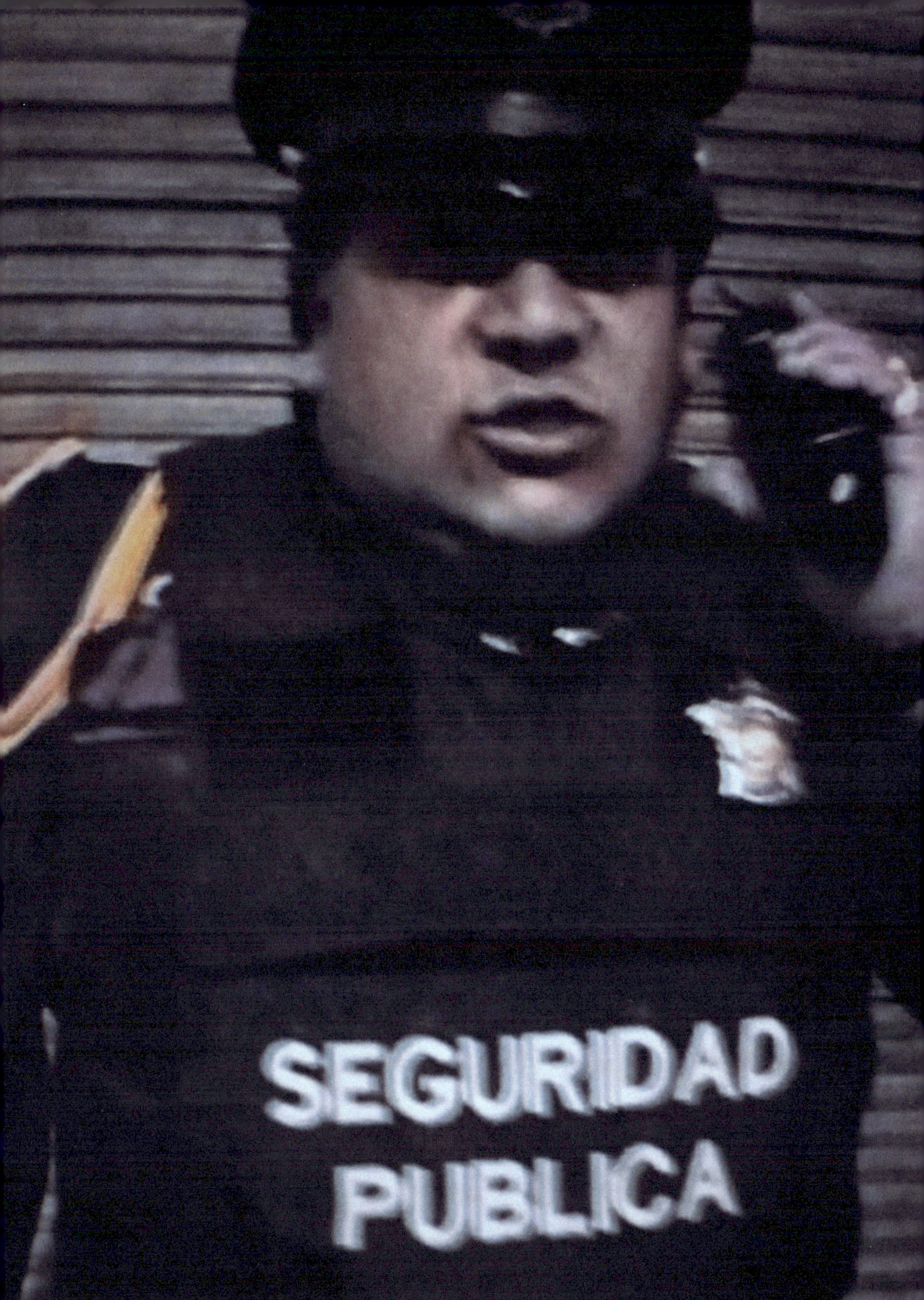

SEGURIDAD
PUBLICA

Gabriel Orozco

Mexico City, Mexico, 1962

Balones acelerados [*Accelerated Balls*], 2005

Installation. 165 intervened balls
Variable dimensions
Acquisition, 2006

For the 2005 re-inauguration of the Museo Experimental El Eco, Gabriel Orozco presented a set of used soccer balls intervened with die-casting molds, which he had been working with for several years. As the story goes, Orozco found some of these balls in a neighbor's yard; tired of returning them to the middle school next door when they landed on her property, she had simply started to keep them. The collection was completed with balls belonging to the UNAM soccer team known as the Pumitas. As a trade, Orozco offered one new ball for every two old ones.

More than the timeworn confrontation with a found object, *Balones acelerados* proposes a confrontation with time. The everyday sight of a deflated ball enters an emotional terrain, triggering childhood memories of pick-up games.

As in this piece, Orozco's work stimulates our relationship with our memories in response to compact, seemingly ordinary gestures. At the same time, it reflects on sculpture in association with social structure and plays with the scale of the individual in relation to the object and one's own memory.

A. d. C.

Detail

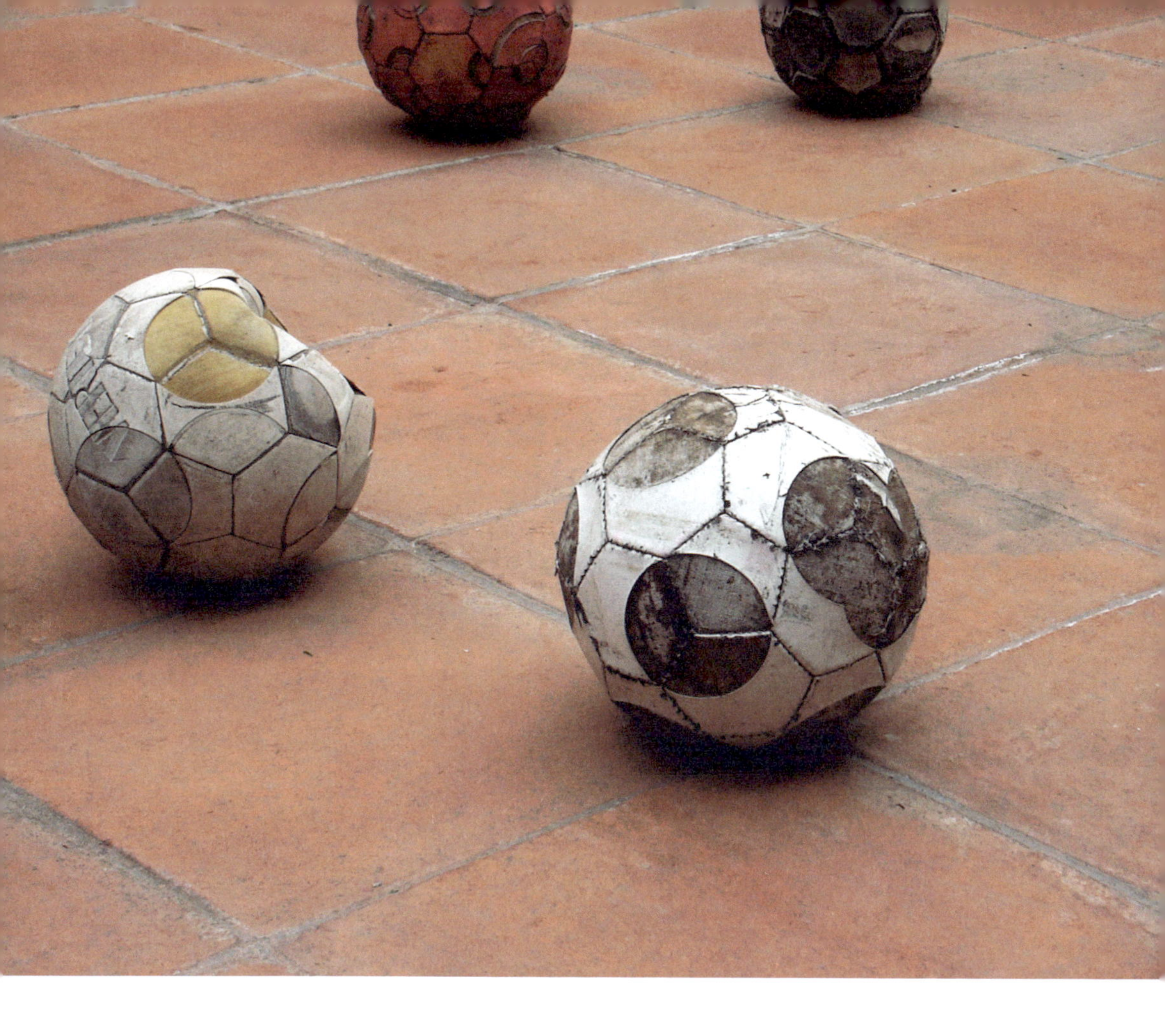

Damián Ortega

Mexico City, Mexico, 1967

América Letrina
[*Letrine America*], 1997

Ceramic, epoxy plasticine, and enamel
89.5 × 93 × 43 cm
Acquisition with funds from the Patronato
Arte Contemporáneo A.C., 2014

Five years before Ortega made this sculpture, the North American Free Trade Agreement went into effect—at the same time as "Latin American identity" was being debated in the cultural sphere. With a Duchampian air, Ortega avails himself of strategies from conceptual art to resignify and alter a utilitarian object, offering ironic commentary on the reductionist notion of Latin America as a kind of drop box, drain, or secondary channel at the service of "the northern powers." In this piece, the artist uses objectified humor to provocatively critique the geopolitical perception of Latin America.

S. H.

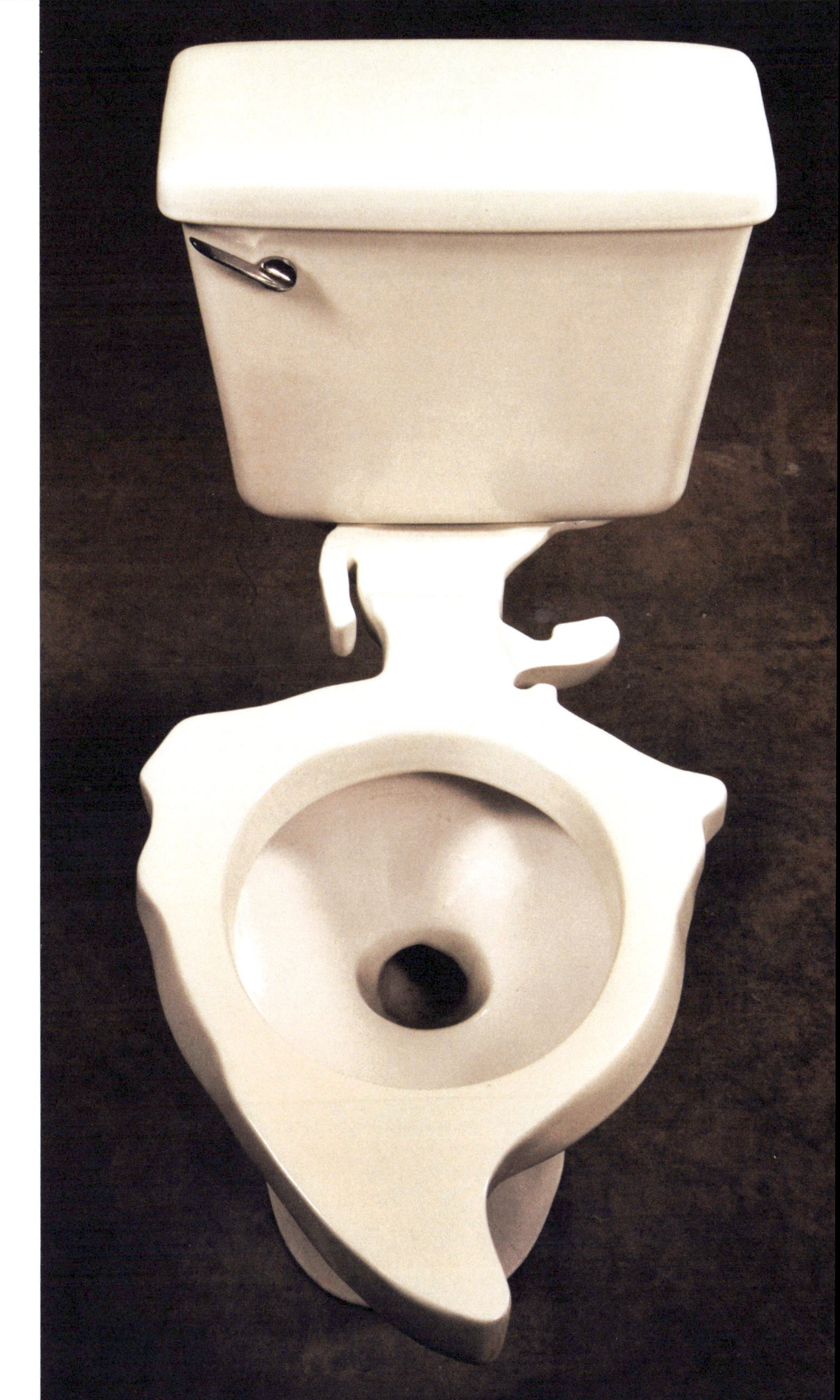

Rubén Ortiz Torres

Mexico City, Mexico, 1964

Rompiendo el código maya, Guatemala
[*Breaking the Maya Code, Guatemala*], 1995

Video installation. CCTV, clay model,
2 videos, and 2 monitors
Variable dimensions
Gift of the artist, 2000

Ortiz Torres's work frequently explores depictions of the past in different images of contemporary culture from the Americas. In this installation, the artist questions the forms of consumption of historical artifacts, contrasting a video of tourists climbing up a Maya pyramid with the image of a camera focusing, in real time, on a souvenir shaped just like the building as people observe it in the museum. The artist ironically presents different ways of viewing a past that has been reinterpreted and instrumentalized by discourses of cultural identity.

J. G. S.

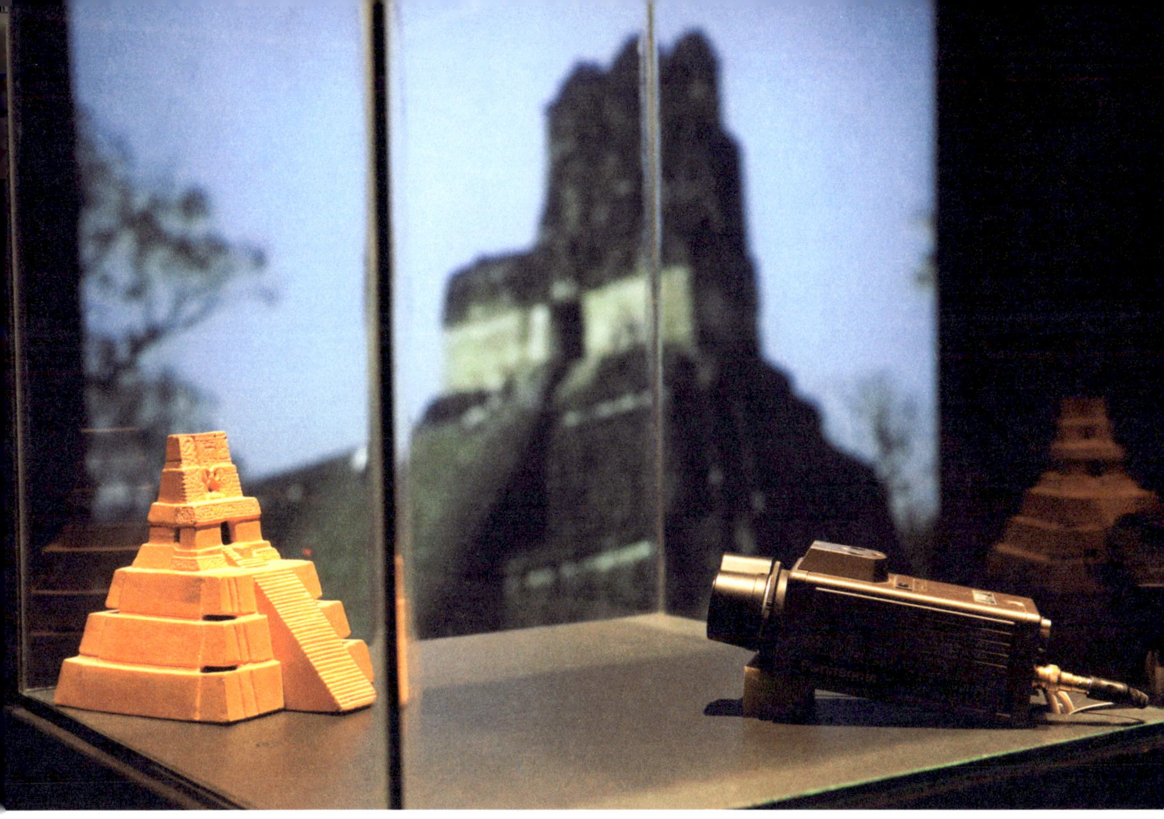

Martha Pacheco

Guadalajara, Mexico, 1957

Sin ningún pudor
[*Shameless*], 1996

Charcoal on paper
43 × 65 cm
Acquisition, 1999

Whether in painting, photography, or drawing, Martha Pacheco's work has continuously depicted corpses, especially those left unidentified in Mexican morgues. In 1993, she began taking photographs in Mexico's Servicio Médico Forense (Semefo), today called the Instituto de Ciencias Forenses (Incifo). During this period, she also received many images from Teresa Margolles, founder of the Semefo artist collective. Her virtuosic realism, approaches, and framing all confront the viewer with the rawness and violence of a death in which the individual is reduced to a forgotten object. Her work, testimony to the state of incessant violence in Mexico, harnesses morbid fascination as a strategy to show how every life lost means, too, the deprivation of intimacy.

E. P.

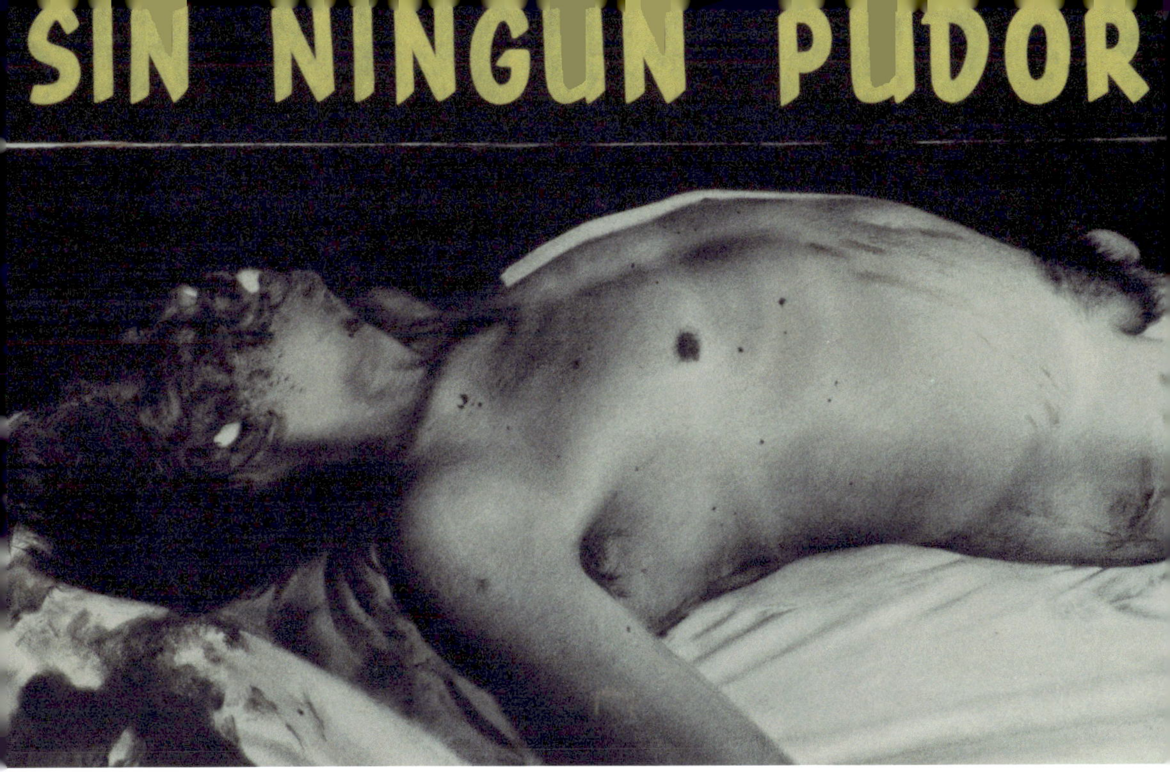
SIN NINGUN PUDOR

Marta Palau

Lérida, Spain, 1934

Cascada [*Waterfall*], 1978

Installation. Nylon and textile fibers
400 × 1000 × 470 cm
Acquisition, 2005

In the late 1960s, Marta Palau abandoned the two-dimensionality of prints and oil paintings in favor of constructing environments and sculptures out of organic fibers (like henequen, corn husks, *ixtle,* wool fiber, and coir), which she proceeded to weave, combine, unravel, and graft without preconceived notions. During the 1970s, she moved away from the format of the wall and instead presented her work as large-scale sculptures: heavy, matterist textile pieces that become powerful installations and invite the viewer to move around inside them. Her work in this period successfully reclaimed textile work, historically associated with women's handicrafts, and introduced it into the artistic sphere. These sexualized sculptures ambiguously express female corporeal forces through folds, creases, and hollows, like bodiless genitals.

Cascada is her most important installation from those years, and one of her most crucial works in general: a transmission of female desire that explores new sensory ways of depicting the body. Shown in 1978 at the Museo de Arte Moderno in Mexico City, this enormous installation intervened in the space through a torrent of translucent tubes of white nylon stockings containing small plush nodules. As a piece without any rigid structures at all, its mounting defied the museography of the era: anchored to the ceiling, it flows and overflows—much like an ejaculatory impulse—before falling to the floor. The artist herself remarked in an interview years later: "I see *Cascada* as a river of sperm."

P. G.

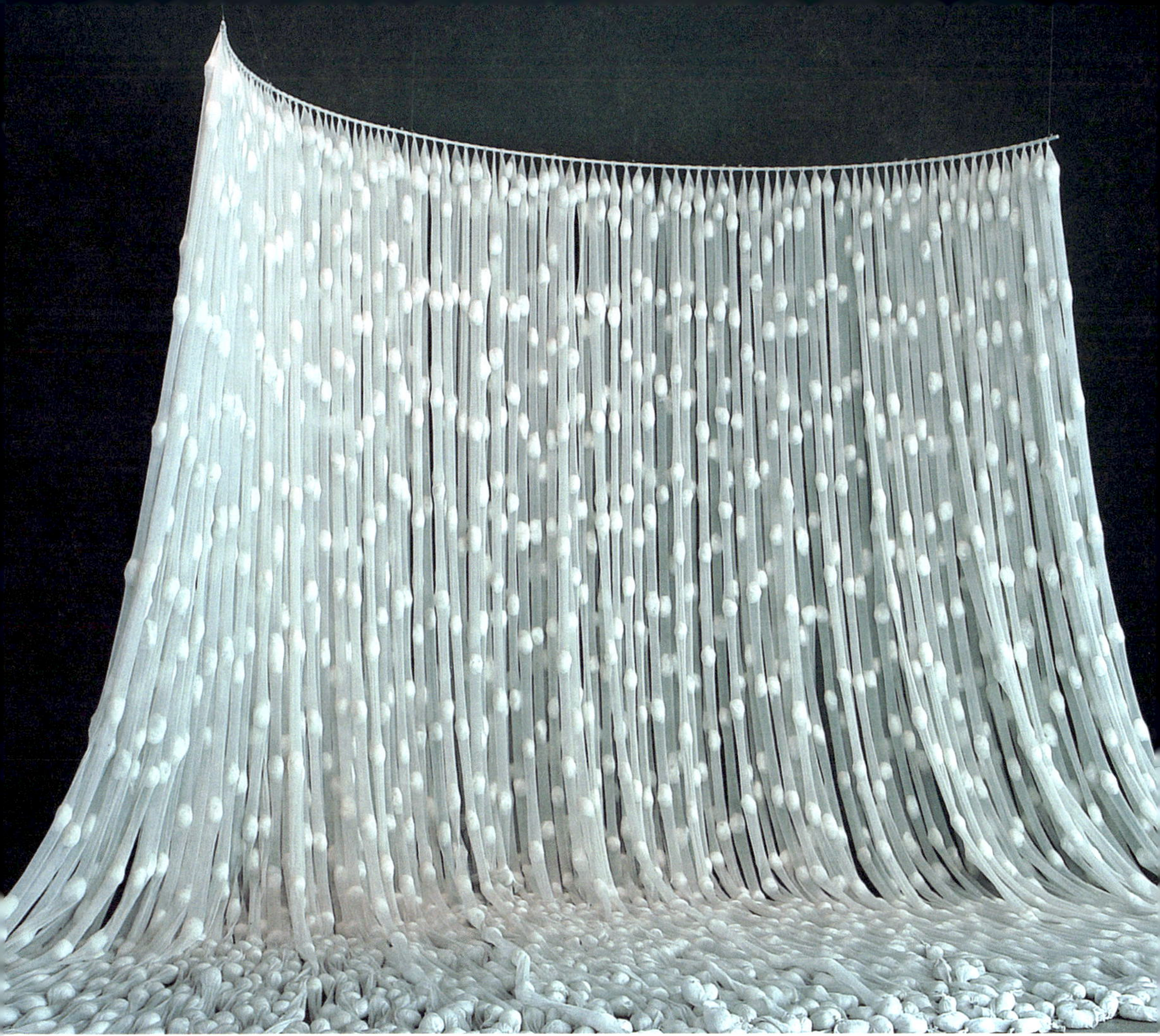

Marta Palau

Lérida, Spain, 1934

Ilerda V, 1973

Spanish jute, high-warp cotton
160 × 100 × 20 cm
Acquisition, 2005

This piece is representative of Palau's work, both in its materiality and in its allusions to femininity. In her final years, the artist acknowledged that the shape of the piece formally evokes a large vagina, although she continued to describe it as an unconscious outcome. *Ilerda* references an old toponymy of the Catalan city where Palau was born; she used it to title a series of textile-based pieces. These "soft sculptures," as critics called them at the time, given their use of textiles and tapestry, characterize Palau's volumetric œuvre of the 1970s and distinguish her from the reigning trends in Mexican sculpture, which strived for geometric monumentality.

E. P.

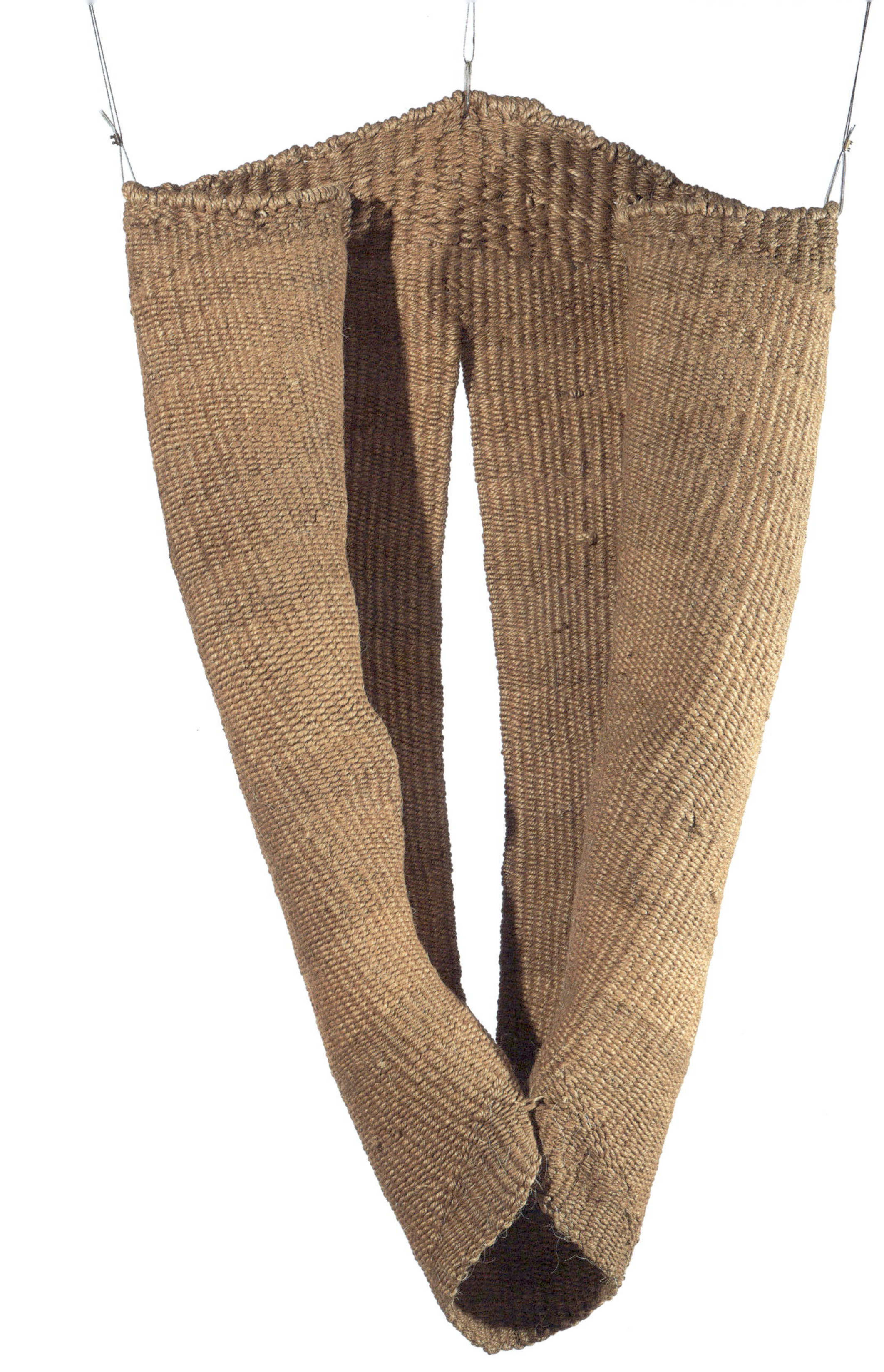

Fernando Palma Rodríguez

Mexico City, Mexico, 1957

Greetings, Zapata Moles, 1994

Installation. 4 intervened sewing machines,
lucha libre masks, cables, sensors, corn seeds,
paper bag, and religious icon
Variable dimensions
Piece made for the Rijksakadamie Open Studies
Acquisition with funds from the
Government of Mexico State, 2012

An early installation made by Palma as a resident artist at the Rijksakademie in Amsterdam. This is one of his first robotic-mechatronic devices, combining elements that directly allude to the uprising of the Ejército Zapatista de Liberación Nacional that same year, as well as to the memory of the seamstresses killed in the 1985 Mexico City earthquake, and to the artist's own family history. Each of these sewing machines, intervened with wrestling masks, represents a member of a family; through sensors, a kind of communication emerges among them.

Palma's work engages in the constant resignification of many different tactics and technologies, participating in a form of indigenous cultural and political recognition. He maintains a position of resistance and cultural invention in his advocacy for indigenous cultures, particularly for the survival of his own Nahua ethnicity. This orientation encompasses both his artistic practice and Calpulli Tecalco, the civil society organization he co-founded in the Mexico City borough of Milpa Alta (*Malacachtépec Momoxco,* in the Nahuatl language).

S. H.

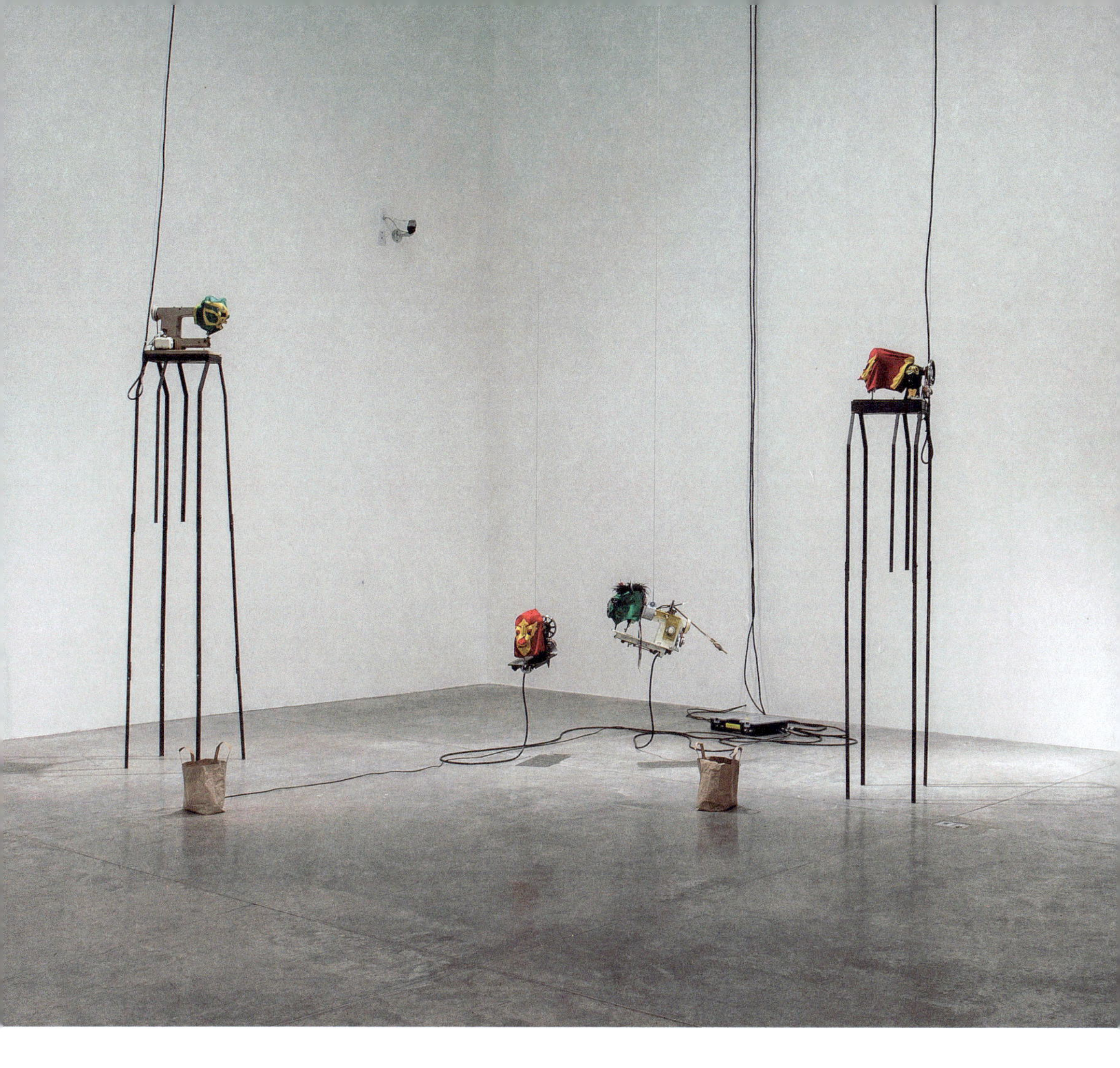

Adolfo Patiño

Mexico City, Mexico, 1954–2005

Jugando con la historia
[*Playing with History*], 1990

Installation. 435 plastic
figures on wooden base
25 × 145.5 × 244.5 cm
Gift of the artist, 2002

During the 1990s, Patiño (also known as "Adolfotógrafo," or Adolphotographer) critically inscribed everyday elements with military or religious imagery: references associated with the bilateral tensions between Mexico and the United States during the North American Free Trade Agreement era, as well as with liberating forms of cultural migrations, which he described as "transfusions." This ensemble, like much of his work, adheres to a Duchampian logic of appropriation, which led the artist to create work based on acquiring, juxtaposing, and exhibiting objects and images of popular consumption. The 435 plastic soldiers that make up this piece are arranged in a grid formation on a white wooden base, forming the American flag in a show of pop-style anti-imperialist critique.

J. G. M.

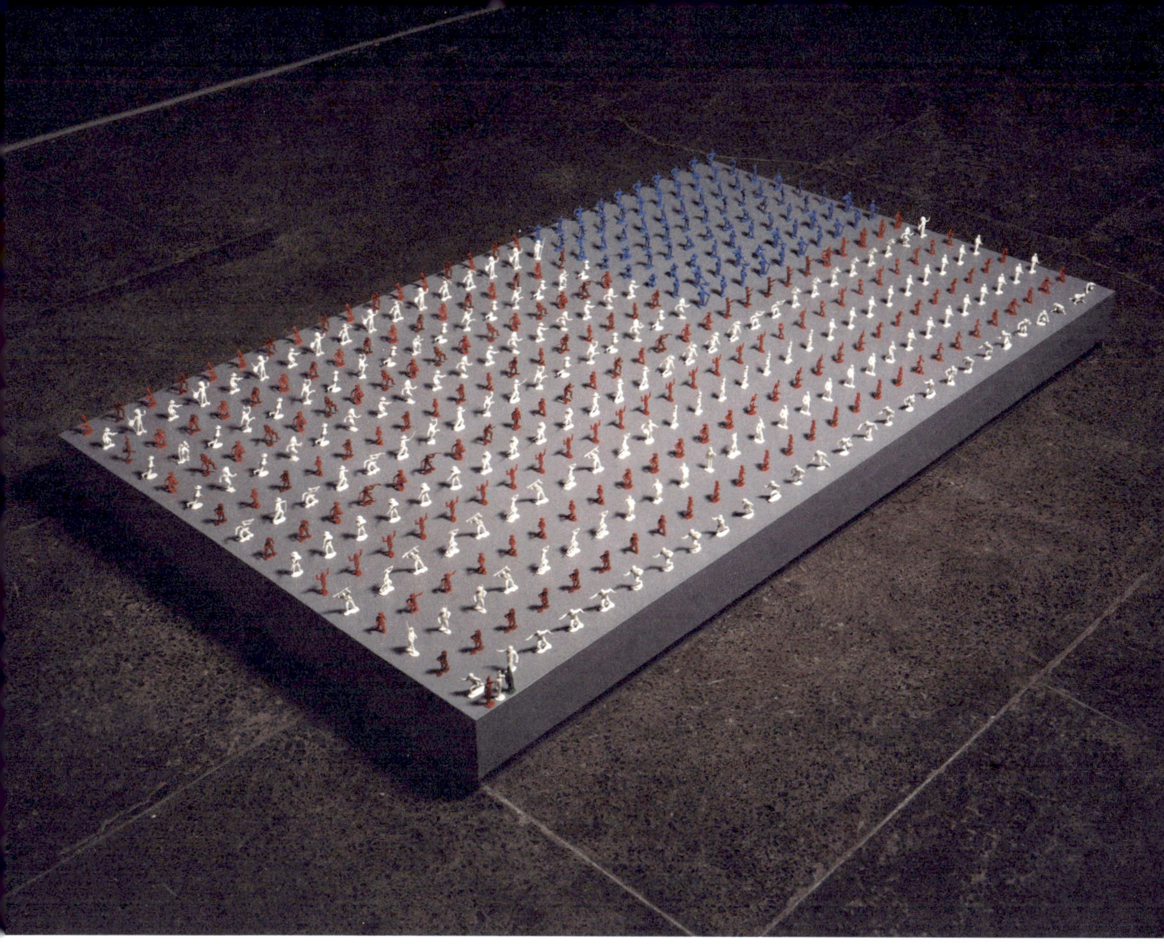

Grupo Proceso Pentágono

—

Active 1976–2015
Felipe Ehrenberg, Mexico City, Mexico, 1943–Ahuatepec, Mexico, 2017; **Miguel Ehrenberg**, Mexico City, Mexico, 1952–2006; **Carlos Finck**, Mexico City, Mexico, 1946; **Lourdes Grobet**, Mexico City, Mexico, 1940; **José Antonio Hernández Amezcua**, Mexico City, Mexico, 1947; **Víctor Muñoz**, Mexico City, Mexico, 1948; with the collaboration of **Carlos Aguirre**, Acapulco, Mexico, 1948

***1929: Proceso* [*1929: Process*], 1979**

Replica, 2015, with the collaboration of the artists
Environment
Variable dimensions
Gift of Grupo Proceso Pentágono, 2018
Replica funded by the Ford Foundation

Since its founding in 1976, Grupo Proceso Pentágono has made art in times of sociopolitical conflict. Creating pieces that express dissent through debate and disagreement among its members, the group has always maintained a critical stance toward repressive state policies.

In January 1979, the INBA inaugurated the sole Sección Anual de Experimentación [Annual Experimentation Section] of the Salón Nacional de Artes Plásticas at the Galería del Auditorio Nacional, Grupo Proceso Pentágono presented an environment, over 400 m² around, that recreated a police station: a series of rooms with closed doors that allowed for glimpses of different scenes condemning the "dirty war" and the use of torture in bureaucratic proceedings. The title alludes to the fiftieth anniversary of the official political party, the Partido Revolucionario Institucional.

The environment addresses state violence in Latin America: it employs signs of human rights-violations perpetrated by dictatorships, exposes continuous forced disappearances and murders, and confronts and engages spectators in an emotionally affecting, fear-inducing aesthetic experience. At the end of the "tour," viewers were given a survey that included questions on the meaning of the word "disappeared" and the name of one of the hundreds of people who had vanished in Mexico under political circumstances.

The group decided to participate outside of contest itself, as they believed that the topic in question—suppression, forced disappearance, and political prisoners—should not be evaluated within an aesthetic framework.

P. G.

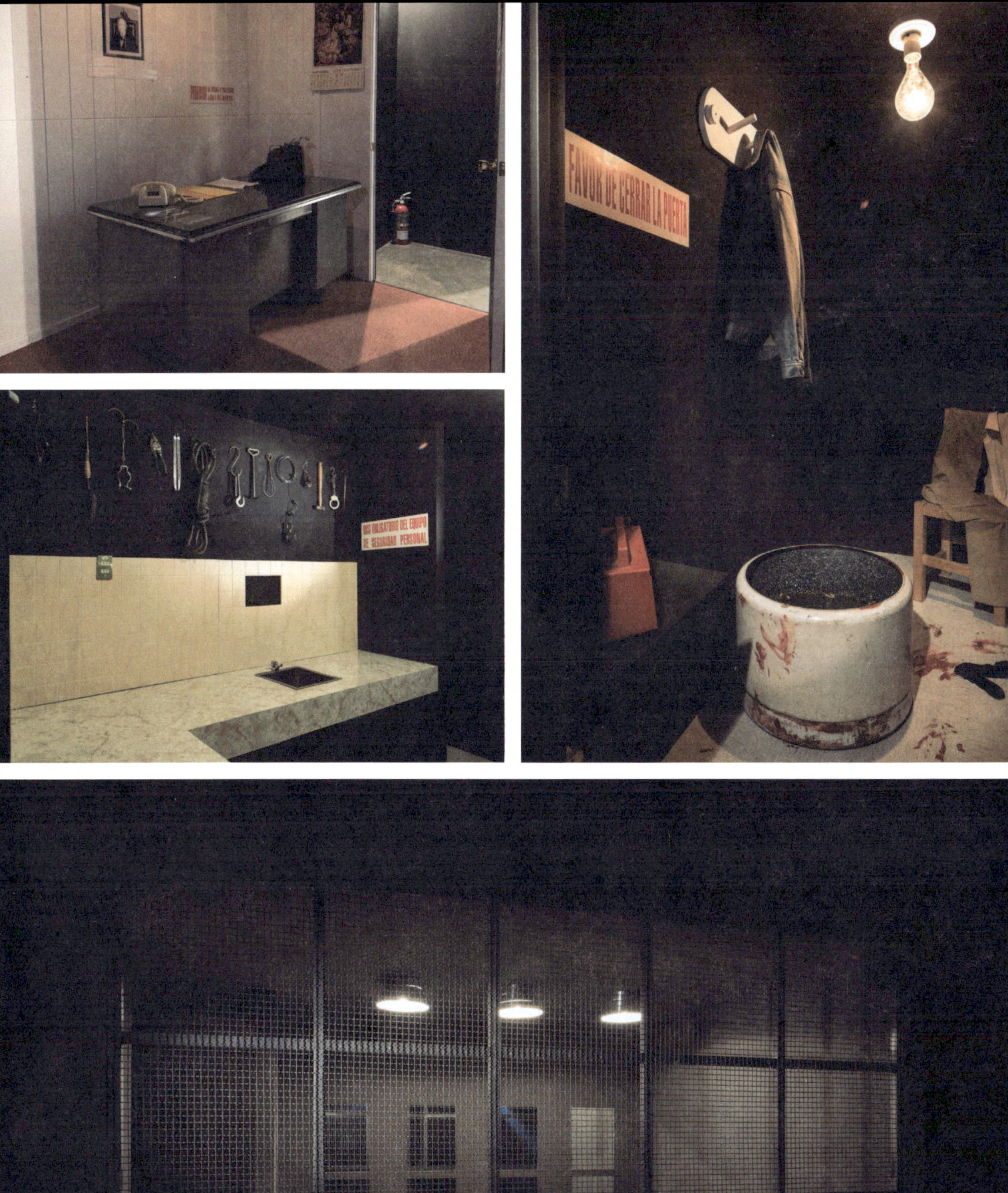

FAVOR DE CERRAR LA PUERTA
USO OBLIGATORIO DEL EQUIPO DE SEGURIDAD PERSONAL

Vicente Razo

Mexico City, Mexico, 1971

Museo Salinas [*Salinas Museum*], 1996

364 pieces. Piñatas, masks, photographs, books,
magazines, newspapers, stickers, audio cassettes,
compact discs, mugs, packs of gum, glass
miniatures, plastic toys, and lead figurines
Variable dimensions
Acquisition, 2007

In early 1995, Vicente Razo was captivated by the way in which thousands of craftspeople in Mexico began to direct their rage against the counterproductive effects of economic integration, organizing attacks against the ex-president Carlos Salinas de Gortari (1988–1994). His fascination had a precedent: in prior years, the artist had toyed with the idea of creating objects of power that would enact a form of symbolic justice. Razo thus interpreted the fetishes of the so-called "salinophobia" as a collective act of witchcraft, and he rushed to amass a collection of the hundreds of toys, piñatas, printed materials, clothing, and images marked with anti-presidential gestures that had emerged from society's rage against the failure of "modernization." And so, by the spring of 1995, Razo set up his collection in the bathroom of his apartment and announced the inauguration of the Salinas Museum, opening it to the public.

Razo declared: "If Duchamp put a urinal in a museum, we have to put the museum in the bathroom." His museum was a kind of inverted ready-made that mimicked the cultural institution by usurping its hierarchy. Razo declared himself director, founder, spokesman, conservator, and chairman of the board of this imaginary institution. His initiative was defined by the museum's "Organic Regulations and Statues," which culminated in the slogan: "STOP MAKING READY-MADES AND START MAKING MUSEUMS."

Active for three years, the Salinas Museum embodied an alternative institutional critique: an institution focused on destabilizing cultural and political legitimacy, but also on disrupting the supposed neutrality of contemporary art.

C. M.

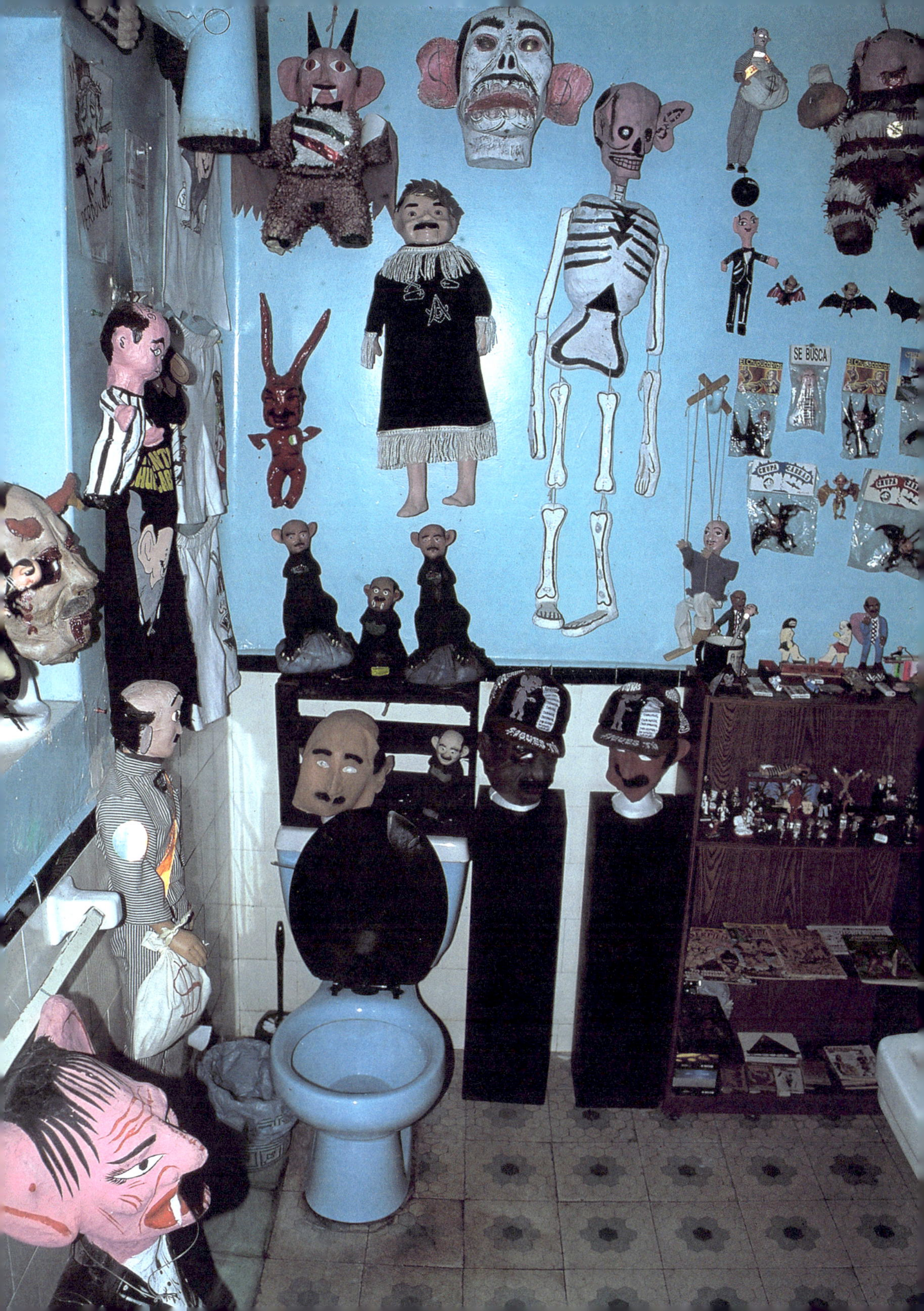

Ricardo Regazzoni

Mexico City, Mexico, 1942

Homenaje a Jean Genet, Homenaje a Yukio Mishima, Homenaje a Pier Paolo Pasolini [*Homage to Jean Genet, Homage to Yukio Mishima, Homage to Pier Paolo Pasolini*], 1977

Graphite, soils, rabbitskin
glue, and glitter on chipboard
1.70 × 85 × 2.5 cm each
Gift of the artist, 2018

This triptych evokes to the figures of Yukio Mishima, Jean Genet, and Pier Paolo Pasolini as intellectuals opposed to social norms and prejudices. The work celebrates the homoerotic sensibility that Regazzoni shares with these three artists, a theme that was practically absent in the local art of his time. This piece was part of the exhibition *Retrato de familia* [*Family Portrait*] at the Galería Pecanins; critics deemed it scandalous. The triptych was shown along with 16 other "erotic male nudes," encompassing portraits both of intellectuals and unknown faces taken from tabloid newspapers, at a time when police blotters and crime-related press expressed widespread homophobia.

These tributes combine an academic treatment with materials like gold leaf and glitter that incorporate camp values, in terms of affect and class, into the frame. Regazzoni had previously used materials like plush and sequins to depict a feminized sensibility. The naked figure appearing repeatedly behind the writers, both implicitly angelic and openly eroticized in his nakedness, is Joe Dallesandro, a model and actor in the films Warhol shot at the Factory. Dallessandro's beauty and sculpted body made him a sex symbol of underground film in the 1960s and '70s. To Regazzoni, the actor's image was an "inspiring" symbol in terms of the classical iconography referenced in his painting: Nicolas Poussin's *The Inspiration of the Poet* (1629–1630), translated into a homoerotic code.

P. G.

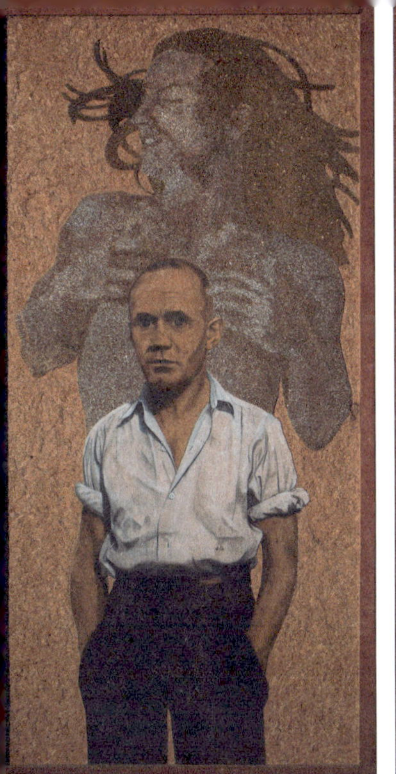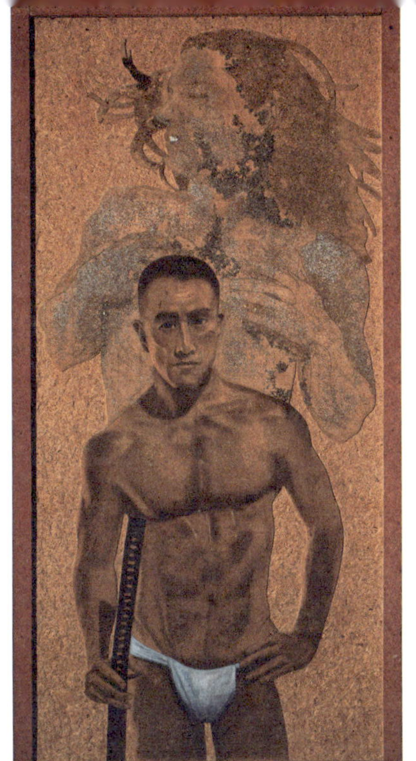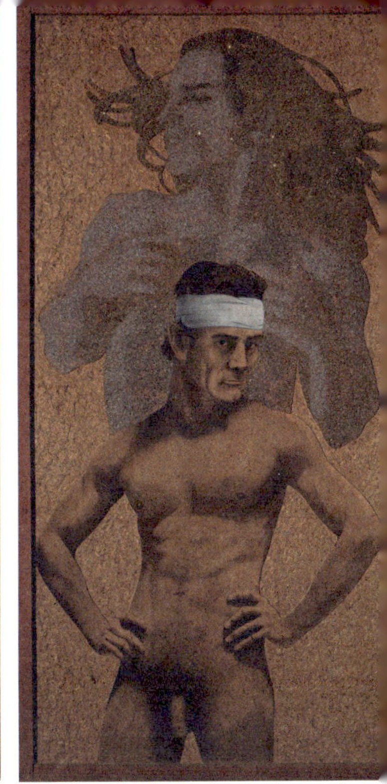

Pedro Reyes

Mexico City, Mexico, 1972

Palas por pistolas
[*Shovels for Guns*], 2007

10 shovels cast from surrendered guns
160 × 22 × 15 cm each
Acquisition through the SHCP
Pago en Especie program, 2019

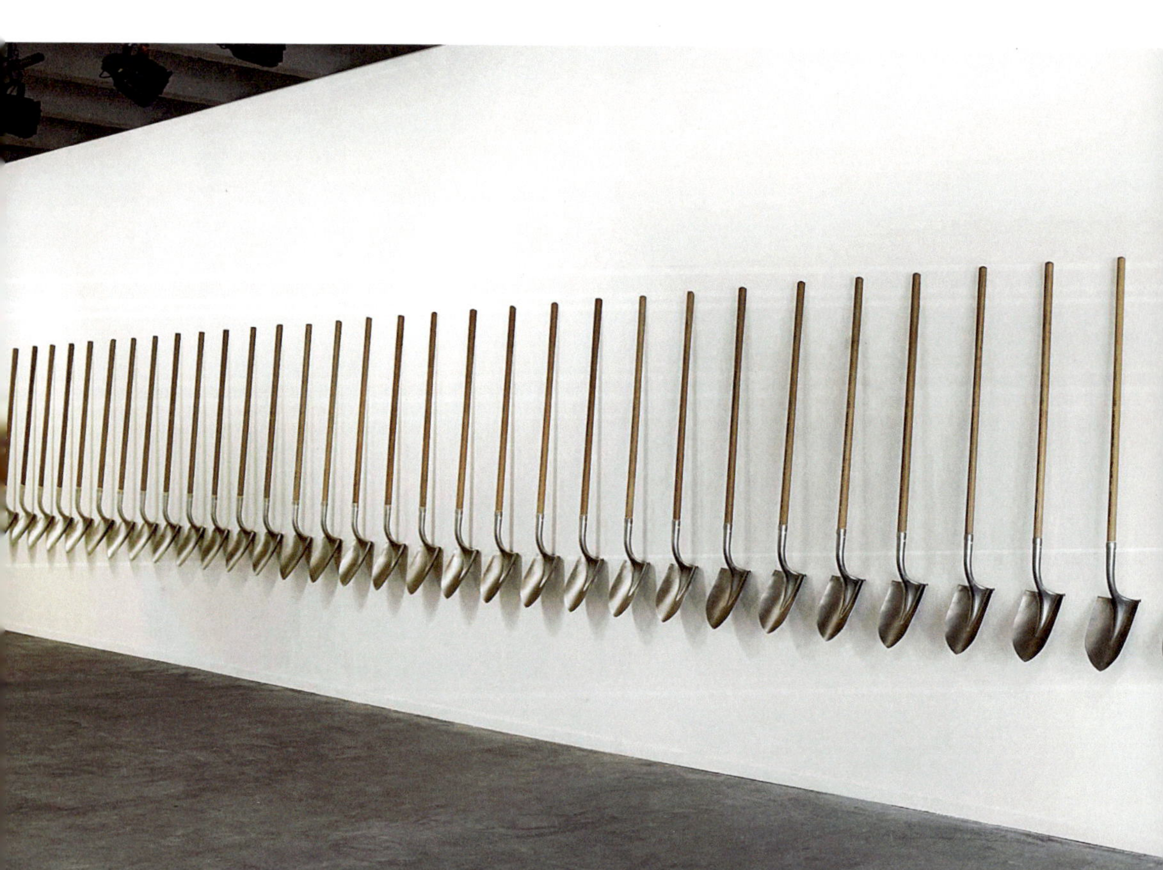

On commission from the Jardín Botánico de Culiacán, Pedro Reyes addressed the violence stemming from the so-called "war on drugs" with a large-scale social intervention. Through ads on local television, he called on the population to donate their firearms in exchange for coupons to obtain household appliances. 1527 guns were collected, 40% of which were legally defined as "for exclusive military use." The steel was publicly melted down under the supervision of the Secretaría de la Defensa Nacional, then used to create 1527 shovels, one for each donated firearm. The same number of trees was planted as a contribution to reforesting the region, transforming an object designated for violence into one that enables life.

A. d. C.

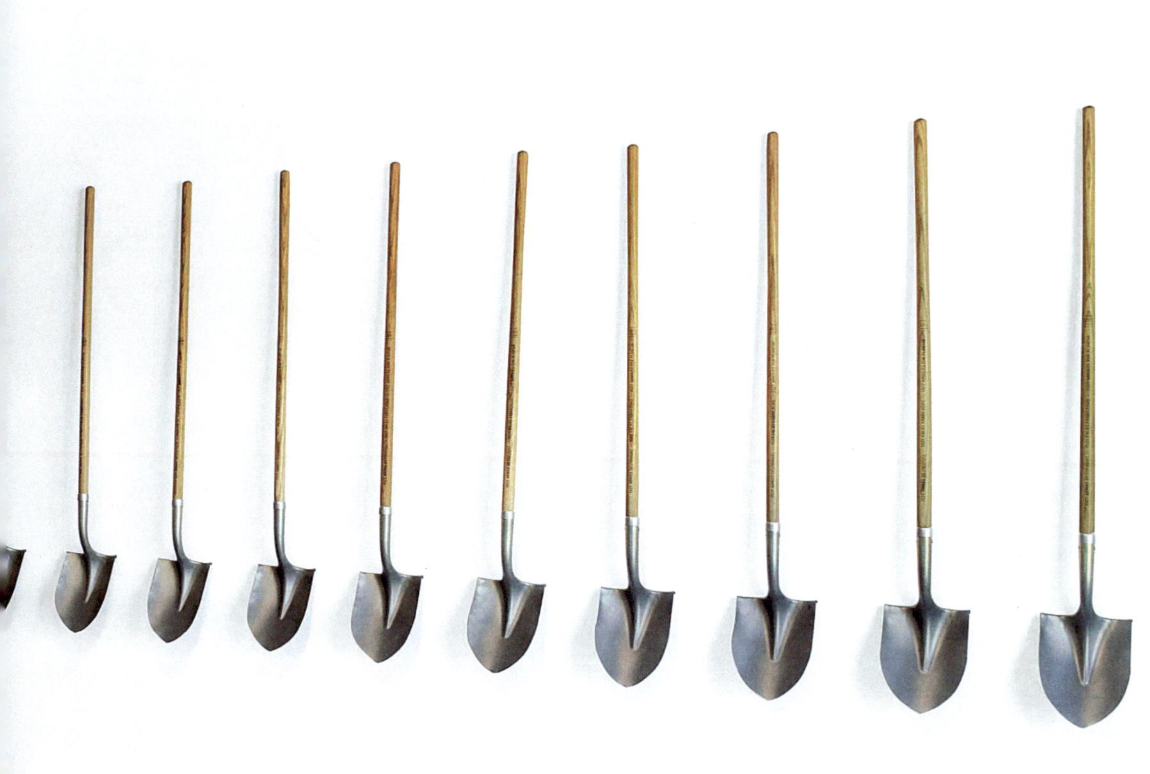

Carla Rippey

Kansas City, United States, 1950

La vidente [***The Seer***], 1987

Graphite and colored pencil on paper
174 × 70 cm
Acquisition with funds from the Presupuesto
de Egresos de la Federación, 2016

In this drawing, Carla Rippey uses elements from two iconographic sources to produce a self-portrait expressing her pain. The image of Pavlova, the famous early-twentieth-century ballerina, is combined with the seven swords and the heart corresponding to the popular Catholic devotion of Our Lady of Sorrows. Dyed with colors much like those of the Mexican flag, these icons help Rippey present herself as an artist/medium who uses the surface of the canvas as an instrument of self-exploration. Like much of her work, this piece is marked by the reuse, copying, and manipulation of images, as well as the creation of her own allegories to depict her emotional states.

E. P.

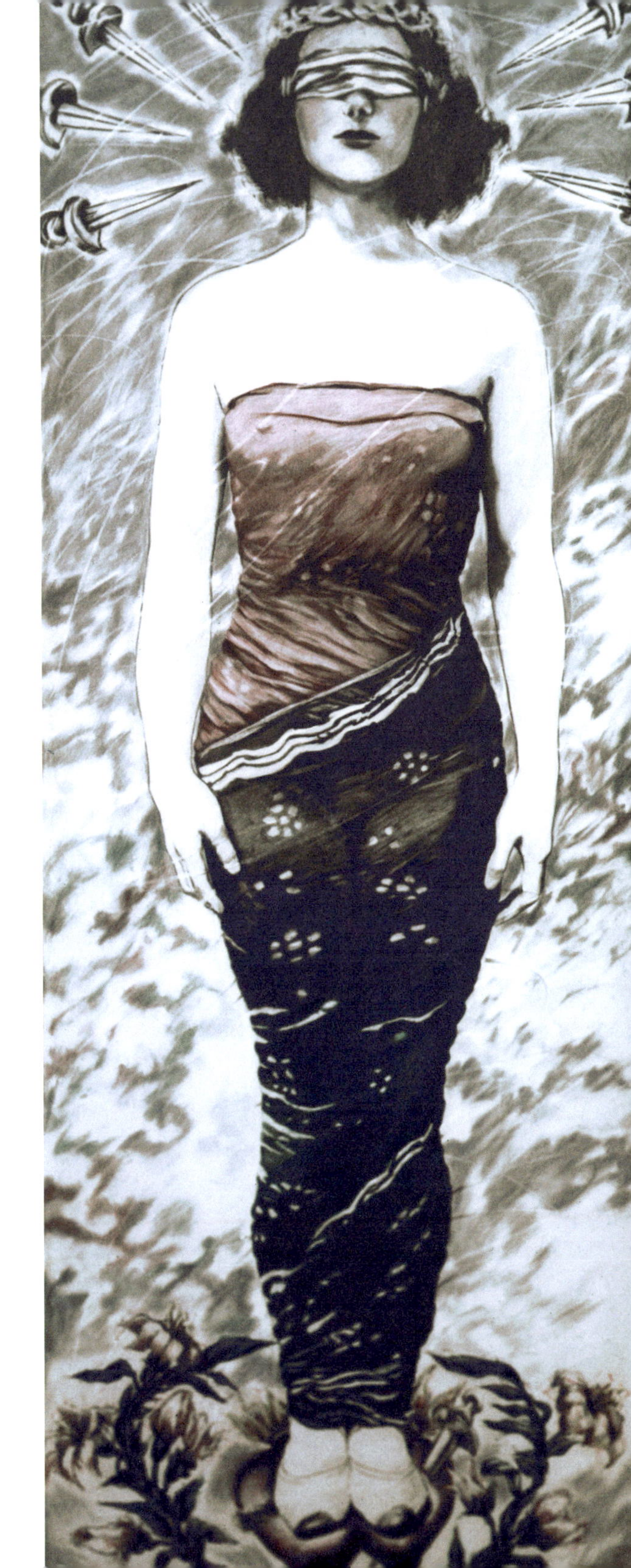

Manuel Rocha Iturbide

Mexico City, Mexico, 1963

Ping Roll, 1997

Aluminum table, 6 speakers,
and 3 audio recordings
76.3 × 192.5 × 92 cm
Gift of the artist, 2015

Several ping-pong balls rest on a table; below are six speakers
evenly distributed to cover the entire area. When the sound piece
activates, the speakers emit sounds and silence that produce
vibrations—which, in turn, make the initially static balls jump
and roll around.

In this installation, Rocha finds a playful and tangible way to
present a quantum paradox associated with the two qualities
of an electron: being a particle that emits discontinuous photons
and simultaneously behaves like a wave. This sound sculpture,
one of his first, was shown at the Biennale of Sydney in 1998.

A. d. C.

Detail

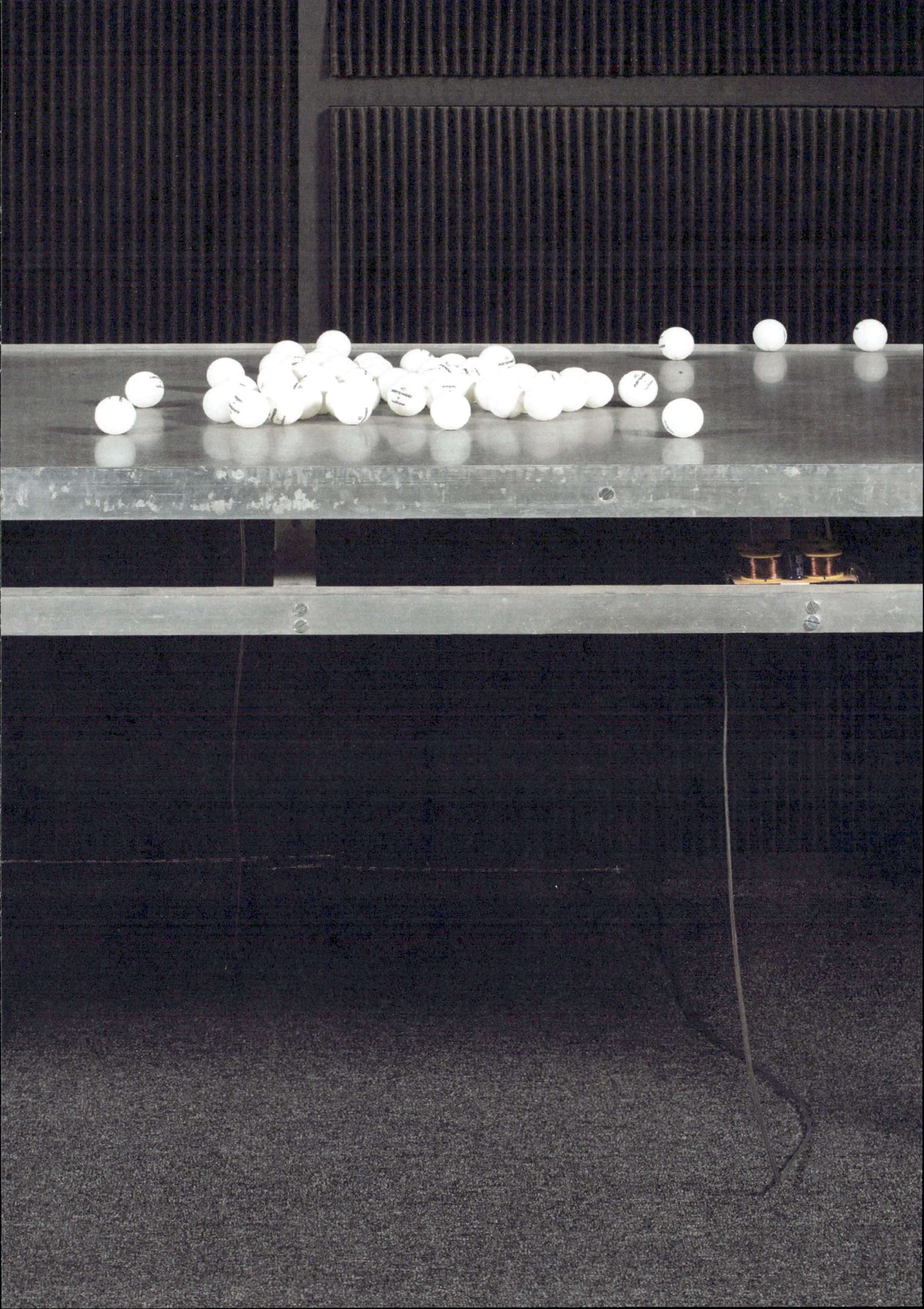

Miguel Rodríguez Sepúlveda

Tampico, Mexico, 1971

Instrumento [*Instrument*], 2012

Sound sculpture. 100 machetes,
metal structure, and electric fan
138 × 150 × 30 cm
Ed. 1/5 + 1 AP
Gift of the artist, 2018

A hundred sharpened machetes are suspended in mid-air: a mobile of sorts. As they shift with the wind blown by a fan, they knock into each other, releasing a gentle, constant noise. This sound sculpture was part of the project *Una historia de machetes* [*A Machete Story*, 2012], presented at the museum Ex Teresa Arte Actual in Mexico City.

By stripping them of their utilitarian function, Rodríguez Sepúlveda subverts the image of the machete as a tool of labor and as a symbol of political protest and uprising. Instead of slogans and clamoring for justice, the clacking of the metal now gives off a soft, even fragile sound. The machetes, sharpened down until they are almost useless, are suspended blade-down. *Instrumento* thus offers a metaphor for social exhaustion and numbness in the face of the country's political situation.

A. d. C.

Detail

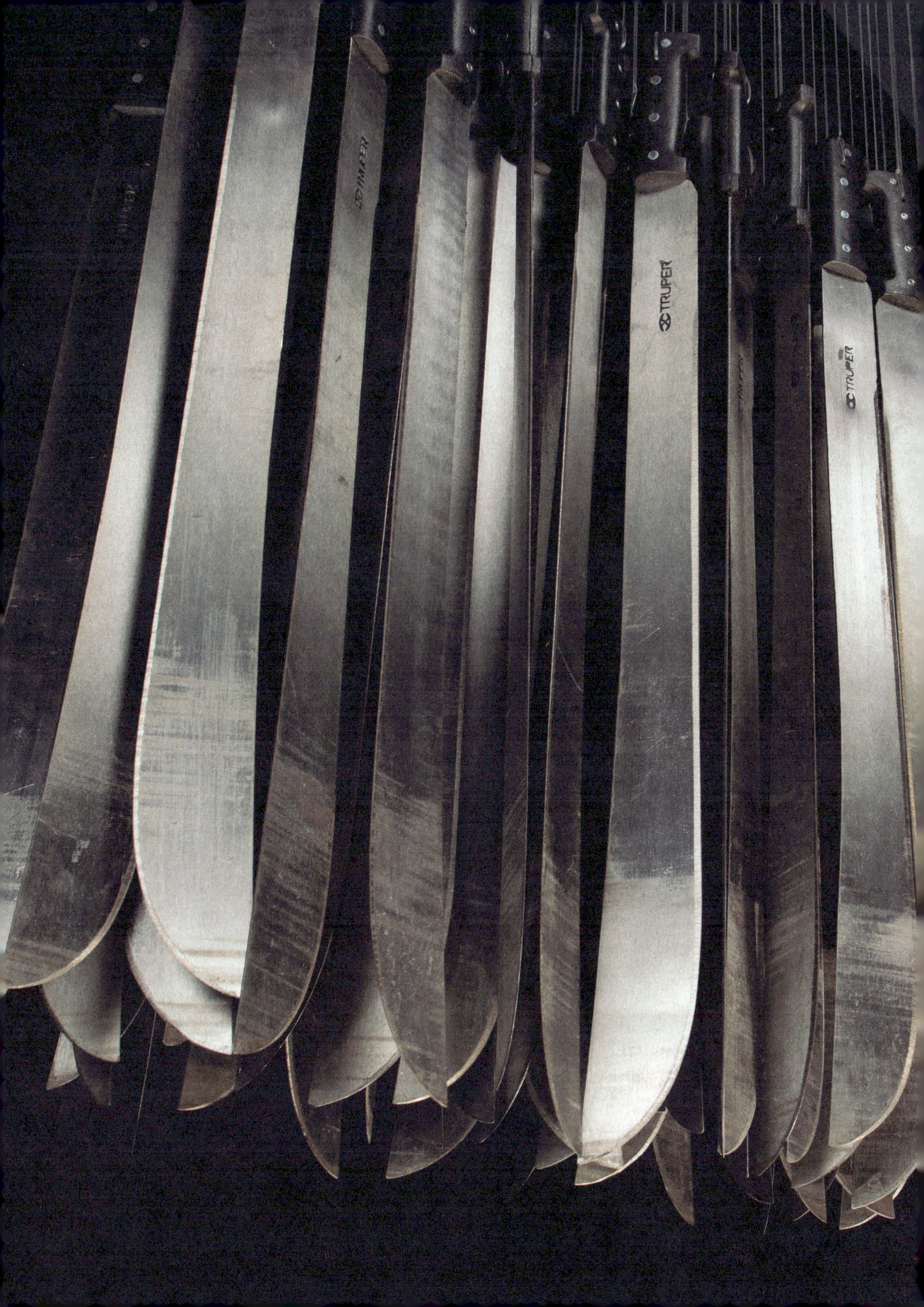

TRUPER
TRUPER

Vicente Rojo

Barcelona, Spain, 1932

Destrucción del orden
[*Destruction of Order*], 1965–1966

Acrylic and latex bath mat on canvas
141 × 182 cm
Acquisition with funds from the Presupuesto
de Egresos de la Federación, 2014

In 1964, Vicente Rojo abandoned figurative language and the use of brilliant colors, turning his work instead toward painting's underlying foundational crisis. From that point forward, self-criticism became the creative storyline of his work. In subsequent years, he created works titled or inscribed with the phrase *Destrucción del orden,* in which he sets out to challenge established artistic "values." In doing so, he attaches objects to his paintings, immersing them in paint. The objects in question are banal, everyday items he selects without trying to retain their connotation or utility (bath mats, plastic objects, lengths of wood stuck together or suspended with rope), boldly integrating seams and slashes into the canvas. This version involves two canvases united by a single frame, the structure of which serves as an antimony to the concept of painting itself. The flat treatment of the canvas on the right side, which focuses on simple geometric shapes that lend it structure, contrasts with the textured finish of the left canvas, which has a bath mat stuck to it. Pursuing a mirrored composition, the artist fills the canvas with scribbles and strike-outs as if it were a desecration. This piece inaugurates Rojo's interest in introducing radical contrasts of gesture and matter in his work. It also represents the initial seed of the working method—sequential, systematic, and structuralist—that he would apply to the series *Señales* [*Signs*], beginning in 1966, and continuing to the present day.

P. G.

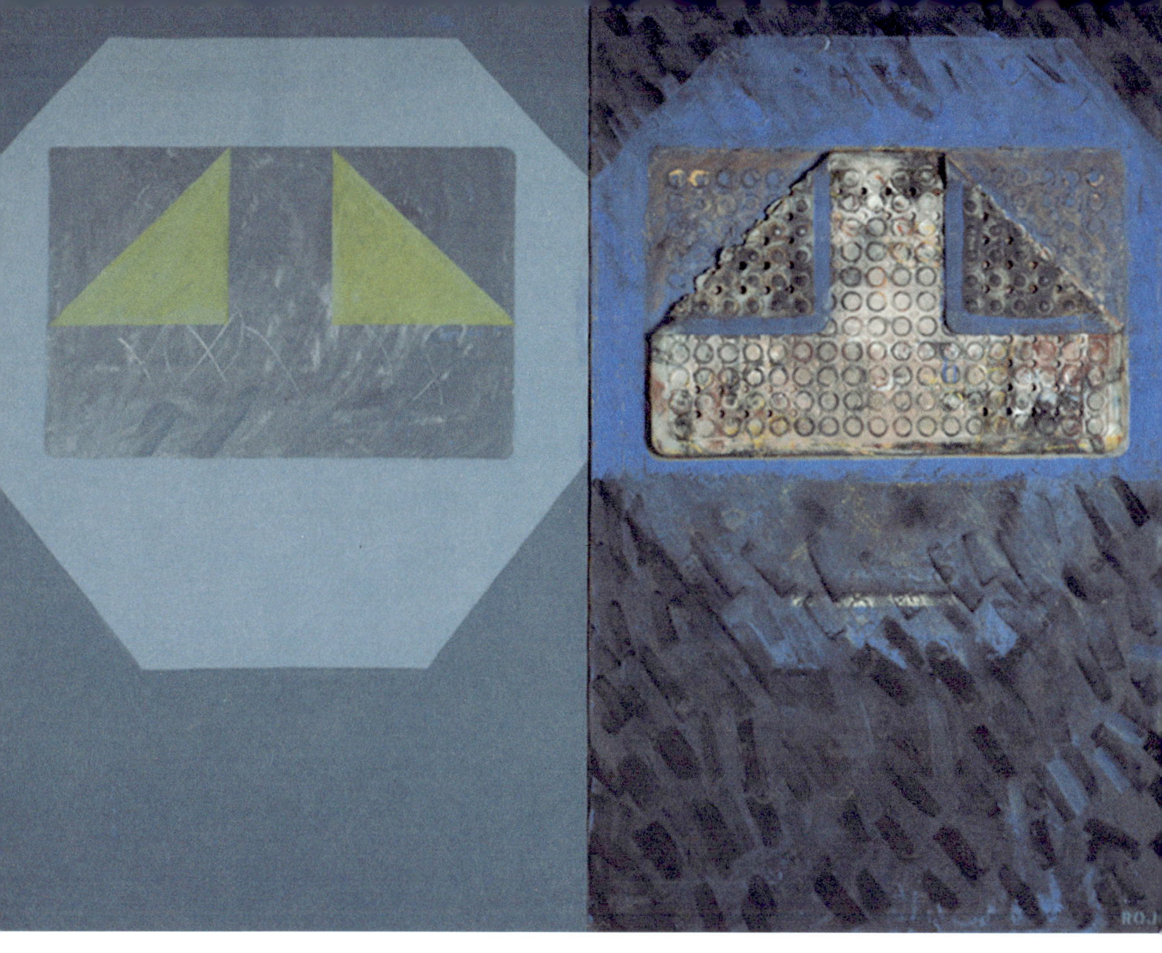

Vicente Rojo

Barcelona, Spain, 1932

México bajo la lluvia 106
[*Mexico in the Rain 106*], 1982

Acrylic on canvas
100 × 100 cm
Acquisition, 2005

The popularity of this series in Rojo's work is partly due to its status as an original icon of Mexican landscape: a rigorous sequence of paintings of varied perspectives, depicting progressions of shapes falling diagonally, left to right, across the colorful surface of the image. According to Rojo, the series evokes the curtains of rainfall he observed from the heights of the observatory of Tonanzintla, Puebla, in 1953. In any case, these works represent an original variant of op art; the set is marked by thrilling visual activity, while each painting maintains its own significant individuality. The synthesis of this gesture—the active diagonals, their suggested movement—makes for an unusual case in the history of twentieth-century abstraction, where meticulous structural execution takes on the signifying value of a collective whole.

C. M.

Graciela Sacco

Rosario, Argentina, 1956–2017

Matorrales [*Thickets*], 1996–2015

From the series *Cuerpo a cuerpo* [*Body to Body*]
Photographic inlay on 43 wood fragments
181 × 550 cm
Gift from Fundación Espacio V, in process, 2020

Sacco's work addresses the reproducibility of images and their circulation in the media, questioning visual hegemony through the critical power of stories.

In *Cuerpo a cuerpo,* Sacco works with heliography, a largely obsolete printing technique, using this method to transfer images onto everyday objects. In this case, Sacco prints photos of protests from newspapers onto found ribbons of wood, placing special emphasis on light projection to create a specific presence. The fragmentation of the captured images often renders the protests unrecognizable, lending the piece a certain timelessness and granting it a universal air.

V. R. L.

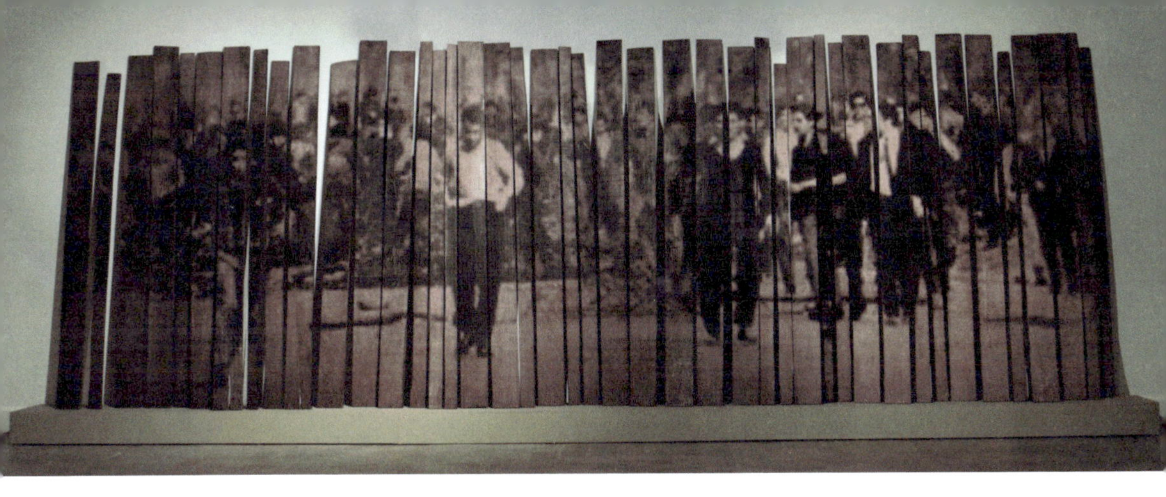

Kazuya Sakai

Buenos Aires, Argentina, 1927–Dallas, United States, 2001

Aus den sieben Tagen (K. Stockhausen)
[*From the Seven Days (K. Stockhausen)*], 1976

Diptych. Acrylic on canvas
198 × 498 cm
Acquisition, 2006

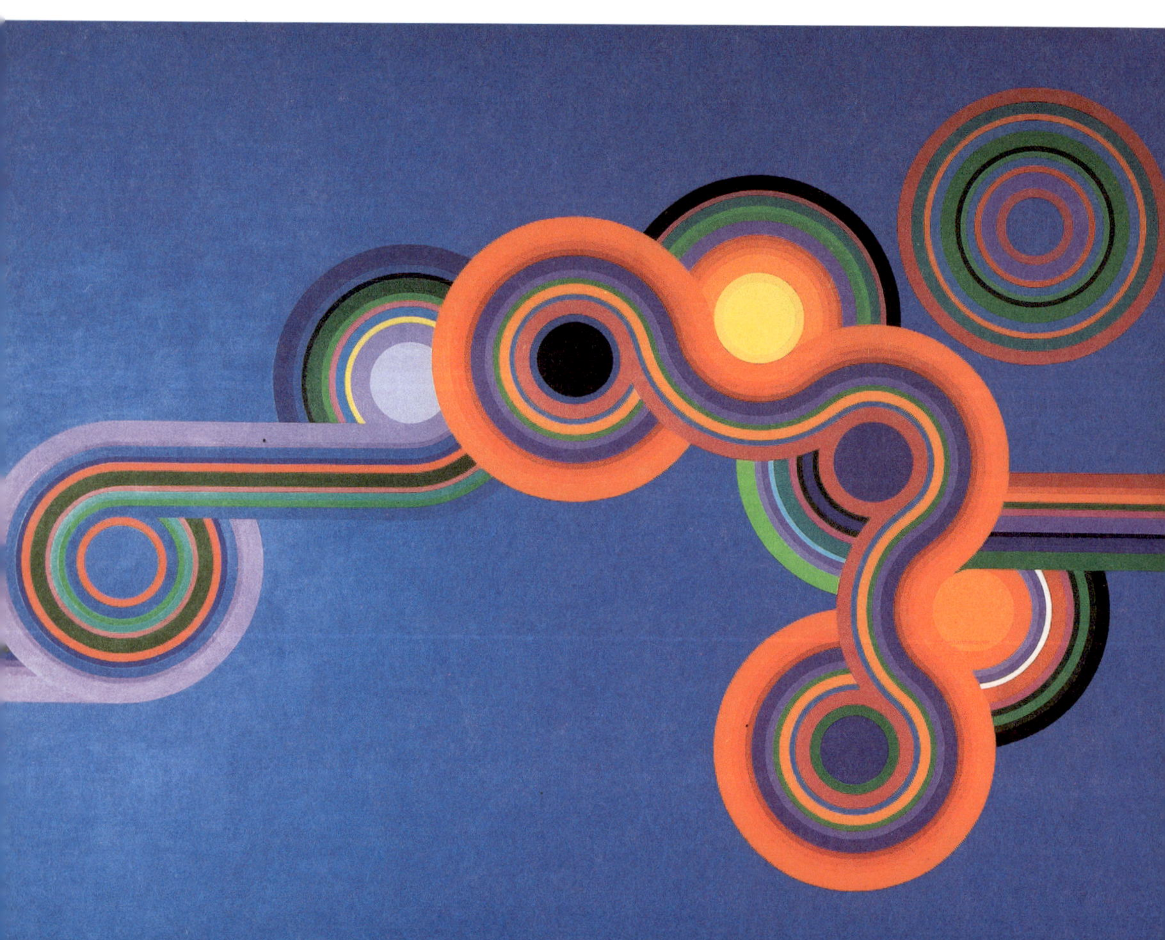

Aus den sieben Tagen refers to the eponymous piece of music by the German composer Karlheinz Stockhausen (1928–2007), involving 15 poetic instructions to be performed freely. The title alludes to the seven days of the week and the creation of the world in the Judeo-Christian narrative. The piece is part of a series of polyptychs that Sakai developed, in varying formats, throughout the 1970s. They are grounded in a system of formal rules for deploying geometric and chromatic elements, practically bands of colors and concentric circles, structured according to jazz and experimental musical compositions.

Sakai intuitively arranges 15 concentric circles across the plane of the painting, corresponding to the German composer's fifteen instructions, which offer Sakai a kind of pictorial score. The hard-edged style is characteristic of the era's industrial orientation toward geometrism: a school that treats the pictorial plane as a formal unit in which brushsrtoke and color are juxtaposed with geometric masses.

J. G. M.

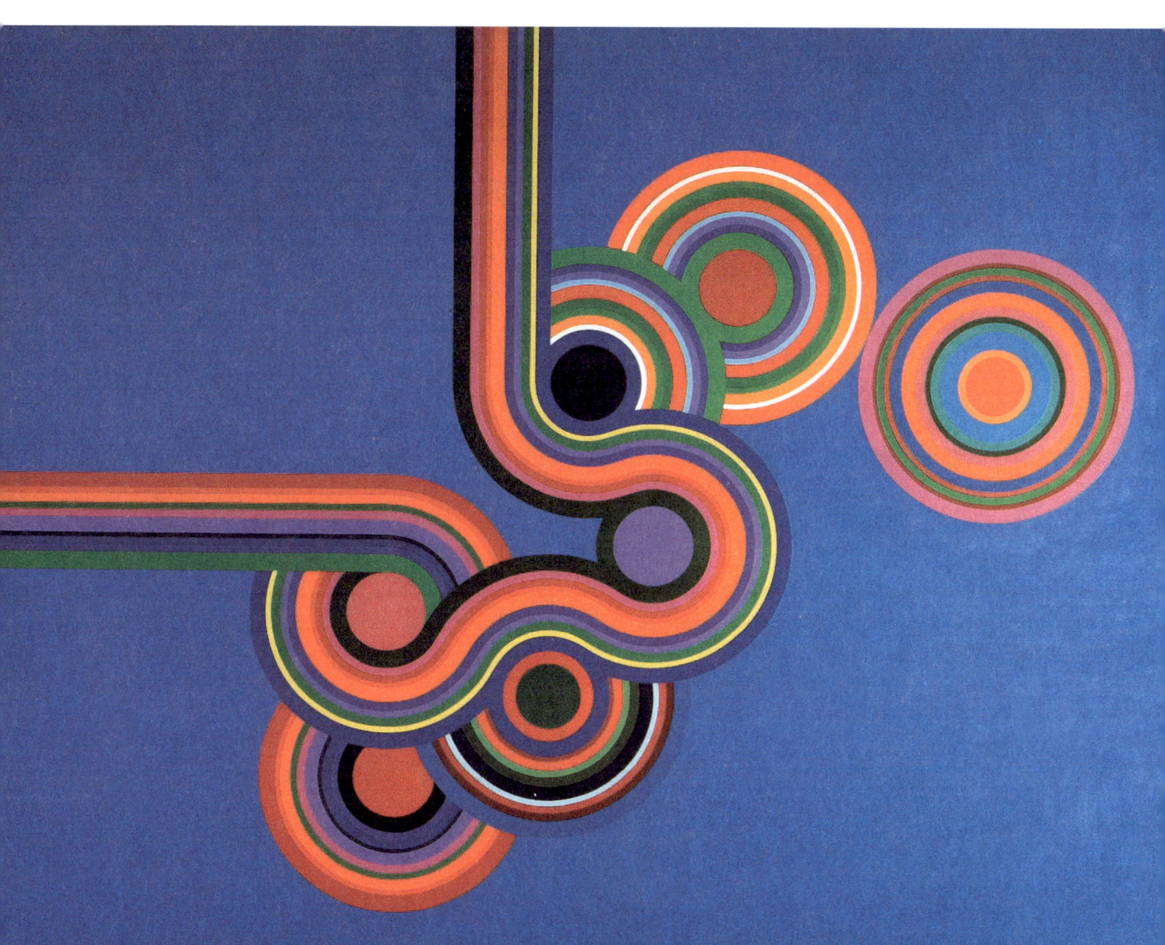

José Luis Sánchez Rull

—

Mexico City, Mexico, 1964

Jekyll & Hyde Club, 2006

Oil on canvas
200 × 400 cm
Acquisition with funds from the Presupuesto
de Egresos de la Federación, 2014

The title of this piece alludes to a New York restaurant so jam-packed with pop culture references that it saturates the senses—much like this canvas. At the same time, the title also refers to the gothic novel by Robert Louis Stevenson, *The Strange Case of Dr. Jekyll and Mr. Hyde* (1886), which employs the contrast between two characters to describe the human duality of good and evil.

Sánchez Rull makes visceral use of the canvas, amassing references from a vast visual, musical, and literary repertoire; together, they chronicle a generation marked by punk aesthetics and underground comix. Here, pop satisfies the gaze's need for constant stimulation, and it serves as a narrative that synthesizes the artist's references: the Sex Pistols, William Blake, and *MAD Magazine,* among others. The texts appearing here and there allude to the songs "Hello Stranger" by Barbara Lewis, "New York Mining Disaster 1941" and "First of May" by the Bee Gees and "B.C. 1675" by the experimental musician Raymond Scott.

This monumental canvas, primarily concerned with intertextuality, offers a proposal of "anti-culture." Through the saturation of images, which comes to resemble a pen drawing, the piece occupies an ambiguous middle ground between "fine" and "popular" art. Deep down, Sánchez Rull seeks to elevate his idea of "anti-cultured painting" to replace the obsolete project of "the end of painting."

P. G.

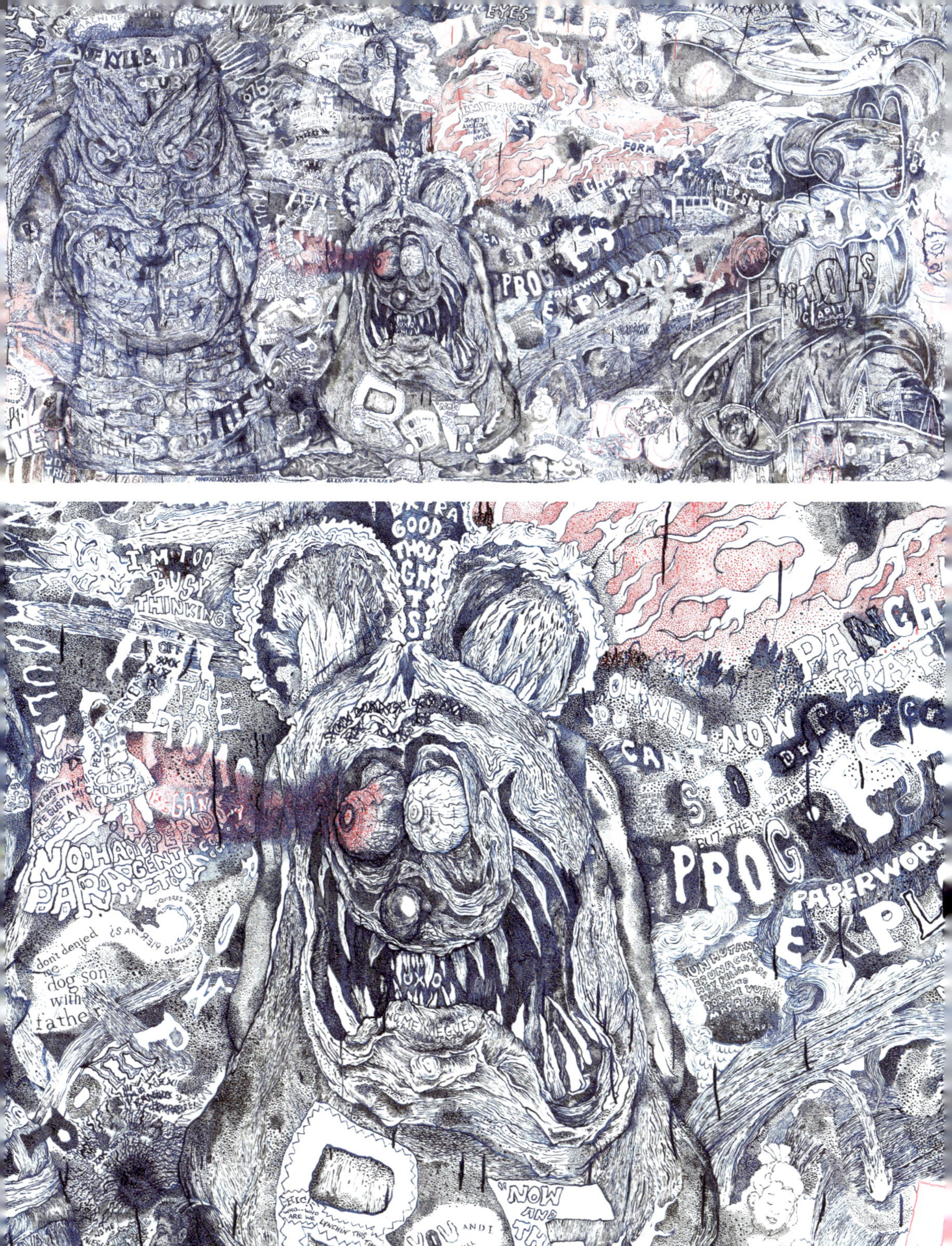

Guillermo Santamarina

Mexico City, Mexico, 1957

Frei von jedem Schaden! [*Unstained by Evil!*
Free from Prejudice! Unharmed!...], 2006–2013

Action/performance
Vinyl LP records on wall
Variable dimensions
Acquisition with funds from the Presupuesto
de Egresos de la Federación, 2014

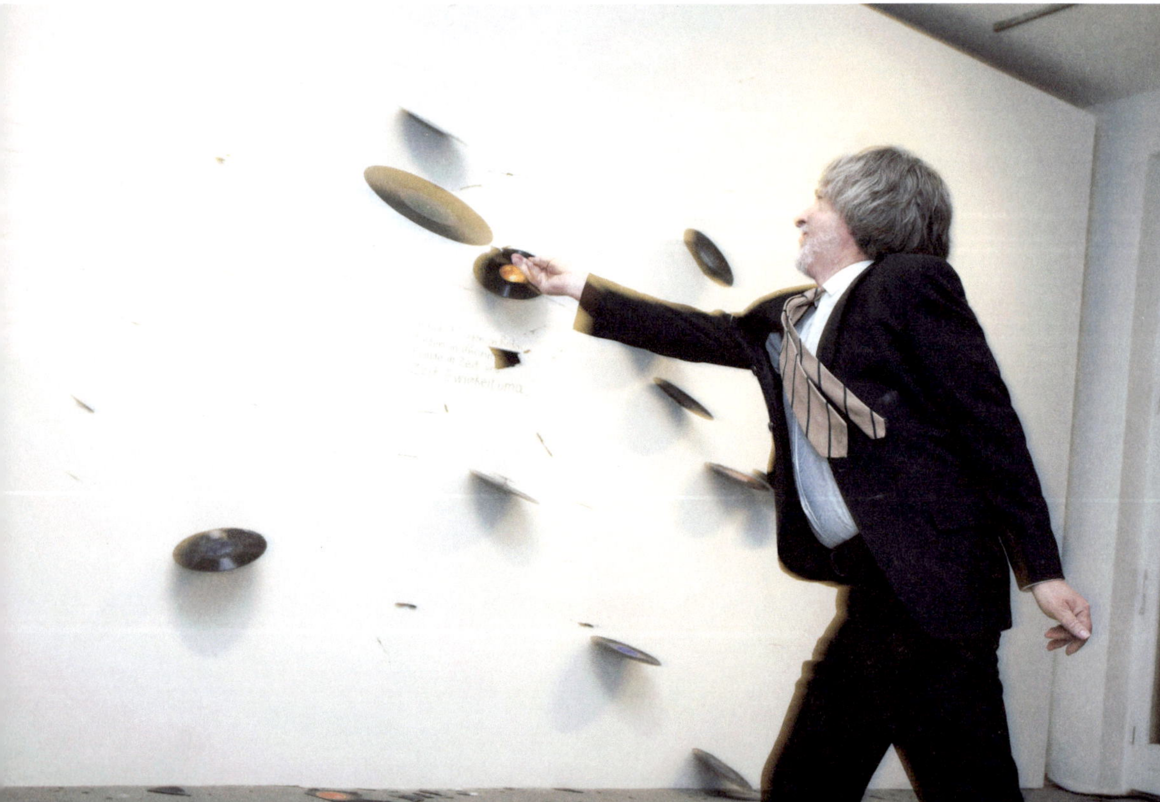

The role of music in the work of the artist and curator Guillermo Santamarina, also a promoter of sound art, has taken many different forms. In this piece, Santamarina creates an uncontrolled sculpture derived from the action of flinging dozens of LP records against a drywall barrier, playing various musical tracks during the hours it takes him to tackle the wall. This Dada-evoking destructive/constructive action is dedicated to deceased friends and colleagues in the art world, such as María Guerra, Mario Rangel Faz, and Olivier Debroise. The resulting installation—the sculpture on the wall and the broken fragments scattered across the floor—is the fruit of the artist's cathartic act.

S. H.

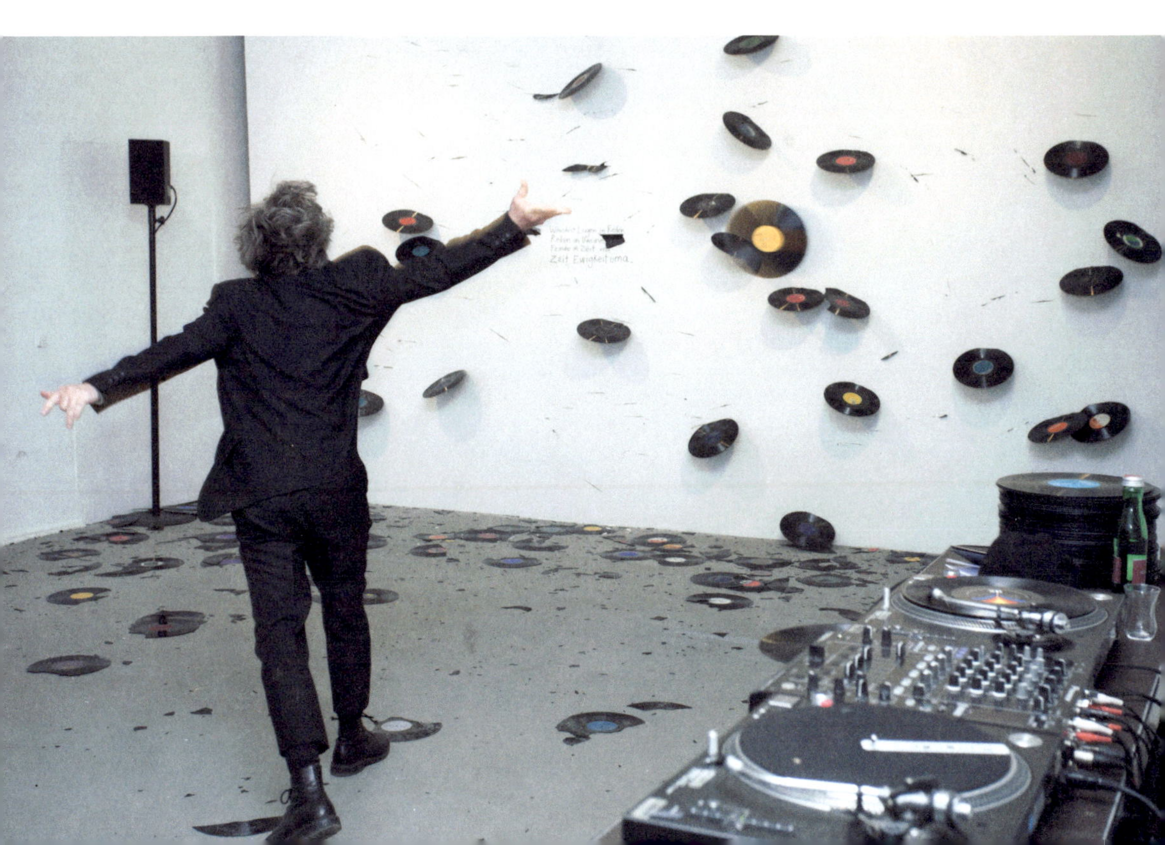

Semefo

Active 1990–1999
Arturo Angulo Gallardo, Mexico City, Mexico, 1965; Juan Luis García Zavaleta, 1961; Carlos López, 1963; Teresa Margolles, Culiacán, Mexico, 1963; Juan Manuel Pernás, Mexico City, Mexico, 1969; Mónica Miroslava Salcido, 1970

Larvarium, 1992

Exhumed coffin, chains,
and metal coat hangers
200 × 70 × 60 cm
Acquisition, 2006

This object was the sinister submission made by the Semefo group (the acronym of Mexico's then-Servicio Médico Forense) to the 1992 Encuentro Nacional de Arte Joven [National Congress of Young Art], where it received an honorable mention. This sarcophagus, shown at the Museo de Arte Carrillo Gil with lingering remnants of soil and rust, represented Semofo's decisive leap from the underground death metal scene to the contemporary art world. It simultaneously symbolizes a gothic monstrification of the Duchampian ready-made and the transfiguration of the field of practices that suggest the death knell of aesthetics.

C. M.

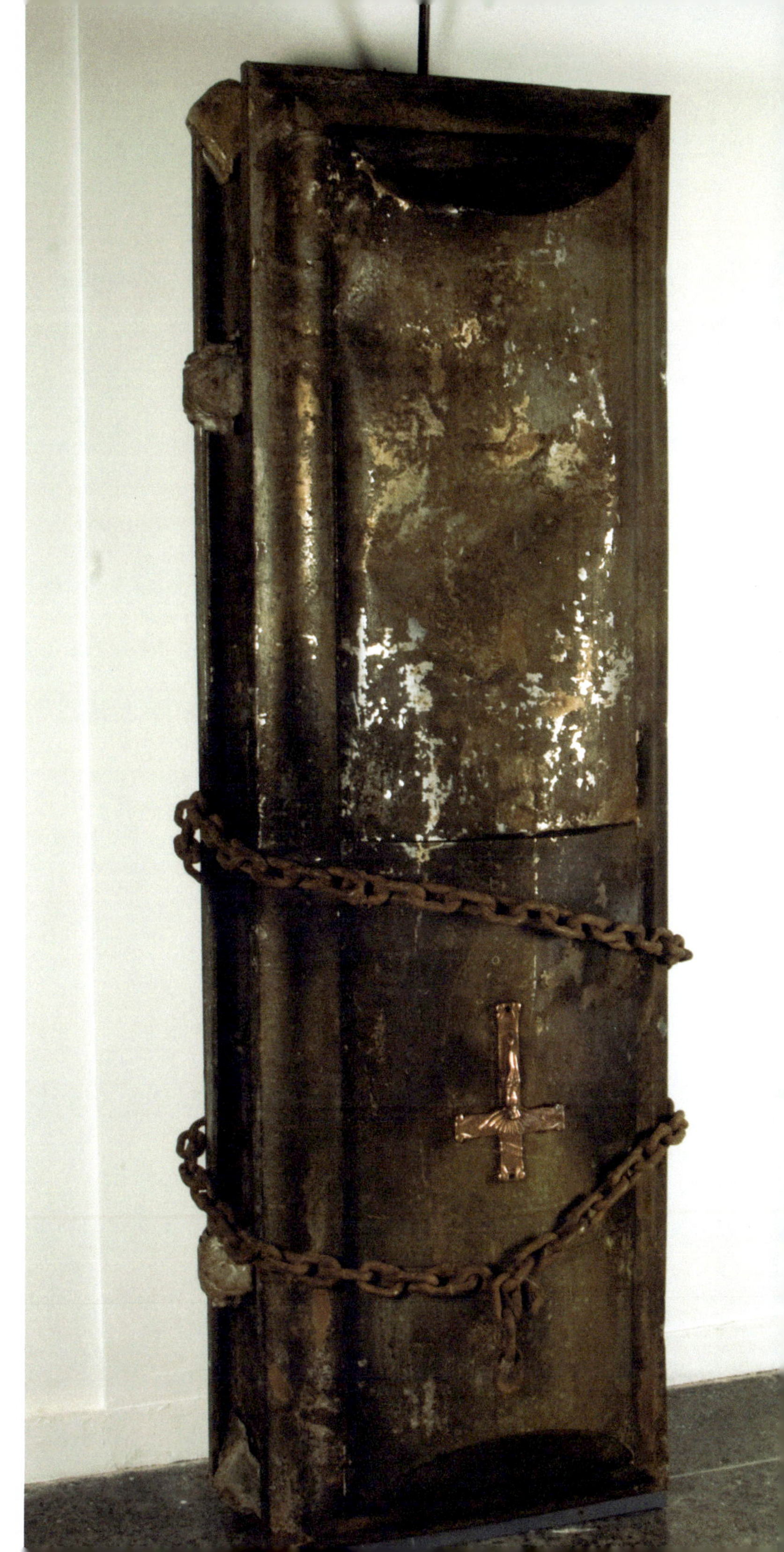

Teresa Serrano

Mexico City, Mexico, 1936

Goddess of Fertility, 1993

Iron, wire, and fiberglass
300 × 300 × 40 cm
Gift of the artist, in process, 2020

The fertility gods of Anatolia were represented as voluminous figures with ample bosoms. Evoking this imagery, the goddess depicted by Serrano is covered in a cascade of fiberglass breasts. The sculpture, designed for exterior spaces, offers a modern-day reflection on motherhood, fertility, and artificial reproduction, recurring themes in her work.

Serrano made this piece for the Primer Certamen de Escultura al Aire Libre [First Open-Air Sculpture Competition], held in Mexico City's Corredor Cultural de la Roma [Roma Cultural Corridor] in 1994. The sculpture was exhibited in Plaza Río de Janeiro and won second place. Adolfo Patiño, disgruntled by the results, destroyed the work in front of the audience. Serrano rebuilt the piece almost immediately.

A. d. C.

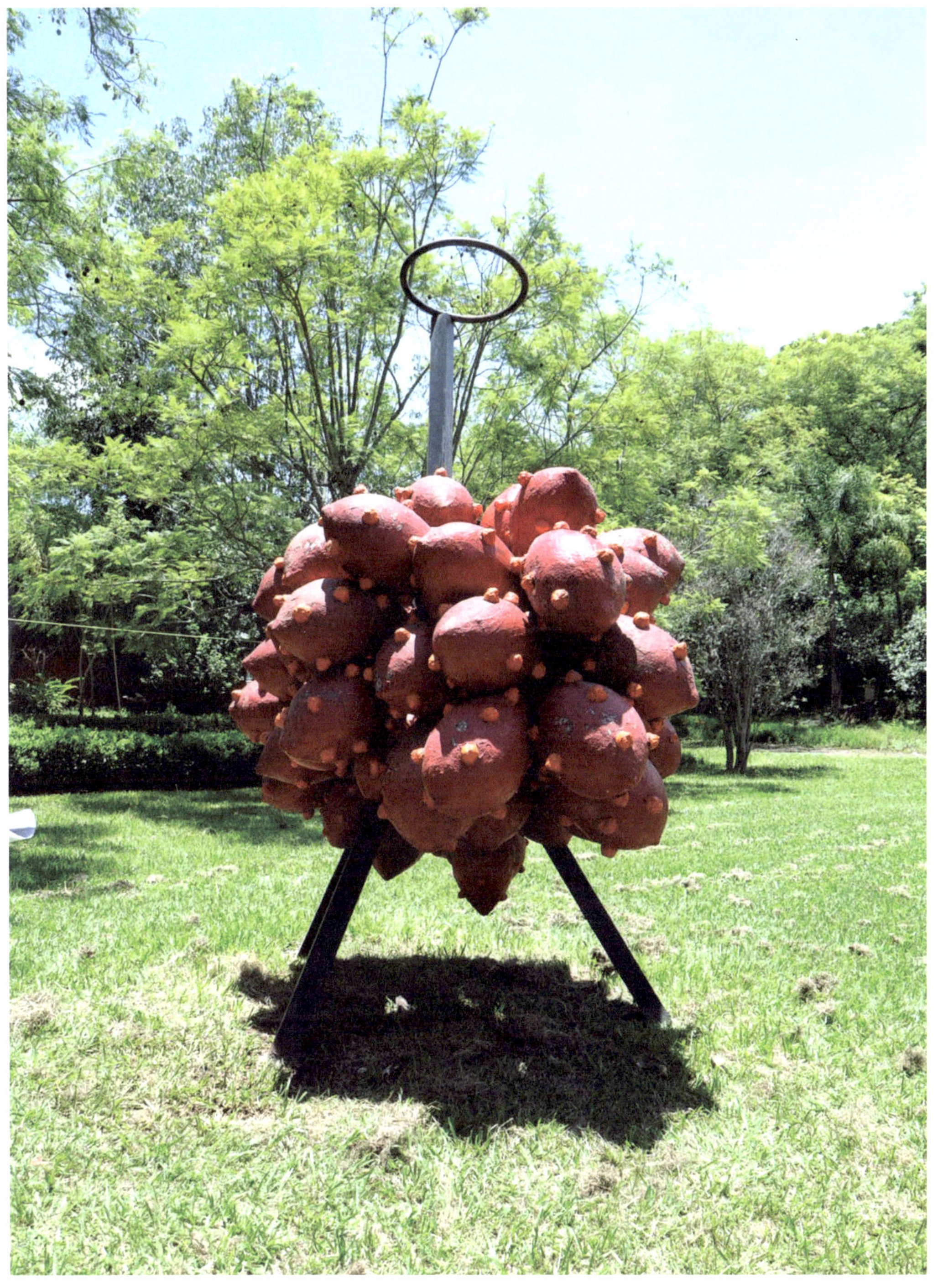

Santiago Sierra

—

Madrid, Spain, 1966

*465 personas remuneradas. Museo Rufino Tamayo,
Sala 7. México D.F. Octubre de 1999* [*465 Paid
People, Museo Rufino Tamayo, Sala 7. Mexico City.
October 1999*], 1999

2 prints. B/W photography
42 × 56 cm each
Gift of Francis Alÿs de Smedt, in process, 2019

In the final years of the twentieth century, Santiago Sierra established a practice that, more than exposing concepts of works
of art or phenomenological sculptural relationships, confronted
the viewer with acts of submission derived from wage exploitation. With *Línea de 30 cm tatuada sobre una persona remu-
nerada* [*30-cm Line Tattooed on a Remunerated Person,* 1998]
and *Desmontaje y montaje de un lavamanos* [*Disassembly and
Assembly of a Sink,* 1998] he instated a means of social intervention, hiring people for actions without any use or practical
justification—and which were sometimes outright degrading—as
a form of artistic output. The radical nature of these proceedings
exposed the utter lack of freedom in contemporary capitalism,
exacerbated by the poverty and exploitation that predominated
in the country from which Sierra had emigrated years prior.

The most ambitious of Sierra's early "remunerated actions"
was the one he organized at the Museo Tamayo in Mexico City:
through a staffing agency, he hired 465 men between 30 and 40
years of age to stand in place as objects on display. The piece
propelled Sierra's practice into a new form of institutional critique,
confronting a largely petit bourgeois public with their own fears of
violence rooted in class, race, and sex. In the austere register
of the action, the artist documents the twisted way in which the
staffing company secured participants. Contradictions and all, the
provocative nature of the piece has already made it a touchstone
of contemporary art.

C. M.

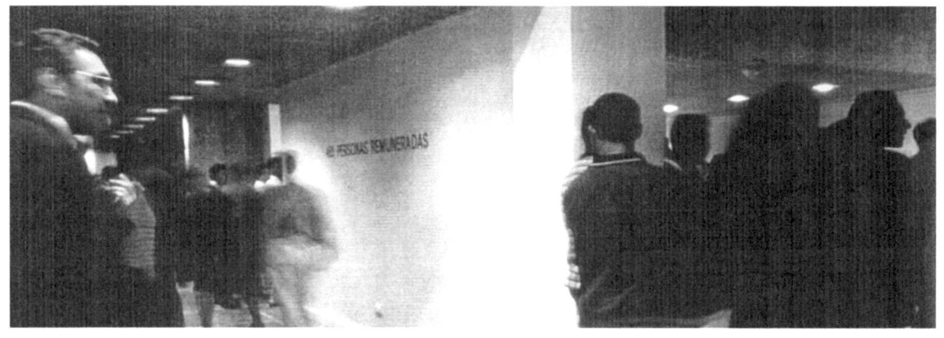

465 PERSONAS REMUNERADAS.

Museo Rufino Tamayo, Sala 7. México D.F. Octubre de 1999.

Para la realización de este proyecto se contrataron los servicios de una empresa especializada en la búsqueda y manejo de tipos humanos, fundamentalmente azafatas o edecanes para congresos, modelos publicitarios, etcétera. Se le pidieron 465 ciudadanos mexicanos varones de 30 a 40 años, de 160 a 170 cm. de estatura y de raza mestiza de amerindio y caucásico. La cifra venía condicionada por la intención de cubrir el espacio con cinco individuos por metro cuadrado. Estos debían permanecer tres horas en pie y de espaldas a los accesos a la sala durante el día de la inauguración. Finalmente la empresa contratada introdujo tantas irregularidades en la pieza que ésta se transformó en una confusión de gentes traida con los más diversos señuelos. Lo más sobresaliente fue que dicha empresa trajo una escuela preparatoria al completo. 150 alumnos con sus maestros a los que se dijo que asistirían a una obra de teatro, lo que obligó a prescindir de estas personas momentos antes de abrir la sala al público. El resto de las supuestas personas remuneradas estuvo integrado por la guardia presidencial mexicana, un batallón de soldados al completo, además de un grupo heterogéneo de amigos de la empresa. Suponemos, no sin razones, que nuestra empresa de contratación pretendió utilizar una masa gratuita de individuos quedándose con sus salarios, lo que no pudimos comprobar al cien por cien.

465 PAID PEOPLE.

Museo Rufino Tamayo, Sala 7. Mexico City. October 1999.

For the realization of this project the services were hired of a company which specializes in stewardesses or aide-de-campes, publicity models, etc. 465 Mexican civilians were requested, males between the ages of 30-40, between 160-170 cm in height and of mixed American-Indian and Caucasian race. The number was determined by the intention to fill up the space with five individuals per cubic meter. These men would have to remain standing with their backs to the room's entrance for three hours on the day of the opening. Finally the company introduced so many irregularities into the piece that it transformed itself into a confusion of people attracted to the most diverse distractions. The most astonishing fact was that the company brought an entire high school for the event. 150 students and their teachers were told they were going to the theater, which resulted in them being ejected moments before opening the museum's door to the public. The rest of the supposed people receiving payment were members of the Mexican National Guard, a complete battalion of soldiers, and a mixed crowd made up of friends of the company. We speculate, not without reason, that the hire company pretended to use a mass of free individuals to keep their salaries, but this we were not able to confirm.

Melanie Smith
and Rafael Ortega

—

Poole, England, 1965; Mexico City, Mexico, 1962

Estadio Azteca. Proeza maleable
[***Estadio Azteca: Malleable Deed***], 2010

Video
10' 30"
Gift of the artists, 2012

Three thousand Mexican public school students were assembled
in Mexico City's Estadio Azteca in Mexico City to make mosaics
depicting a range of images from international art history and
Mexican culture. Together, they encompassed both official narrative and popular mythology. While Smith had already incorporated
the human body into live actions exploring the intersections of
different media, this piece marks a change in scale. The intrinsic
inefficiency of the system she chose to produce the work, along
with the symbolic and historical weight of its spatial and visual
elements, revisits the tension between chaos and modernity that
characterizes Smith's aesthetic interests.

A. L.

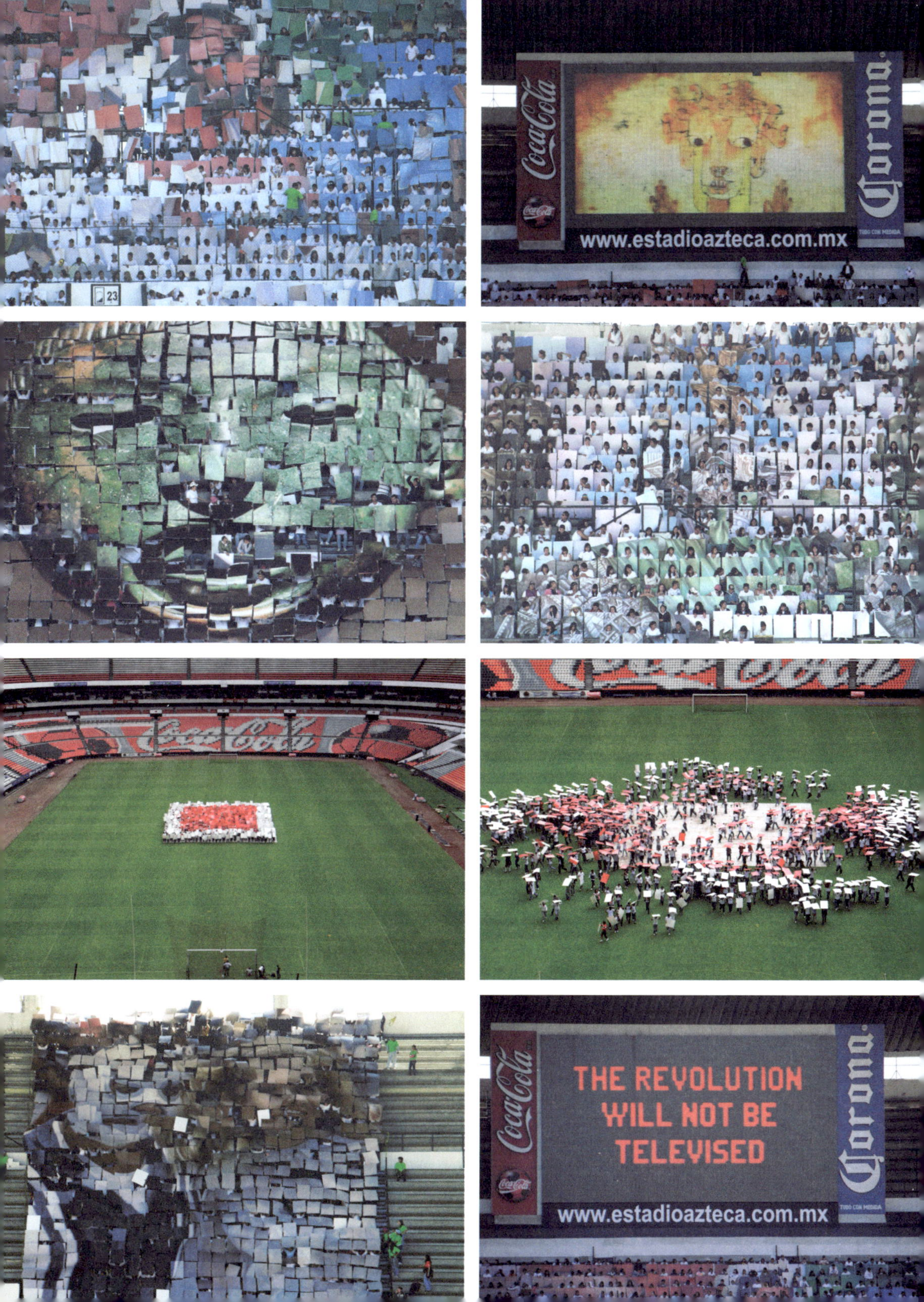

Coca-Cola
Corona.
www.estadioazteca.com.mx
Coca-Cola
Corona.
THE REVOLUTION
WILL NOT BE
TELEVISED
www.estadioazteca.com.mx

Taller Documentación Visual

Active 1984–1999
Antonio Salazar, Mexico City, Mexico, 1956–2016; Gabriel Astror Rocha, Mexico City, Mexico, n.d.; Rubén Gómez-Tagle, Mexico City, Mexico, n.d.; Gustavo Guevara, Mexico City, Mexico, n.d.; Francisco Marcial Castro, Tapalpa, Mexico, 1970; Víctor Hugo Martínez, Mexico City, Mexico, n.d.; Enrique Méndez, Mexico City, Mexico, 1970; Israel Mora Lara, Mexico City, Mexico, 1968; Marco Aulio Prado, Mexico City, Mexico, n.d.; Sergio Carlos Rey, Mexico City, Mexico, 1959; Ricardo Serrano Cornejo, Mexico City, Mexico, 1966; and Carlos Veloz, Mexico City, Mexico, n.d.

Hasta atrás [*In the Back*], 1989

Acrylic on canvas
120 × 90 cm
Gift of Antonio Salazar Bañuelos, 2011

Organized at the Academia de San Carlos, the Taller Documentación Visual [Visual Documentation Workshop, TDV] availed itself of both classical paintings and mass-circulated images to critically address subjects such as inequality, religion, and the HIV pandemic. *Hasta atrás* is a painting that addresses the struggle of marginalized youths in the late 1980s to seek social representation in punk culture. The TDV frequently took up the figure of the so called *chavo banda* as the protagonist of the late-twentieth-century urban revolution, depicting this trope in paintings and rendering it in neo-pop silkscreen prints.

S. H.

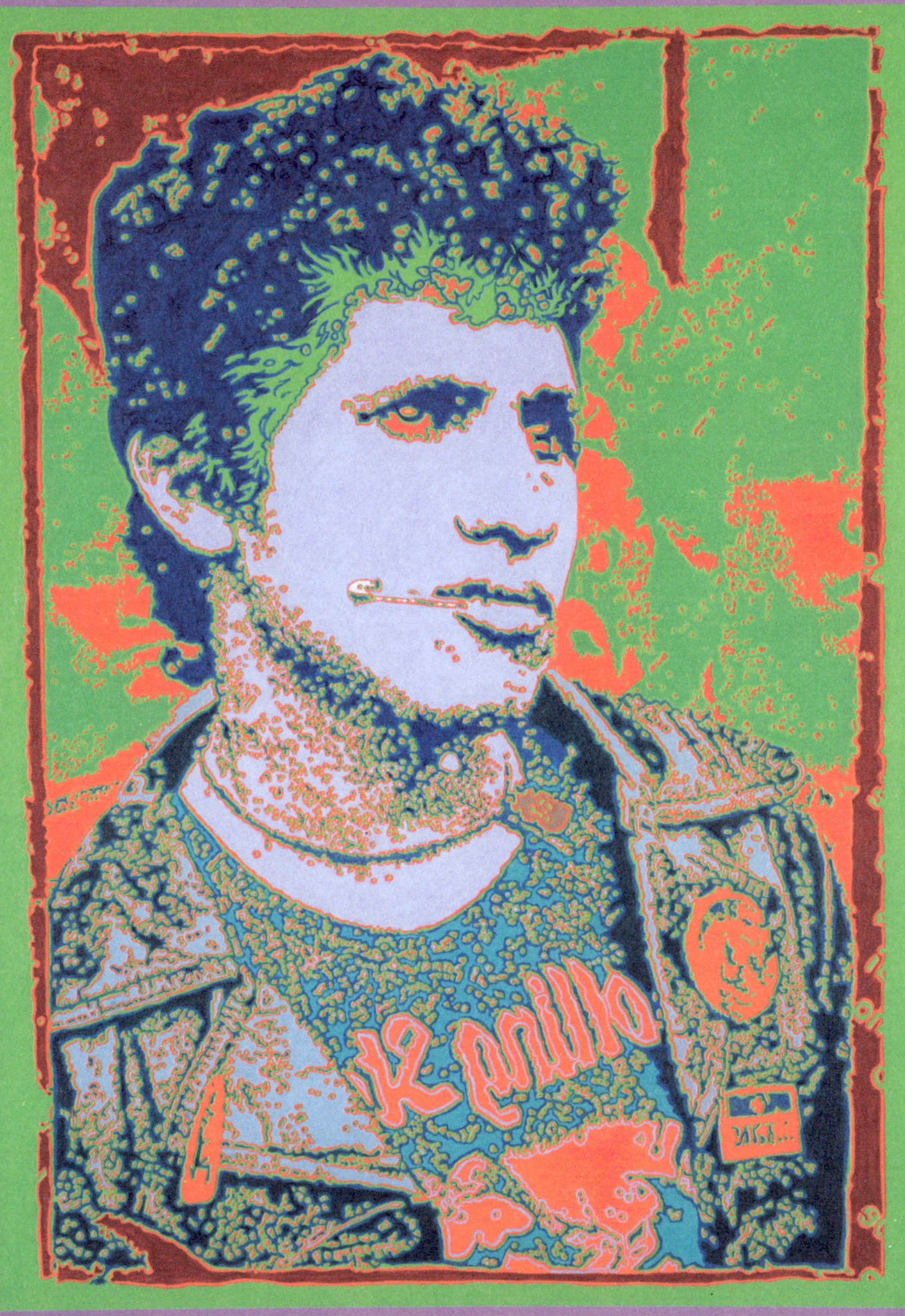

Tercerunquinto

Active since 1998
Julio Castro Carreón (active 1998–2015), Monterrey,
Mexico, 1976; Gabriel Cázares Salas, Monterrey, Mexico,
1978; Rolando Flores Tovar, Monterrey, Mexico, 1975

Restauración de una pintura mural (PRI)
[***Restoration of a Mural (PRI)***], 2004

9 intervened photographs
17.2 × 12.2 cm (4), and 26.7 × 20.3 cm (5)
Acquisition, 2006

This series of intervened photographs marks the first materializa-
tion of a long-term project launched in 2000 by the Tercerunquinto
collective. The sequence reflects on political *pintas* (hand-painted
electoral murals), a common, nearly omnipresent element in the
visual environment of Mexican urban and rural life. In 2010, the
same gesture culminated in the recovery, thanks to a team of pro-
fessional restorers, of a campaign mural painted on a house on the
outskirts of the town of San Andrés Cacaloapan, Puebla. The series
in the museum's possession gestures toward restoring a worn-out
painted sign from downtown Mexico City, using digital intervention
to emphasize the importance of these vestigial murals as a powerful testimony, now veiled, of recent political history.

J. G. S.

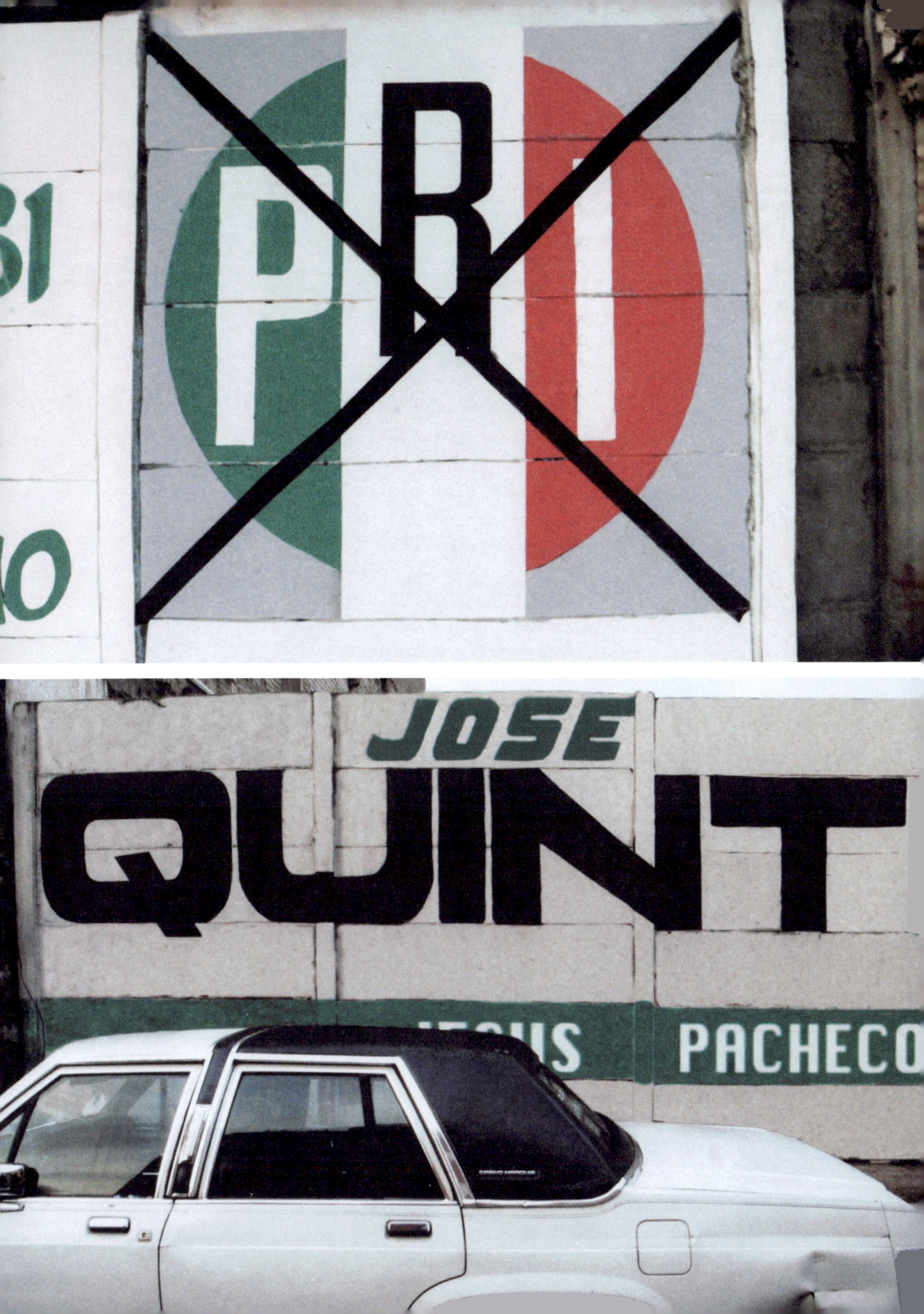
31
10
PRI
JOSE
QUINT
JESUS PACHECO

Francisco Toledo

—

Juchitán, Mexico, 1940–Oaxaca, Mexico, 2019

Sin título 2 [*Untitled 2*], 2015

High-temperature ceramic
47 × 51 × 51 cm
Acquisition, 2018

In 2014, Francisco Toledo worked in the red ceramics studio run by Claudio Jerónimo López, in San Agustín Etla, Oaxaca, to produce a series alluding to the widespread violence across Mexico and the world in the first quarter of the twenty-first century. Most of the pieces were shown in the exhibit *Duelo* [*Grief*, 2015–2016] at Mexico City's Museo de Arte Moderno, which accentuated the drama of the work itself with stark lighting and high contrasts.

The exhibition made a profound impact, both due to the virtuosity of the work and to Toledo's expression of collective mourning for the hundreds of thousands of murdered and disappeared people in Mexico. The decoration of the pieces is a historic accounting: accumulations of bodily fragments of animals and humans; figures in pain, many without eyes; and the combination of bones, cord, tape, and body bags that have become the vocabulary of executions in this country.

Sin título 2 is among the most austere and purist urns in the series. It stands out for the clay's precise emulation of roughly textured wicker and string; a cross on the lid is the sole symbolic gesture. The careful color-dispersion expresses Toledo's obsession with the physical truth of his object. This piece unites his intent to reconcile historical and ethical belonging with the way in which his art makes demands of material and technique as the imprint of a complex cultural history.

C. M.

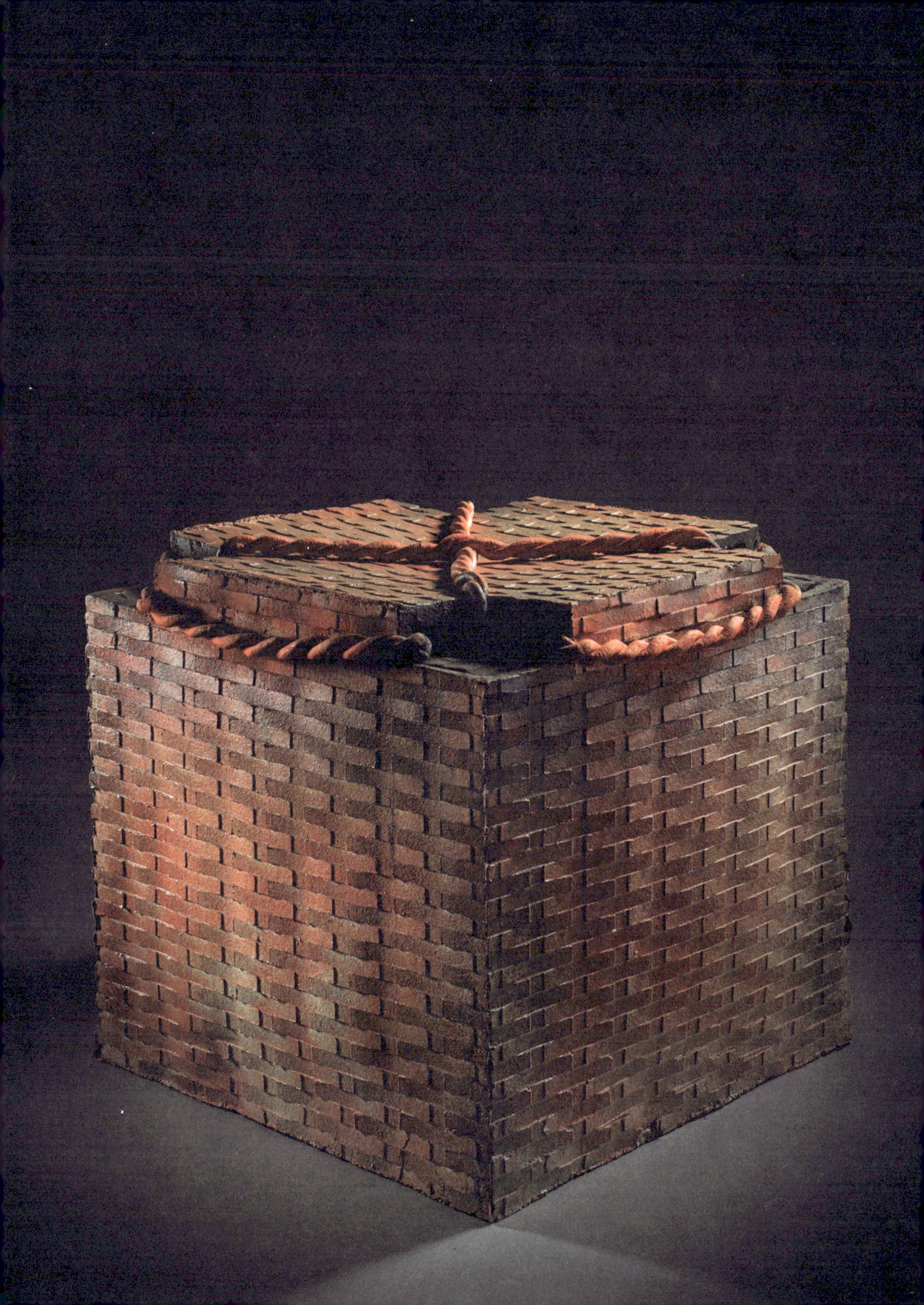

Pablo Vargas Lugo

Mexico City, Mexico, 1968

Relojes I, II, III [*Clocks I, II, III*], 2003

3 monitors and executable program
for PC, Mac, and Linux programs
Variable dimensions
Acquisition through the SHCP
Pago en Especie program, 2014

This piece is part of Vargas Lugo's inquiry into how machines interfere with our perception of time. One sculpture shows three forms of experiencing time on three monitors. All are 24 hours in duration, but time passes at different speeds in each sculpture; most importantly, it is divided into prime numbers. This decision destabilizes the conventions through which we have learned to measure time in manageable, intuitive segments, such as a quarter-hour or half-day. In this way, Vargas Lugo uses the very same technology that permits the control and industrialization of time to perform an unsettling gesture.

A. L.

08 07 12
17:07 53
34:22 39

Germán Venegas

—

Tlatlauquitepec, Mexico, 1959

El triunfo de la muerte
[*The Triumph of Death*], 1988

Four-piece polyptych. Oil, wood
carving, and mixed media on canvas
190 × 300 cm each
Acquisition, 2005

Venegas's early work combines his knowledge of woodcarving
with his training as a painter. *El triunfo de la muerte* is the most
ambitious and renowned relief painting of his early period. Here,
Venegas made use of an enormous dead *ahuehuete* trunk to
carve figures representing divine and earthly battles, suffering,
and diaspora, as well as the barbaric celebration of skeletons and
the dead. The backdrop to these compositions consists of sec-
tions assailed by fire and an authentically apocalyptic landscape
of hazy, colorful masses. The expressive imaginativeness of his
scenes, not to mention his technical audacity, makes this piece
a remarkable example of 1980s neo-expressionism.

C. M.

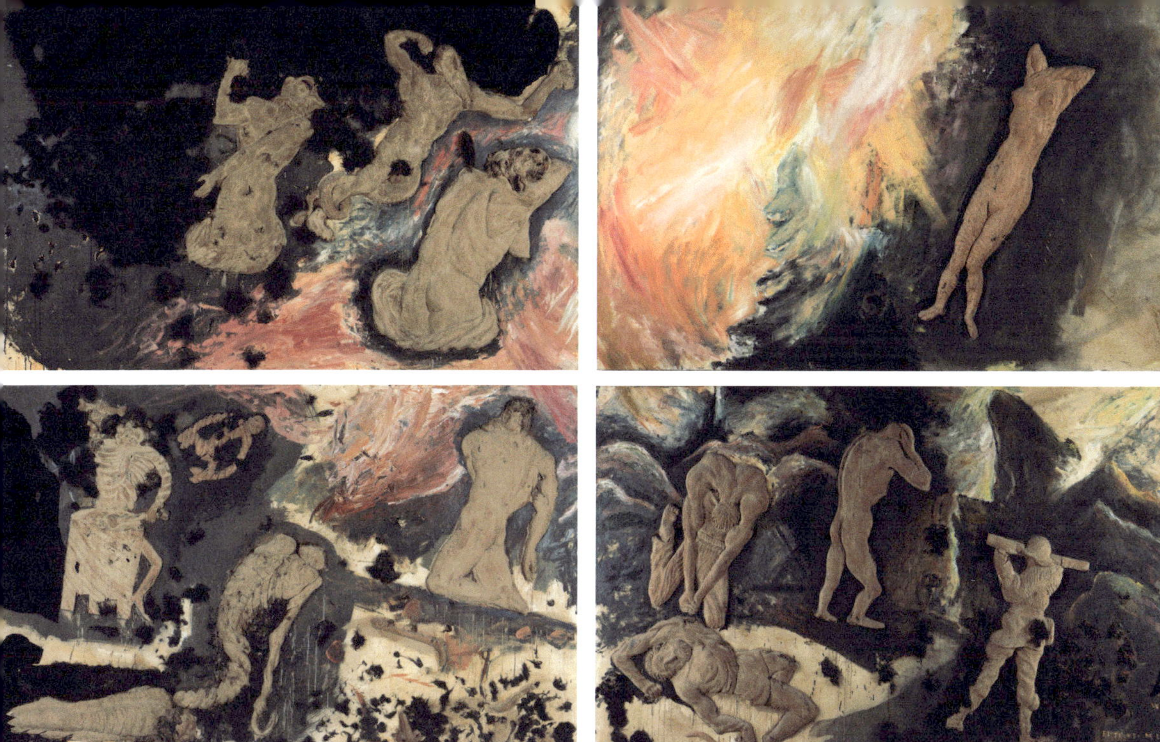

Lorena Wolffer

Mexico City, Mexico, 1971

Evidencias [*Evidence*], 2010–2016

Installation. 237 objects and
their respective testimonies
Variable dimensions
Gift of the artist, 2016

The work of Lorena Wolffer is known for exposing and condemning patriarchal structures. Be it through performance pieces or participatory actions, her work has addressed the many ways in which gender-based violence has been silenced. In doing so, she has also sought to give voice to various feminist struggles.

    Evidencias delves into everyday expressions of domestic aggression. Through a public call, the artist collected different objects—all of which had been used as instruments of violence—from anonymous female donors. Each object is accompanied by the woman's textual account of her own abuse.

V. R. L.

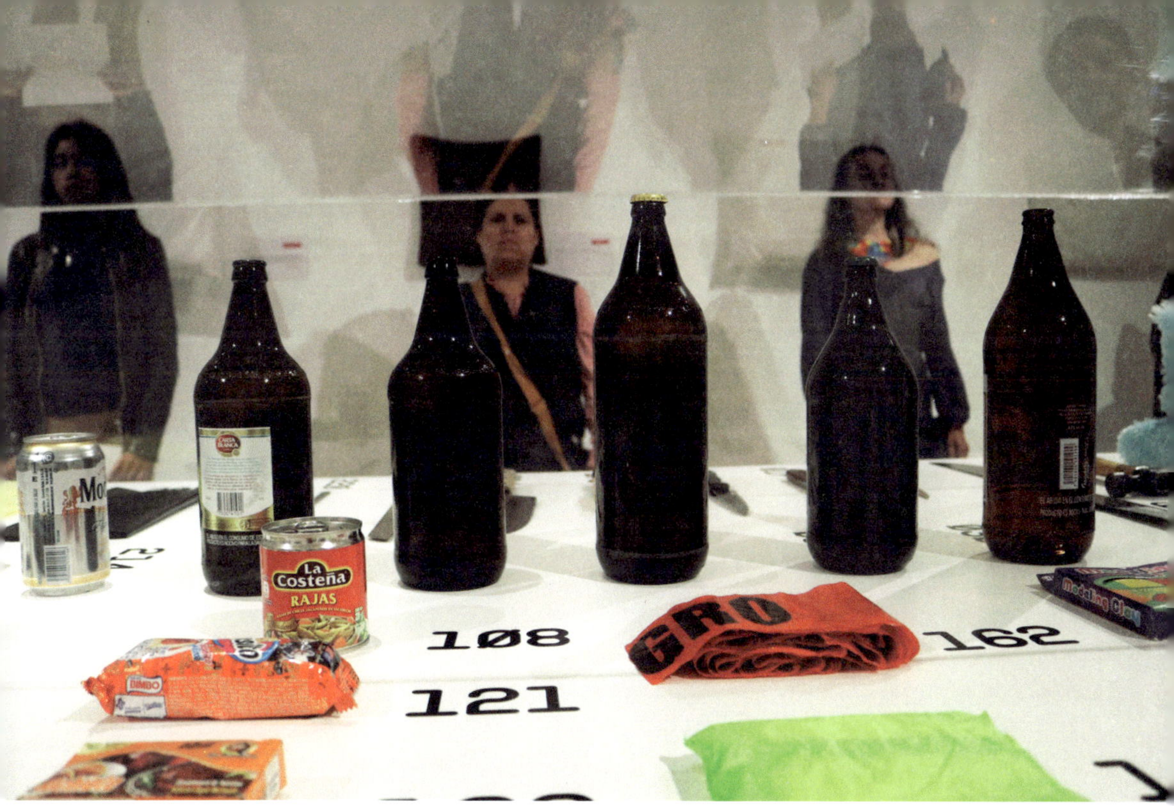

La Costeña
RAJAS

108

121

162

GRO

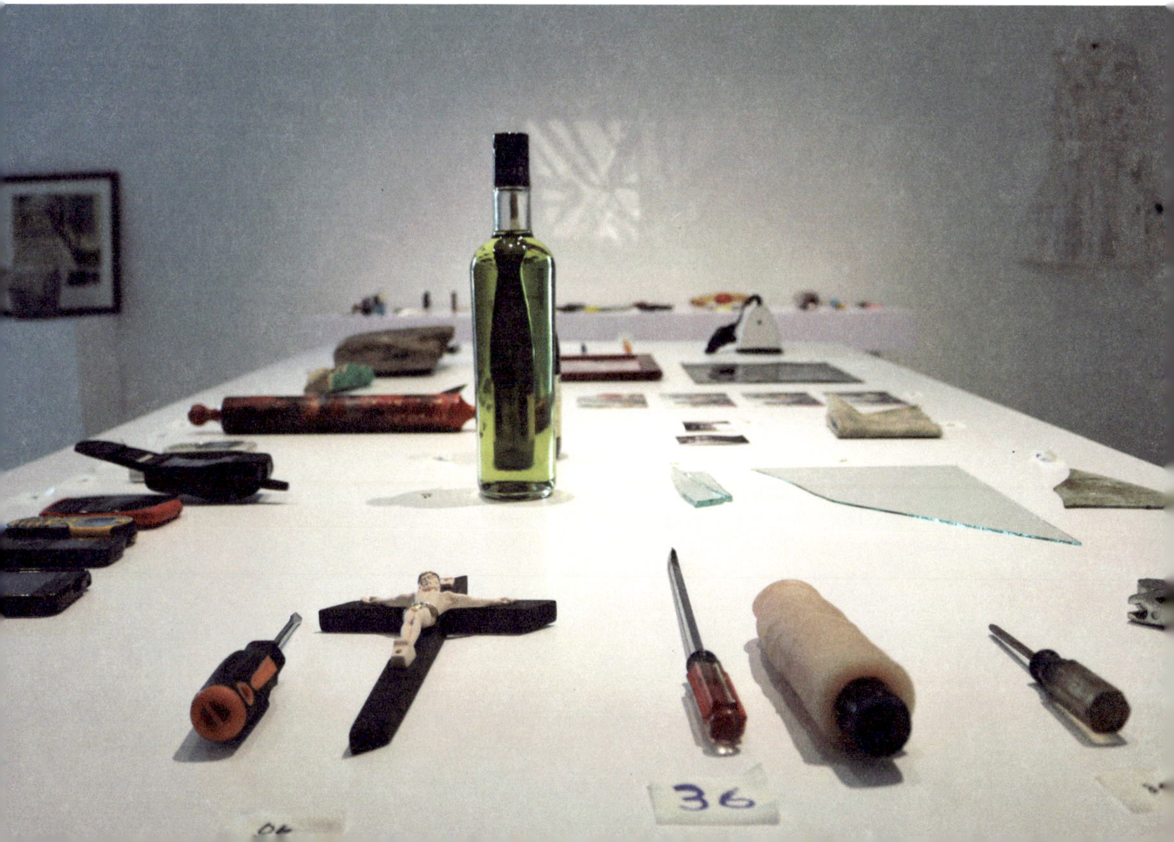

36

Nahum B. Zenil

Chicontepec, Mexico, 1947

¡Oh, santa bandera! (A Enrique Guzmán)
[Oh, Holy Flag! (For Enrique Guzmán)], 1996

Triptych. Ink, acrylic, and oil on paper
238 × 71.5 cm
Acquisition with funds from the Presupuesto
de Egresos de la Federación, 2013

By way of homage, Zenil uses this triptych to reproduce a 1977 painting by Enrique Guzmán's from 1977. In Zenil's version, the flag replaces the Mexican coat of arms with a screaming mouth, and the flagpole penetrates the anus of the painter's self-portrait, metaphorically condemning the consequences of nationalist discourse on the subjectivity of dissident bodies and sexualities. In 1997, the painting was the subject of a public debate during its presentation at the Museo Universitario del Chopo, in the context of the Semana Cultural Lésbico-Gay. Members of the artistic community and LGBTQ+ activists reacted emphatically to protect the work from censorship, as it had been accused of profaning national symbols.

J. G. S.

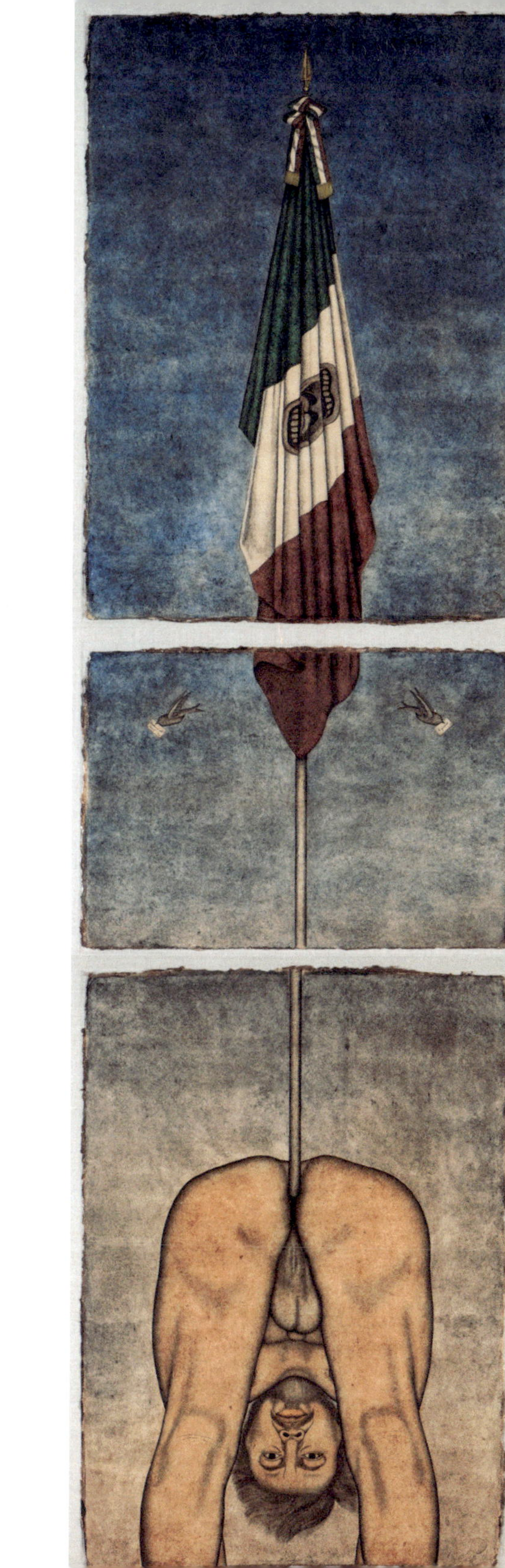

Museum Personnel

DIRECCIÓN GENERAL DE ARTES VISUALES (DiGAV)

Director General
Amanda de la Garza Mata

Executive Assistant
Angélica Hernández

Coordination of Museum Projects
Claudia Barrón

Advisor on International Initiatives
Patricia Sloane

Planning and Data Management
Guadalupe Vázquez

Adjunct Curator
Jaime González Solís

MUSEO UNIVERSITARIO ARTE CONTEMPORÁNEO (MUAC)

CURATORIAL SUBDIRECTION

Curator in Chief
Cuauhtémoc Medina

Adjunct Curators
Alejandra Labastida
Virginia Roy Luzarraga

Assistant Curatorial Coordination
Ana Sampietro Brosa

Artistic Collection
Pilar García

Curatorial Assistant
Andrea de Caso

CENTRO DE DOCUMENTACIÓN ARKHEIA

Curator
Sol Henaro

Research
Elva Peniche

Library
Catalina Aguilar
César González
Julieta Sánchez

COMMUNICATIONS DEPARTMENT
Ekaterina Álvarez

Executive Assistant
Beatriz Angulo

Digital Communication
Ana Cristina Sol

Publicity and Media
Francisco Domínguez

Graphic Identity
Andrea Bernal

Press
Eduardo Lomas

Publications

Editing
Ana Xanic López

Verbal Identity
Vanessa López

CONSERVATION AND REGISTRAR DEPARTMENT
Julia Molinar

Collections in Transit
Elizabeth Herrera

Assistant
Mariana Arenas

Works Registrer and Control
Juan Cortés

Assistant
Alfredo Cuevas
Manuel Magaña

Technician
Cruz Lira

Restoration
Claudio Hernández

Assistant
Mónica Nuñez

EXHIBITIONS DEPARTMENT
Joel Aguilar

Executive Assistant
Edith Ocampo

Design and Producer
Cecilia Pardo

Exhibition Designers
Triana Jiménez
Rafael Milla

Exhibition Technicians
Enrique Castillo
Javier Lira
Víctor Vidal
Alberto Villaruel

IT and Audiovisual Media
Salvador Ávila

Technicians
Antonio Barruelos
Edgar Carbo
Mario Hernández
Alberto Mercado

PUBLIC PROGRAMS DEPARTMENT
Julio García Murillo

Academic Program

Lecture Series
Isabella Contreras

Seminars
Alejandra Monroy

Pedagogical Program
Beatriz Servín

Communities
Miriam Barrón

Art Networks
Natalia Millán

Mediation
Adán González
Adrián Martínez
Aidee Vidal

Courses and Workshops
Fabiola Fragoso

Auditorium
Mauricio Cueva

OUTREACH DEPARTMENT
Gabriela Fong

Executive Assistant
Guadalupe Campos

Fundraising Coordinator
Teresa de la Concha

Strategic Alliances
Carolina Condés
Rebeca Richter

Retail Sales
Alexandra Peeters
Juan Carlos Rojas

José de Jesús Vázquez

Amigos del MUAC
David Montes de Oca

ADMINISTRATIVE UNIT
Pedro Colio

Goods and Supplies
Mirella de la Rosa

Maintenance
Roberto Arreortua

Maintenance and Safety
Maribel Sánchez

Assistant
Mauricio Galván

Staff
Antonio Espinosa
de los Monteros

Budget
Diana Molina

Gross Receipts
Luis Ángel González

General Services
Germán González

Services
Daniel Avilés

COORDINATION OF
FINANCIAL PLANNING
Daniel Correa

**PATRONATO FONDO DE ARTE
CONTEMPORÁNEO, A. C.**

TRUSTEES
Chairman
Gilberto Borja Suárez

Vice-Chairman
Arturo Talavera Autrique

Secretary
Marta M. Mejía

Treasurer
Maribel González de Danel

Alfonso de Angoitia Noriega
María Teresa Borja de Rodríguez
Nicolás Carrancedo Ocejo
Juan Ignacio Casanueva Pérez
Raymundo del Castillo González
María de las Nieves Fernández
José Ramiro Garza Vargas
Andrés Gómez Martínez
Alfredo Harp Helú
Aimée Labarrere Álvarez
Eugenio Madero Pinson
Gabriela Ortiz de Garza
Lulú Ramos Cárdenas de Creel
Jesús Rodríguez Dávalos

HONORARY TRUSTEES
Patrick Charpenel Corvera
Gerardo Estrada Rodríguez
Licio Antonio Minvielle Lagos
José Ignacio Rubio Hidalgo

Executive Coordinator
Graciela de la Torre

Rector | UNAM
Honorary Chairman
Enrique Luis Graue Wiechers

Rector Representative | UNAM
María Teresa Uriarte Castañeda

***Modern and Contemporary
Design in Mexico Collection***

Appointee
Alonso de Garay Montero

Alejandro Legorreta González

**UNIVERSIDAD NACIONAL
AUTÓNOMA DE MÉXICO**

Rector
Dr. Enrique Luis Graue Wiechers

General Secretary
Dr. Leonardo Lomelí Vanegas

Administrative Secretary
Dr. Luis Álvarez-Icaza Longoria

**Secretary of Institutional
Development**
Dr. Alberto Ken Oyama Nakagawa

**Secretary of Prevention, Support
and University Safety**
Lic. Raúl Arsenio Aguilar Tamayo

General Counsel
Dr. Alfredo Sánchez Castañeda

**COORDINACIÓN DE DIFUSIÓN
CULTURAL**

Coordinator
Dr. Jorge Volpi Escalante

Acknowledgements

The Museo Universitario Arte Contemporáneo, MUAC, wishes to thank the following people and institutions whose generous assistance made this publication possible.

Craig Baker, Abraham Bromberg Alterowicz, Elizabeth Calzado, Kerstin Erdmann, Florencia Giordana, Francisco Kochen, Jorge López, Rocío Mireles, Elena Navarro, Odette Paz, Christian Sánchez, Graciela Toledo, Sara Toledo, and Raúl Zorrilla.

Fundación Espacio V, Galería OMR, Galerie Peter Kilchmann, kurimanzutto, LABOR galería, and Morton Subastas

Photo Credits

pp. 1, 10–11 Oliver Santana

p. 15 Reproduction authorized by the Instituto Nacional de Bellas Artes y Literatura, 2020 © David Alfaro Siqueiros/Somaap/Mexico/2020

pp. 20–21 Ohad Matalon

p. 39 Courtesy of Morton Subastas

pp. 57, 73, 92–93, 109, 169 Francisco Kochen

p. 73 © Gunther Gerzso/Somaap/Mexico/2020

p. 75 © Alberto Gironella/Somaap/Mexico/2020

p. 87 Courtesy of Silvia Gruner

pp.184–185 © Kazuya Sakai/Somaap/Mexico/2020

p. 195 Courtesy of Galerie Peter Kilchmann

p. 203 Marcel Rius Baron. Courtesy of Graciela Toledo

p. 205 Courtesy of LABOR galería

p. 209 Larissa Espinosa

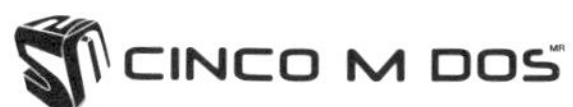

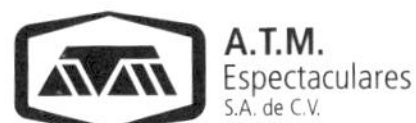

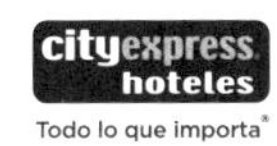

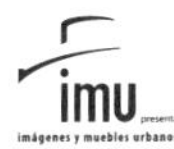